FAMILY-CENTERED MEDICAL CARE
A Clinical Casebook

Edited by
WILLIAM J. DOHERTY, PhD
University of Minnesota

and

MACARAN A. BAIRD, MD
University of Oklahoma Health Sciences Center

THE GUILFORD PRESS
New York   London

© 1987 The Guilford Press
A Division of Guilford Publications, Inc.
200 Park Avenue South, New York, N.Y. 10003
All rights reserved
No part of this book may be reproduced, stored in a retrieval system, or transmitted, in any form or by any means, electronic, mechanical, photocopying, mircrofilming, recording, or otherwise, without written permission from the Publisher

Printed in the United States of America

Last digit is print number: 9 8 7 6 5 4 3 2 1

LIBRARY OF CONGRESS CATALOGING-IN-PUBLICATION DATA

Family-centered medical care.

   Bibliography: p.
   Includes index.
   1. Family medicine—Psychological aspects—Case studies. 2. Family medicine—Case studies. 3. Family psychotherapy—Case studies. I. Doherty, William J. (William Joseph), 1945- . II. Baird, Macaran A.
[DNLM: 1. Family—case studies. 2. Family Practice—case studies. WA 308 F198]
RC66.F23 1987 610 86-27146
ISBN 0-89862-070-8

FAMILY-CENTERED MEDICAL CARE

*We dedicate this book with love to our parents,
Elizabeth M. Doherty and the late William A. Doherty,
and
Hugh A. Baird and Marie Baird*

CONTRIBUTORS

MACARAN A. BAIRD, MD, Department of Family Medicine, University of Oklahoma Health Sciences Center, Oklahoma City, Oklahoma

LISA C. BAKER, PHD, Department of Family Medicine, University of Oklahoma Health Sciences Center, Oklahoma City, Oklahoma

KARLOTTA L. BARTHOLOMEW, PHD, Philadelphia Child Guidance Clinic, Philadelphia, Pennsylvania

MARTY BARTOLAC, MD, Resident, Department of Family Practice, University of Iowa, Iowa City, Iowa

ROGER P. BERMINGHAM, MD, Private practice, Family Physician Associates, Lamar, Colorado

EDWARD T. BOPE, MD, Acting Director, Family Practice Program, Riverside Methodist Hospital, Columbus, Ohio

STEPHEN A. BRUNTON, MD, Associate Director, Family Practice Residency Program, Memorial Medical Center of Long Beach, Long Beach, California

ALVAH R. CASS, MD, Department of Family Medicine, University of Oklahoma Health Sciences Center, Oklahoma City, Oklahoma

JANET CHRISTIE-SEELY, MD, MSc, Department of Family Medicine, Ottawa University, Ottawa, Ontario, Canada

KATHERINE COLE, MD, Private practice, Wapello, Iowa

MICHAEL A. CROUCH, MD, MSPH, Department of Family Medicine and Comprehensive Care, Louisiana State University, Shreveport, Louisiana

JOHN J. DALLMAN, PHD, MD, Head, Department of Family Medicine, Wayne State University, Detroit, Michigan

WILLIAM J. DOHERTY, PHD, Departments of Family Social Science and Family Practice, University of Minnesota, St. Paul, Minnesota

KARL B. FIELDS, MD, Nantahala Health Services, Andrews, North Carolina

JOSÉ FRIEYRO, MD, Unidad de Medicina de Familia, Ruber Hospital Internacional, Madrid, Spain

BARRY L. R. GILBERT, MD, CCFP, Department of Family Medicine, University of Toronto, Toronto, Ontario, Canada

THOMAS GILBERT, MD, Department of Family Medicine, Brown University, Pawtucket, Rhode Island

MICHAEL L. GLENN, MD, Department of Family and Community Medicine, University of Massachusetts, Worcester, Massachusetts; Private practice, Medford, Massachusetts

PETER A. GOODWIN, MD, Department of Family Medicine, Oregon Health Sciences University, Portland, Oregon

JEFFREY GRABENSTEIN, MD, Private practice, Rogers Park Family Practice Center, Chicago Illinois
PETER ROBERT GRANTHAM, MD, Chief, Department of Family Practice, University of British Columbia, Vancouver, British Columbia, Canada
THOMAS J. GRAU, MD, Sioux Falls Family Practice Residency, Sioux Falls, South Dakota
JERI HEPWORTH, PHD, Department of Family Medicine, University of Connecticut, Storrs, Connecticut
GEORGIANNA S. HOFFMANN, RN, MA, CS, Department of Family Practice, University of Iowa, Iowa City, Iowa
DAVID O. HOUGH, MD, Department of Family Practice, Michigan State University, East Lansing, Michigan
CLARK A. JOHNSON, MD, Department of Family Medicine, Texas Tech University Health Science Center, Lubbock, Texas
S. LAWRENCE LIBRACH, MD, FCFP, Family Medicine Residency, University of Toronto, Toronto, Ontario, Canada
TERENCE MCCORMALLY, MD, Private practice, Wapello, Iowa
JAMES J. MCCOY, MD, West Suburban Hospital Medical Center, Oak Park, Illinois
DENNIS M. MCCULLOUGH, MD, Wingra Family Medicine Center, University of Wisconsin Medical School, Madison, Wisconsin
SUSAN MCDANIEL, PHD, Department of Preventive, Family, and Rehabilitation Medicine, University of Rochester, Rochester, New York
MARK MENGEL, MD, Robert Wood Johnson Family Medicine Fellow, University of Washington, Seattle Washington
WILLIAM L. MILLER, MD, Department of Family Medicine, University of Connecticut, Hartford, Connecticut
JAMES W. MOLD, MD, Department of Family Medicine, University of Oklahoma Health Sciences Center, Oklahoma City, Oklahoma
ELIZABETH NAUMBURG, MD, Department of Preventive, Family, and Rehabilitation Medicine, University of Rochester, Rochester, New York
J. M. PONTIOUS, MD, Private practice, Madill, Oklahoma
RUTH POWELL, MD, CCFP, Department of Family Medicine, University of Western Ontario, London, Ontario, Canada
ALEXANDER PREKER, MD, Geriatric Medicine, St. Pancras Hospital, London, England
HARLEY J. RACER, MD, Family Practice Clinic, Hennepin County Medical Center, Minneapolis, Minnesota
DANIEL P. RAINS, MD, Private practice, New Castle, Indiana
GODFREY D. RIPLEY, MD, Department of Family Medicine, Texas Tech University Health Science Center, Amarillo, Texas
E. LEONARD ROBERTS, MD, Department of Family Medicine, Bowman Gray School of Medicine, Wake Forest University, Winston-Salem, North Carolina
JOHN S. ROLLAND, MD, Department of Psychiatry, Yale University, New

Haven, Connecticut; Center for Illness in Families, New Haven, Connecticut

ANTHONY ROSTAIN, MD, Robert Wood Johnson Foundation Clinical Scholars Program, University of Pennsylvania School of Medicine, Philadelphia, Pennsylvania

GEORGE W. SABA, PHD, Division of Family and Community Medicine, University of California, San Francisco, California

RUSSELL J. SAWA, MD, CCFP, Department of Family Medicine and Social Welfare, University of Calgary, Calgary, Alberta, Canada

A. PATRICK SCHNEIDER II, MD, MPH, Private practice, Burlington, Iowa

THOMAS L. SCHWENK, MD, Department of Family Practice, University of Michigan, Ann Arbor, Michigan

SUSANA SEGRE, PHD, National Institute of Mental Health and Private practice, Buenos Aires, Argentina

MILTON H. SEIFERT, JR., MD, Private practice, Excelsior, Minnesota

CHARLES E. SHIELDS, MD, Department of Family Medicine, Texas Tech University Health Science Center, Lubbock, Texas

STEPHEN J. SPANN, MD, Department of Family Medicine, University of Oklahoma Health Sciences Center, Oklahoma City, Oklahoma

HOWARD F. STEIN, PHD, Department of Family Medicine, University of Oklahoma Health Sciences Center, Oklahoma City, Oklahoma

G. GAYLE STEPHENS, MD, Department of Family Medicine, University of Alabama, Birmingham, Alabama

YVES R. TALBOT, MD, FRCP(C), Family Practitioner-in-Chief, Family Practice Unit, Mount Sinai Hospital, Toronto, Ontario, Canada

DAVID TANNENBAUM, MD, CCFP, Department of Family and Community Medicine, Mount Sinai Hospital, Toronto, Ontario, Canada

STEPHEN TAPLIN, MD, MPH, Group Health Cooperative of Puget Sound, Seattle, Washington; Department of Family Medicine, University of Washington, Seattle, Washington

ROBERT B. TAYLOR, MD, Chairman, Department of Family Medicine, Oregon Health Sciences University, Portland, Oregon

KAREN WEIHS, MD, Department of Family Medicine, Brown University, Pawtucket, Rhode Island

W. WAYNE WESTON, MD, CCFP, FCFP, Department of Family Medicine, University of Western Ontario, London, Ontario, Canada

PAUL S. WILLIAMSON, MD, Department of Family Practice, University of Iowa, Iowa City, Iowa

ACKNOWLEDGMENTS

A number of people deserve special credit and thanks for the making of this book. Jeanne Corbin skillfully and enthusiastically guided the mechanics of the project from start to finish, and provided many insightful comments on the cases. Laine McCarthy, whose task was to copyedit cases and make the book's style hold together, worked with amazing skill and grace. We feel indebted to the authors of the cases in this book; they shared their souls along with their cases. Finally, we want to thank our life partners, Leah Doherty and Kris Baird, for supporting us during the distracted and busy period during which this book was created.

CONTENTS

Editors' Introduction   1

LEVEL TWO CASES
Ongoing Medical Information and Advice   9

A Family-Aided Diagnosis. *Macaran A. Baird*   11
A Family Discharge Conference. *E. Leonard Roberts*   13
The Symptom Is the Father's, but the Voice Is the Son's.
Howard F. Stein   16
A Treatment Failure. *Michael L. Glenn*   19
Critical Illness while on Vacation. *John J. Dallman*   28

LEVEL THREE CASES
Feelings and Support   33

Complications of Diabetes. *Dennis M. McCullough*   35
Acute Vertigo in a Homemaker. *Godfrey D. Ripley*   39
The Delivery of an Abnormal Baby. *Peter Robert Grantham*   43
A Patient with Chronic Headache. *Daniel P. Rains*   47
Death as a Part of Family Life. *Peter A. Goodwin*
with *Robert B. Taylor*   49
A Family with Alzheimer's Disease. *Harley J. Racer*   53
Patient–Physician Bonding during Long-Term Chronic
Hematologic Illness. *Charles E. Shields and
Clark A. Johnson*   57
Physician Home Visit with a Terminally Ill Patient and
Her Family. *Stephen J. Spann*   61
Family Support in Terminal Illness. *Peter Robert Grantham*   64
The Stoic Caretaking Sister with Congestive Heart Failure.
John J. Dallman   68
It's How You Listen: A Boy with Diplopia.
Jeffrey Grabenstein   70

An Overweight Adolescent. *Milton H. Siefert, Jr.*	73
A Family Coping with Death. *David Tannenbaum*	77
A Family with a Dying Son. *Lisa C. Baker*	79
Clyde and Betty: Problems of the Heart. *A. Patrick Schneider II*	82
Dignity in Death. *Russell J. Sawa*	85
Pain in a Terminally Ill Patient. *S. Lawrence Librach*	87
Missing Data: A Boy with Gastrointestinal Problems and Hyperventilation. *James W. Mold*	90
A Woman Learning to Live with Osteoporosis: Making Lemons into Lemonade. *Stephen A. Brunton*	94
Parkinson's Disease and the Aging Patient. *Edward T. Bope*	98
Birth of a Down's Syndrome Baby. *Karl B. Fields*	101

LEVEL FOUR CASES
Systematic Assessment and Planned Intervention — 105

Behind the Mask: "Unnecessary" Pediatric Visits. *William L. Miller*	107
The Death of a Teenager. *G. Gayle Stephens*	110
Leukemia and the Reluctant Husband. *James J. McCoy*	115
A Therapeutic Family Disruption after Cancer Surgery. *Thomas L. Schwenk*	119
The Ventriloquist: Fear that Father Will Die. *Yves R. Talbot*	122
Outpatient Care of a Newly Diagnosed Adolescent Diabetic. *David O. Hough*	125
A Deteriorating Family. *Russell J. Sawa*	130
Dementia or Alcohol Intoxication?: A Case for Home Evaluation. *J. M. Pontious*	133
A Mother's Pain: The Son Who Stayed Too Long. *James W. Mold*	136
A Hyperactive Child. *E. Leonard Roberts*	139
A Hospice Patient and Her Family. *Roger P. Bermingham*	143
Father and Daughter Alcoholics Move toward Recovery. *Terence McCormally and Katherine Cole*	149
The Family Seizure. *William L. Miller*	152

The Symptomatic Aged. *Alexander Preker* 155
A Woman Prepares to Die. *Ruth Powell and W. Wayne Weston* 160
Death Brings a "Cutoff" Daughter Back. *Russell J. Sawa* 164
A Family with Chronic Crisis. *Barry L. R. Gilbert* 167
A Boy with Recurring Abdominal Pain. *Godfrey D. Ripley* 170
Life after Death. *William L. Miller* 174
And Baby Makes Three. *Thomas Gilbert* 178
A Husband with Dementia, a Wife with Terminal Cancer, and a Caretaking Sister. *José Frieyro* 182
A Patient with Stomachache. *W. Wayne Weston* 185
Lower Abdominal Pain in an Adolescent. *Mark Mengel* 189
Family Dysfunction and Peptic Ulcer Disease. *Stephen J. Spann* 194
Enuresis: A Dog Is a Boy's Best Friend. *Thomas J. Grau* 198
Functional Symptoms in Response to Stress. *Anthony Rostain* 202
A Girl with Uncontrolled Diabetes. *Daniel P. Rains* 209
A Family with Recent Loss. *Alvah R. Cass* 212
A Woman with Fibromyositis. *Alvah R. Cass* 215

LEVEL FIVE CASES
Family Therapy 221

Family Intervention in Failure to Thrive. *Karen Weihs* 223
A Patient with Alopecia Areata. *Mark Mengel* 228
Ventricular Tachycardia and Family Explosions. *Janet Christie-Seely* 232
A Suicide Gesture: The Youngest Child Brings Her Family to the Doctor. *Georgianna S. Hoffmann and Paul S. Williamson* 239
A Boy with Abdominal Pain. *Jeri Hepworth* 244
A Family's Headache. *Thomas J. Grau* 249
Chronic Headaches and a Couple Who Knew Better. *Georgianna S. Hoffmann and Marty Bartolac* 253
Overutilization of the Medical System and a Teenage Suicide Attempt. *Thomas L. Schwenk* 257

Who's on First: Problems in Parenting. *Michael A. Crouch*   260

A Teenager with Brittle Diabetes. *Karlotta L. Bartholomew*   264

A Husband and Wife with Backaches. *Stephen Taplin, Susan McDaniel, and Elizabeth Naumberg*   267

"Bypass Surgery" on the Doctor–Patient Relationship. *George W. Saba*   275

Sexual Problems and Unresolved Grief. *Janet Christie-Seely*   281

Prematurity and the "Vulnerable Child Syndrome." *Anthony Rostain*   285

A Patient with Aphasia. *Susana Segre*   291

Triangulation, Fear, and Uncertainty in Treating an AIDS Patient. *John S. Rolland*   296

CONCLUSION
The State of the Art in Family-Centered Medical Care   303

References   313

Index   315

EDITORS' INTRODUCTION

The idea for this book was born in 1982 after we finished *Family Therapy and Family Medicine: Toward the Primary Care of Families* (Doherty & Baird, 1983). While writing that book, we became aware of the lack of adequate case material illustrating family-centered medical care. About the same time, we were meeting and corresponding with family physicians and family therapists who were working with families routinely and creatively in medical settings across the country. We became convinced that the beginnings of a practical knowledge and experience base already existed in the field, and we decided to tap it in a book of cases.

The case study approach seems well suited to garnering the experience of physicians who involve families in their practice. As Howard Stein (1983) has pointed out, case studies illuminate clinical practice in a special way that no other method offers. They offer richly textured information about the practitioners, the patients and their families, and the context in which they all live and work. Cases reveal what people do and how they feel about what they do in a way that theory and empirical research, indispensable as they are, can never reveal.

Having decided to do a casebook, we puzzled for a number of months about how to find the cases. We already knew a core group of 10–15 family physicians, mostly in academic settings, who actively involved families in their practices. Similarly, we knew a handful of family therapists who were working collaboratively with family physicians. But we also wanted to find people whom we didn't already know, especially those in community practice settings. The problem we faced was akin to that of researchers studying people with highly unusual lifestyles: The population of interest is not easily available through normal sampling procedures. Eventually we opted for the following chain sampling approach to solicit case studies.

First, we wrote to the people we already knew were practicing family-centered medical care, and to family physicians who attended the 1984 Society of Teachers of Family Medicine Conference on Working with Families. Respondents were asked to nominate three other colleagues, especially community-based family physicians who regularly worked with families. We then sent invitations to these nominees, and asked them to nominate three more people. Through this procedure, we were able to obtain case reports from a diverse group of physicians and family therapists from across the country.

The letter of invitation gave guidelines about the kind of cases we wanted, namely those in which a physician dealt directly with the patient's family in diagnosing or treating a problem that family physicians see in their practices. The range of patient problems was deliberately broad, but we said that we were especially interested in cases in which the family was involved in the management of routine medical problems. After reaching agreement with the author on the proposed topic for the case, we sent guidelines for writing it. Basically, we asked authors to write a four- to five-page narrative of their experience with the patient and family, including the presenting biomedical and psychosocial information, diagnosis, approach to treatment, outcome, and follow-up. We wanted to know specifically how the author involved the family in the case, and what family therapy consultants, if any, were used. We asked authors to use the first person "I" or "we" in recounting the case, and to write in personal terms about their own reactions to the patient and family.

As editors, we reviewed the cases, accepted some with no substantive changes, sent others back for revision, and decided that some were not suitable for this book. We then wrote commentaries on all the cases in order to draw general themes and connections throughout the book. Our focus in the editors' comments is on the physician's part of the interaction with the patient and family. The result, we believe, is a collection of compelling accounts of encounters between physicians and families. We were impressed by all these cases and emotionally moved by many of them. Furthermore, we believe that they represent the state of the art in family-centered medical care as practiced by family physicians in North America. We are aware of a similar movement in family-centered nursing, and we look to the day when the whole health care team is trained to be sensitive to families. Although this book may be of interest to nurses and other health professionals and therapists, the primary audience we wish to reach and influence is composed of family physicians and medical students.

Since both the editors and the authors are invested in showing the usefulness of this approach to medical care, most of the cases naturally present "successes." However, there are some failure and "hitting a brick wall" cases in the book, and we want to acknowledge openly that involving families in patient care is no panacea. Nor is direct interaction with families always the treatment approach of choice; it obviously is not when the patient does not want family involvement or when the physician is overwhelmed with immediate biomedical responsibilities for the patient. Most of the case authors, however, would probably agree that *thinking* about the patient's family and other psychosocial contexts is nearly always feasible and important over the course of an ongoing doctor–patient relationship. Like all other *intervention* approaches, however, the appropriateness, timing, and usefulness of family meetings depends on the unique context of the patient, family, health professional, and treatment setting.

These cautions aside, we unabashedly view family-centered care as a reasonable, humane, and exciting way to practice medicine. One purpose of this book is to communicate this view and this enthusiasm to readers. The other purpose is to put flesh on the abstract concept of family-centered medical care by showcasing skillful applications of the approach. We realize that case reports do not provide convincing evidence of the usefulness of an approach to diagnosis and treatment. As Edwin Friedman (1985) observed, "Case histories always seem to offer more promise than any approach to healing can truly deliver" (p. 137). But we believe that taken together, the cases in this book do help build the argument for the attractiveness and feasibility of a family-centered approach to patient care.

At the end of the book, in a concluding chapter, we attempt to describe the state of the art in family-centered medical care using three sources: the cases, a questionnaire completed by physician case authors about their practices and orientations, and our own observations and experience.

FRAMEWORK FOR ORGANIZING THE CASES

The cases are organized around a conceptual model we developed in 1984 to describe qualitatively different levels of physician involvement with families. The model has been described in Doherty (1985) and Baird and Doherty (1986); implications for education are described in

Doherty and Baird (1986). The levels represent a range of ways in which physicians are involved with families in medical practice. The levels can also be applied to other health care professionals, but for the purposes of this book will be restricted to physicians.

Just as physicians' level of involvement with biomedical treatment depends on the severity of the disease and the physician's level of knowledge and skill, so does physicians' involvement with families. Beyond level one, which generally ignores family issues, all the other levels represent potentially helpful physician–family interactions, ranging from dealing exclusively with medical information (level two), to also dealing supportively with feelings and stress (level three), to working in a primary care mode for change in family interaction patterns (level four), to providing family therapy for dysfunctional family patterns (level five). The appropriate level of physician involvement with a family in a particular case must be determined not only by the needs and desires of the patient and the family, but also by the skill, motivation, time, and other resources of the physician.

Table 1 delineates in detail the knowledge base, personal development level, and skills that we believe are required at each level. Level one represents the minimal level of involvement with families practiced in many tertiary care medical school programs. Level two is the beginning of family-centered medical care, in which the physician actively collaborates with families around the patient's medical problem by creating a dialogue about the medical diagnosis and treatment plan.

Level three builds on the medical collaboration of level two and goes beyond its cognitive focus to address the emotional reactions of family members and the ways they deal with the stress of an illness or lifestyle problem. Some families presumably neither need nor want to discuss these personal issues with their physician, in which case level two involvement would be more appropriate than level three. A similar preference for level two would be indicated when the physician does not have time to open up discussion of family members' feelings and stress. These exceptions notwithstanding, it appears that level three ideally would be a common style of involvement of family physicians with patients and families who are under stress that is related to medical or other problems. At level three, the physician is able to move back and forth between medical and personal conversation, between facts and feelings, and does not censor family members' expressions of strong emotions such as grief, anger, and fear. A hallmark behavior of the physician operating at level three would be temporarily shifting the focus of a family conference from the identified patient to other family members who are hurting.

Level four represents a more sophisticated involvement with families when the agenda is the need for change. Here part of the focus of a family conference, in addition to sharing information and talking about feelings, would be on helping to change interaction patterns in the family system. For example, in dealing with the family of an adolescent diabetic who is locked into a battle with her parents over her insulin injections and diet, the family physician might attempt to help the parents and the adolescent mutually negotiate a new set of procedures to remove the diabetes care from the family power struggle. Knowledge of family systems theory, and experience with primary care family counseling interventions would prepare the physician to counsel families who had not yet become chronically conflicted over these issues. As at all the preceding primary care levels, the physician can refer this family if he or she does not feel qualified to counsel them or if the primary care counseling attempt is not successful.

Level five represents family therapy as opposed to primary care family counseling (Doherty & Baird, 1983). Only a small number of family physicians are likely to have the time, interest, and training to engage in level five family therapy. Level five is distinguished by the intensity of the therapist's engagement with a family that is "stuck" in a dysfunctional pattern. In the case of the diabetic family mentioned above, level five family therapy would be indicated if the family engages in chronic conflict about managing the disease, is not responsive to supportive and educational interventions, or has rigidly stabilized, despite the physician's best efforts, around recurring episodes of ketoacidosis. The best use of primary care skills with such families lies in assessment and referral to a therapist. However, some of the family physicians who wrote case studies for this book are fully qualified to handle level five involvement with families, and other physicians with a special interest in family therapy might serve as assistant therapists with a trained family therapist. We suspect that most family physicians, however, will be pleased to function at level three most of the time, and some will want to be trained at level four primary care systems interventions.

This book uses the levels of involvement, beginning with level

TABLE 1. Levels of Physician Involvement with Families

Level one: Minimal emphasis on family	Level two: Ongoing medical information and advice	Level three: Feelings and support
This baseline level of involvement consists of dealing with families only as necessary for practical and medical–legal reasons, but not viewing communicating with families as integral to the physician's role or as involving skills for the physician to develop. This level presumably characterizes most medical school training in which biomedical issues are the sole conscious focus of patient care.	*Knowledge base:* Primarily medical, plus awareness of the triangular dimension of the physician–patient relationship. *Personal development:* Openness to engage patients and families in a collaborative way. *Skills* 1. Regularly and clearly communicating medical findings and treatment options to family members. 2. Asking family members questions that elicit relevant diagnostic and treatment information. 3. Attentively listening to family members' questions and concerns. 4. Advising families about how to handle the medical and rehabilitation needs of the patient. 5. For large or demanding families, knowing how to channel communication through one or two key members. 6. Identifying gross family dysfunction that interferes with medical treatment, and referring the family to a therapist.	*Knowledge base:* Normal family development and reactions to stress. *Personal development:* Awareness of one's own feelings in relationship to the patient and family. *Skills* 1. Asking questions that elicit family members' expressions of concerns and feelings related to the patient's condition and its effect on the family. 2. Empathically listening to family members' concerns and feelings, and normalizing them where appropriate. 3. Forming a preliminary assessment of the family's level of functioning as it relates to the patient's problem. 4. Encouraging family members in their efforts to cope as a family with their situation. 5. Tailoring medical advice to the unique needs, concerns, and feelings of the family. 6. Identifying family dysfunction and fitting a referral recommendation to the unique situation of the family.

Level four: Systematic assessment and planned intervention	Level five: Family therapy
Knowledge base: Family systems.	*Knowledge base:* Family systems and patterns whereby dysfunctional families interact with professionals and other health care systems.
Personal development: Awareness of one's own participation in systems including the therapeutic triangle, the medical system, one's own family system, and larger community systems.	*Personal development:* Ability to handle intense emotions in families and self and to maintain neutrality in the face of strong pressure from family members or other professionals.
Skills 1. Engaging family members, including reluctant ones, in a planned family conference or a series of conferences. 2. Structuring a conference with even a poorly communicating family in such a way that all members have a chance to express themselves. 3. Systematically assessing the family's level of functioning. 4. Supporting individual members while avoiding coalitions. 5. Reframing the family's definition of their problem in a way that makes problem solving more achievable. 6. Helping the family members view their difficulty as one that requires new forms of collaborative efforts. 7. Helping family members generate alternative, mutually acceptable ways to cope with their difficulty. 8. Helping the family balance their coping efforts by calibrating their various roles in a way that allows support without sacrificing anyone's autonomy. 9. Identifying family dysfunction that lies beyond primary care treatment and orchestrating a referral by educating the family and the therapist about what to expect from one another.	*Skills* The following is not an exhaustive list of family therapy skills but rather a list of several key skills that distinguish level five involvement from primary care involvement with families. 1. Interviewing families or family members who are quite difficult to engage. 2. Efficiently generating and testing hypotheses about the family's difficulties and interaction patterns. 3. Escalating conflict in the family in order to break a family impasse. 4. Temporarily siding with one family member against another. 5. Constructively dealing with a family's strong resistance to change. 6. Negotiating collaborative relationships with other professionals and other systems who are working with the family, even when these groups are at odds with one another.

two, as a framework for presenting the case material. Our purpose is to show the distinctive usefulness of each level for different kinds of cases. We did not prescreen the cases according to level, but rather rated each case after it came in. Generally, the rating process was straightforward, although sometimes we had difficulty deciding between level three and level four for particular cases. Our purpose was to conceptually organize the book, and to exemplify the levels rather than to provide the most rigorously accurate rating of each case.

How did the cases divide according to level? The bulk of the cases fell into levels three and four. However, we were delighted to attract several fine level two cases and a number of level five cases. Although case authors are mostly family physicians in academic or community practice settings, the book also contains cases authored by family therapists, by a psychiatrist, and by a pediatrician. All but two cases reflect U.S. and Canadian experiences; one case was sent from Spain and one from Argentina. The families in the cases range in setting from rural to inner city and, while mostly white, also include black families and families of Latin American and Spanish origin. Medical topics in the cases run the gamut from otitis media to cancer to acquired immune deficiency syndrome.

CONCLUSION

We invite the reader to browse through these cases in any order, perhaps choosing a title that strikes your interest, or perhaps taking a level at a time. There are rich, complex stories told here as well as some everyday, simple ones. Some are tales of transforming experiences for families and physicians alike, while others tell of reasonable efforts leading to satisfying, and sometimes unsatisfying, results. We are proud to pass these stories on to you. May you enjoy them as much as we have.

LEVEL TWO CASES

ONGOING MEDICAL INFORMATION AND ADVICE

KNOWLEDGE BASE

Primarily medical, plus awareness of the triangular dimension of the physician–patient relationship.

PERSONAL DEVELOPMENT

Openness to engage patients and families in a collaborative way.

SKILLS

1. Regularly and clearly communicating medical findings and treatment options to family members.
2. Asking family members questions that elicit relevant diagnostic and treatment information.
3. Attentively listening to family members' questions and concerns.
4. Advising families about how to handle the medical and rehabilitation needs of the patient.
5. For large or demanding families, knowing how to channel communication through one or two keys members.
6. Identifying gross family dysfunction that interferes with medical treatment, and referring the family to a therapist.

A FAMILY-AIDED DIAGNOSIS

MACARAN A. BAIRD
University of Oklahoma Health Sciences Center

Mrs. B, a 68-year-old widow, presented first to the emergency room at 2 a.m. with complaints of severe upper abdominal and middle back pain. She said it had been present for several weeks but became unbearable this night. She denied recent falls or other trauma. Further history suggested severe peripheral vascular and coronary artery disease, and osteoarthritis. I became concerned about a high aortic aneurysm.

Physical exam revealed a slender, frail, elderly woman with a palpable pulsatile mass in her abdomen. There were decreased femoral pulses in both legs. She had reduced mobility in her neck and back. She seemed to be tender everywhere, but especially in her abdomen and upper back. Vital signs were all normal. Because our small rural hospital had no satisfactory means of evaluating her aorta, I immediately transferred Mrs. B to a nearby referral center via ambulance with uninflated MAST trousers applied.

Mrs. B was evaluated quickly and found to have a normal aorta, significant coronary and peripheral vascular disease, osteoporosis, osteoarthritis, and what appeared to be an old compression fracture of the 12th thoracic vertebra (T_{12}). She was discharged within 48 hours and returned to my care. Her pain persisted. Potent analgesics did not seem to help and the nonsteroidal antiinflammatory agents upset her stomach.

Initially, I felt relieved that Mrs. B did not have the life-threatening disorder I had first suspected. However, her symptoms continued to make her life miserable. Family members who took turns caring for her were convinced that she was going to die from pain and despair if nothing further could be done. She could not sit or lie in any position without severe pain. She did not want to go to the hospital again. After 2 weeks of unsuccessful management and numerous phone calls, I asked for a family interview in the office.

In the staff lounge, I met with Mrs. B and all six of her children, ages 27 through 42. All the children lived on nearby farms and had been involved in caring for their mother. Each expressed frustration over trying to help; they could see that her pain was disabling and persistent. We reviewed her consultant's diagnosis of arthritic pain and the old compression fracture of T_{12}. I asked if anyone could remember if Mrs. B had fallen recently (even though she denied it). No. Did anyone have suggestions for different treatment approaches? Yes. They all felt that she should be admitted to our local hospital for whatever treatment I wanted to try. They were exhausted and unable to bear her suffering any longer. Mrs. B reluctantly agreed to try anything that might help. I agreed to admit her with the understanding that I could not guarantee any improvement but would try absolute bed rest as treatment. This open discussion of the problem, however, had stimulated me to consider the possibility that the compression fracture was new rather than old. This could explain the severe pain that was palpable to everyone in the family. I had neglected that diagnosis in my relief over the absence of an abdominal aneurysm.

Mrs. B improved steadily in the hospital. She was treated with bed rest, gentle physical therapy, and an antidepressant for her chronic pain. She was discharged after 10 days with a diagnosis of compression fracture of T_{12} with delayed healing. Mrs. B had some pain after activity but was much improved. She felt more cheerful and no longer feared random bursts of shooting pain. Follow-up x-rays demonstrated a healing fracture of T_{12}.

A brief family interview was held just prior to discharge, and together we reviewed Mrs. B's recovery. I gave credit to the family for helping me make the diagnosis and for suggesting an appropriate treatment setting. They credited me with being open to their suggestions.

EDITORS' COMMENTS

In this case, the family interview provided information that led to a more helpful diagnosis and treatment plan. As a physician, I (Baird) had been relieved that a very serious problem was not present. Such relief may have blocked my ability to make other diagnostic inquiries. I was following the recommendations of the consultants who had seen the patient briefly in an acute-care setting. I had incorrectly interpreted the series of phone calls as an indication that the patient and family were overreacting to her chronic arthritic discomfort. Only after seeing the patient with her sincere and appropriately frustrated family did the clinical picture make sense. Ultimately, the patient, family, and I were pleased with the outcome and with the process. The technical diagnosis and treatment plan were slow in developing but were not unusual in content. It was the *process* of working with the patient's family that clarified the diagnosis and enriched my relationship with the patient and her family. By asking for and accepting help from each other, we became a team that could face future problems with more confidence. For me, this process was humbling but richly satisfying.

A FAMILY DISCHARGE CONFERENCE

E. LEONARD ROBERTS
Wake Forest University

Mrs. M, an 80-year-old woman, was admitted to the hospital for diagnostic workup of weight loss and hemoccult-positive stools. Her x-ray studies demonstrated a colon carcinoma, which appeared operable. At operation, lymph node and liver metastases were discovered. Mrs. M and her family were told by the surgeons that she "had a tumor." During her second-week postoperative recovery period, I assumed responsibility for her care. It became apparent that neither Mrs. M nor her family knew that "having a tumor" meant cancer of the intestines in her case. It also was evident that the family had unrealistic ideas about her ability to return home and live alone. Despite several telephone calls, the son and daughter-in-law were not available to discuss discharge plans, home care, nursing home placement, and so on. In fact, the son said, "She ought to stay in the hospital until she gets a nursing home bed, and I'm not going to be pushed around by anyone." This cycle of telephone calls and relayed messages continued for 7-10 days.

At this point, I requested a family meeting with all members who were interested and would have a role in her care. Mrs. M's son, daughter-in-law, and I met with the hospital social worker and the physician's assistant, who often helped coordinate discharge planning. Mrs. M was physically too weak to attend, although we discussed plans with her. The family appeared quite anxious and even hostile; they responded briefly, and had few questions. Noting this, I stated matter-of-factly, "We are here to make the best arrangements possible for Mrs. M's discharge. Do you have any suggestions or questions?"

Both the son and daughter-in-law began to express concern about Mrs. M coming home, and asked the following questions: "How can we care for her skin and her diarrhea? What will she be like? What if she gets really sick? How will we know? We have young children. How will this affect them? Will we have to sit with her 24 hours a day? What if she moans all night or is in pain? The insurance will pay for her stay in the hospital but not at home."

We were able to discuss each concern and arrange a plan to deal with each. We also informed the family that the insurance company would not pay for hospitalization if there was no adequate medical reason for Mrs. M to remain in the hospital (such as waiting for a nursing home bed). As part of the arrangement, Mrs. M's daughter-in-law agreed to come and spend several nights in the hospital, aiding in the feeding, turning, and other nursing-care chores, and thus getting some idea of the routine care required. Home health nurse visits were arranged, and a hospital bed, a wheelchair, and supplies were available from the local cancer foundation at minimal cost. Volunteer sitters from a local hospice organization could aid in relief and family support. Meanwhile, the search for a nursing home bed would continue.

Mrs. M's discharge was arranged within 5 days, and she went home with the family. Her course at home was that of gradual medical decompensation and decreasing mental status. She died at home within 2 months still awaiting nursing home placement. Visits by the physician's assistant revealed that the family was caring for Mrs. M wth the help of the support services mentioned (hospice, home health nurses, etc.). In addition, a local church supported the family by maintaining regular contact with them and offering appropriate help (relief sitters, minister visits, etc.).

Discharge planning is often best done face-to-face with the people who are involved. In families with a dying member, it is too easy for all of us to delay facing the issues realistically. At the family meeting, the concerns were expressed, and a plan to deal with each was developed. Also, the family meeting provided the opportunity to cultivate a certain spirit of support and cooperation that enabled all of us to break through the collective denial and fears that surround our dealings with dying patients. With the advent of changes in hospital and insurance policy (DRGs, PPOs, HMOs, etc.) the family meeting to facilitate hospital discharge planning may become more feasible and important. Both families and physicians often do not know all that is available, and both are concerned that quality care may end with hospital discharge. This concern aids "foot-dragging" by both parties. The family meeting offers the opportunity for information to be shared and misinformation corrected. Once a clear plan is set, the foot-dragging usually stops, and all involved feel the satisfaction of having cooperated in the patient's best interest.

EDITORS' COMMENTS

This case illustrates the value of meeting with the patient's family to discuss the patient's medical status and to plan realistically for posthospital care. The family was fearful that the physician was going to dump Mrs. M on them. Therefore, they persistently avoided talking with the physician. Instead of giving up at this point, Dr. Roberts called a conference with the family, the social worker, and the physician's assistant. Through this informational conference, the family was able to accept Mrs. M's terminal status and learn ways to care for her at home. The family conference also helped the physician to avoid angrily rejecting the family, and in the process accepting too much responsibility for deciding about Mrs. M's future care.

THE SYMPTOM IS THE FATHER'S, BUT THE VOICE IS THE SON'S

HOWARD F. STEIN
University of Oklahoma Health Sciences Center

As the behavioral science consultant with two community-based family medicine residency training programs, I often assist the physician by observing the clinical interaction and offering a brief comment to the physician following the encounter. The following vignette is the product of that context.

Mr. D, Sr., a long-standing family medicine clinic patient, was at the clinic for a return visit to have his blood pressure checked, and to have the discoloration and scaling on his skin bilaterally above the ankles rechecked. He was a 70-year-old white male, neatly dressed in a long-sleeve western shirt and jeans and clean boots. He was accompanied in the examining room by his 35-year-old son, who was rather pot-bellied, with scruffy beard, slightly torn T-shirt, and clearly worn jeans. The impression the pair made was that the father was clean-cut while the son resembled a bum. The father was seated on the exam table, and the son was seated in a chair against the wall when the physician and I entered the room. The son drove the father to all his medical appointments (although the father did drive), and has been present in the examining room (with the physician's endorsement) in all past visits his father has paid to this family medicine clinic. Throughout the encounter, the father responded briefly to questions the physician asked. The son, although deferential to his father, voluntarily contributed information or amplified what the father tended to minimize.

On the previous appointment, the physician had prescribed an ointment and now wanted to check the patient to see if any change had taken place. (It had not.) The physician shared with father and son his thinking: that he had originally thought the skin problem to derive from decreased peripheral circulation, but now thought that the problem was nummular psoriasis. He prescribed a cream for Mr. D, Sr. to use.

Thus far, the discussion had centered around Mr. D, Sr.'s presenting complaint—itch. The physician then asked Mr. D, Sr. how his drinking had been lately: "Oh, you know, I drink a little. That's all." he responded matter-of-factly. He had a long history of alcoholism, but he tended to minimize his (*whose?*) problem. The physician gently enjoined him to try to ease up on his drinking. The encounter had concluded from the father's viewpoint, whereupon the son asked the physician to take a look at his father's right forehead, which the father had hit when he sustained a fall earlier that morning. Before the physician could get to the forehead, Mr. D, Sr. protested, "It wasn't nothing, just a little bump." The son replied: "I thought you [the doctor] ought to take a look at it." The physician strategically replied to the father: "Everybody's entitled to *one* fall. But I want you to let me know if you have another fall, so that we can make sure nothing's going on." The son followed this with a question: "Do you think my dad needs to have his liver x-rayed again this year?" The physician replied that he thought it would be a good idea. They made an appointment for 2 weeks hence, when they would return and have the scaling checked. The alcoholism issue was out in the open.

From this brief, 10-minute encounter, several issues in clinical and family communication are illustrated: (1) The patient's presenting complaint is not necessarily the companion's or family's primary complaint or interest. (2) A family member other than the one afflicted (or seen as afflicted) may serve as the mouthpiece for the family's concerns. (3) Although the family physician is privy to little family interaction in the examining room, much can be gleaned about the family of Mr. D, Sr. from this interaction between father, son, and physician. (4) It is easy to read the wrong meanings into people's dress (e.g., the sloppily dressed son was interested in controlling his father's drinking, whereas the neatly dressed father was the drinker, at least in my impression). (5) If it is necessary to make quick or emergency family interventions, one must identify who is the most reliable or stable member of the family. In this case, the son would be a good bet. (6) Likewise, since families tend to have secrets (e.g., denial in the case of problems with alcohol), it is important to identify who is (are) a fairly reliable source of medical and interactional data. Again, at least for a start, the son is also a good bet. (7) Clinical encounters are full of surprises, upsetting our own clinical agendas, plans, expectations, and sense of closure. They can also be welcome opportunities to obtain new types of clinical data and to rethink our interventions (e.g., *what* kind of intervention, and *with whom* we wish to intervene). The son's remark about his father's recent fall dramatically redefined the symptom and problem—and at a point in the clinical encounter when physician and father were ready to walk out the door. (8) Finally, none of the above data and perspectives would have been accessible had the identified patient been seen exclusively alone.

EDITORS' COMMENTS

This case illustrates a number of issues, which are fully discussed by the author. We shall address somewhat different aspects of the case. Denial of a complex and socially uncomfortable issue did not rest solely with the patient or family, but also with the physician. When the physician in this case had offered ineffective advice (cut down on drinking), the family member raised the issue of alcoholism by referring to its physical consequences. With that direct assist, the physician moved a little closer to the more serious medical issue. As discussed by the author, this interaction was possible only because the son was encouraged to be present for the medical interview. Therefore, the resident physician moved one step closer to being helpful. Perhaps with further training, this physician will learn more effective ways to relate to the problem of alcoholism and to the general issue of how to collaborate with patients and families. It was fortunate that a skilled observer, in this case Dr. Stein, was present to encourage further discussion.

A TREATMENT FAILURE

MICHAEL L. GLENN
University of Massachusetts
Private practice, Medford, Massachusetts

Some teach by their successes. I'll tell about a failure and hope we both learn from the telling. My narrative history follows. My notes are in a separate section at the end, each comment keyed to the superscript numbers.

Mary M, an 85-year-old Irish woman, entered my practice in September 1983. She was referred by the chiropractor down the street. In her first visit, she had many complaints, including bad nerves, pains in the stomach, arthritis, back pains, ulcers, gallstones, ringing in the ears, an "upside-down stomach," burning in the legs, sense of having a hot face, feeling cold all over, and a past history of vaginal bleeding. She had been to a surgeon who had performed a D&C, but she stopped being his patient because there seemed little else he could do for her. She was still angry at him because he didn't have any time for her. She had then seen the chiropractor. He had helped her arthritic pains somewhat, but, as she had continued to have many different problems, he referred her to me for a more thorough evaluation.[1]

Mary M lived with her husband who had had a stroke and was quite ill. They had no children, and she was the only person who could care for him. At our first meeting, I sensed a lot of restless chatter on her part, most of it vague and unfocused, and presented with extreme anxiety. I undertook to sort out her physical and emotional problems and began a full workup. At the same time, I offered to treat

---

[1] The reason a patient leaves her physician often foreshadows the main problem that will arise in a new relationship. The manner, the style in which a patient leaves a physician is also highly predictive. In Mary M's case, (a) she felt the surgeon didn't have enough time for her, and (b) she had been subtly "turfed" by the surgeon to the chiropractor, and from the latter (not so subtly) to me.

her "bad nerves" with a mild sedative.[2] She had already been treated with 15 mg of oxazepam, but it was "not strong enough." Her other medications included cimetadine (for dyspepsia, I think) and a thiazide diuretic (for fluid accumulation?).

Blood tests showed she had a low sodium level, so I asked her to stop the diuretic. She did and said she felt a bit stronger. Soon afterward, however, she phoned with severe abdominal pain. When she came in, she complained bitterly: "My nerves is all gone, my stomach feels sick, I couldn't take the Tigan, I feel depressed, I'm so weak. . . . " I prescribed vitamins and an antacid, took an electrocardiogram, which was normal, and commiserated with her over the situation with her sick husband.

Over the next few months, she often complained about being tired and worrying about her husband. Mainly though she complained about upsetting bodily sensations—burning in the legs, burning in the stomach, feeling "all in," numb and cold legs, constipation, ringing in the ears. I encouraged her to talk about her situation and continued my workup, in the process uncovering diverticulosis and sciatica, which I treated with medicine.

By January 1984, we had established a pattern: Mary M would come in for her appointment, starting to talk before she had even gotten through the door. Once inside, she would chatter nonstop, reciting one complaint after another in a monotone, giving me little time to write them all down, and still less time to respond. When I tried to respond, she seemed not to hear. She wouldn't stop her talking, wouldn't acknowledge what I said, wouldn't engage me in a discussion. She'd just ramble on to another set of symptoms. When I brought this to her attention, she'd apologize perfunctorily, then continue the same behavior. I wrote in one of my notes, "Doesn't listen, just talks."[3]

---

[2] She had offered "bad nerves" and "depression" as problems in her very first session. If I had pursued this right away, rather than going into an investigation of her medical condition, I might have had a better chance of short-circuiting her ensuing somatic obsessiveness.

I prescribed the initial sedative because her agitation made me uncomfortable, and I felt she must also have been very uncomfortable. I might have done better just to acknowledge her feelings, and plan to explore them with her the next time we met.

[3] This was already a challenge. Had I persevered, focusing on "what she was doing" rather than on what she was saying, I might have been able to help her look at her illness behavior. By withdrawing from this attempt, I allowed her to direct our interaction, and focus it around her somatic complaints.

She stayed on her sedative, and continued her regular visits. Yet soon she upped the ante. She asked for more frequent visits, and interspersed these with many phone calls, inquiring about one or another physical complaint. She also visited the emergency room several times. "I had to go to the emergency room last week," she'd say, and then pour forth a torrent of obsessive rumination.

In 1984 she visited me 23 times:

January (one visit): She had a bad cold, aches and pains, was nervous, felt she had sinus trouble, and felt her legs were icy.

February (one visit): "I get that awful sick feeling now'n'again, tired, weak, I had it bad in the back, from my head to my chin. . . . "

March (one visit): "Doing well, but a lot of worries about my husband. He needs a lot of attention." She still had headaches, cramps in the legs, cold feet.

April (three visits): This month marked an intensification of her visits. First visit: Her abdomen ached. She thought she might have cancer. Her physical exam and blood tests were normal, but she worried she was ill with something terrible. Not sensing anything new was happening, I refilled her medicines and asked her to return in a month.

Second visit: She insisted on being seen. "I'm not feeling good. I had to come back for a visit. I'm weak, can't get out of bed." Her neck hurt, her stomach was aching, the house was cold, her knees hurt, and (finally) "Is it my heart?" I tried to talk to her about her depression, attempted to reassure her about her heart, even started her on an antidepressant.

Third visit: She came back a week later. The arthritis medicine gave her heartburn, and she refused to take the antidepressant because she feared it would make her weak. I was so dismayed that I wrote in the chart, "Patient in impossible situation, is not likely to be helped."[4]

---

[4]Once the physician says the patient is "not likely to be helped," a problem has developed. If the physician continues trying to help, efforts are doomed by the self-fulfilling prophecy. Furthermore, the patient will sense the lack of hope. In retrospect, it might be better to tell the patient something like, "Gee, I don't know if I can help you at this point." Or, "It must all seem pretty hopeless to you, doesn't it." The Mental Research Institute people call this assuming the one-down position. It also entails telling the patient, not the chart, what I was thinking, thus taking a meta-approach to the relationship—that is, standing alongside it instead of in the middle of it. This pushes the discussion to the level on which things are happening. Avoiding this does two things: (1) it makes treatment a charade, because no one is really convinced of its

May (two visits): No pills agree with her. She is "wobbly and weak. . . . Something's wrong with my heart, and the pains, and my legs, and the feet." She appeared severely agitated, and talked nonstop in a croaky voice. Both sessions were filled with constant complaining, darting from one topic to another. She would not discuss her husband now, but instead focused monomaniacally on her aches and pains. She rejected antidepressants and refused all arthritic medications. Now she started refusing to leave my office. When I rose to usher her to the door, she simply kept talking. I literally had to guide her out of the room. Frequently, she would then rush back with another question just as I was about to see my next patient.[5]

At this point, I raised the question of psychotherapy to her.[6] I explained that she seemed very upset, and I wondered if she might like to talk to a counselor in our office who was skilled in helping people deal with such feelings. She refused. Instead, she insisted on phoning, coming in more and more frequently with complaints of burning stomach, constipation, arthralgias, cold feet, and weakness, and wanting more frequent appointments.[7]

I said I would see her every 3 weeks, defining this as "supportive therapy." In spite of this, she phoned more frequently, insisting on coming in every 2 weeks, then every week, then every few days.[8]

---

value; (2) it takes away from the physician a chance to ask the patient what she'd want to do if the situation couldn't change, thereby shifting the burden of treatment off the physician's back and offering to redefine the relationship rather than get mired in it. I did not seize this chance.

It also raises the question of goals. Mary M's goal was relief of her pains; mine was to stop her complaining. Were they the same?

[5]This was another missed opportunity. As I saw this pattern develop, I might have brought her back into the office, sat her down, and discussed her actions with her, commenting that she seemed to need more time, noting how upset she'd been with her previous doctor not giving her more time, and then asking what she wanted. Instead, I was so glad when she finally left the office, I strongly resisted any thought of bringing her back for more.

[6]This had to be taken as a rejection, which it was.

[7]Mary M was not consciously behaving in this way. She was not deliberately trying to make my life miserable. Her behavior pointed at her problem. By reacting to her naggy behavior as others had, I missed the chance to step outside it, observe its pattern, and intervene to change it. I became part of the problem.

[8]Simple sympathy was not going to work. First, I was angry, not sympathetic, and she had to sense this. Second, there was no concrete basis on which I'd agreed to see her "supportively" because we disagreed about what we were supposed to be doing. We each had a different agenda. We each felt jammed and cheated. This was the process that needed attention, and there was no need for superficial expressions of sympathy.

In July, she appeared with a sister who was visiting from Ireland. The sister said Mary M seemed in a state of exhaustion from caring for her husband, yet rejected any efforts to get help. She agreed that Mary M's physical complaints reflected chronic stress and exhaustion, but she felt Mary wouldn't listen to anyone. "She's a worrier," the sister commented. "Now she thinks she has cancer."[9]

In early July, Mary M asked for a urine culture. In mid-July, she asked for a throat culture. In late July, she demanded to come in as an emergency. She was having heartburn. She'd stopped taking her sedative. She rambled from system to system in a fervor. I tried to listen, tried to link her complaints to her worry and her exhaustion, but it was no use. She would pause for a moment, then quickly switch to complain about another part of her body. She was driving me crazy. It was all I could do to get her to stop talking long enough to get her out of the room.[10] In August, she complained about her legs. She was sick all over, distraught. I ran through one home remedy after another—oil of peppermint, charcoal, antacids, heat, rest, tea . . . all to no avail.[11]

In late August, I hit again upon the idea of referring her to our counselor. Medicare would pay for it. I told her I felt it was important to try and talk about her worry and depression, because I felt it was her nerves that were causing so many of her bodily problems. I was at the end of my rope, and, probably sensing this, at this point she agreed.[12]

She saw Dr. Cohen, one of our therapists, four times in late August and September.[13] His notes comment (in part):

8/27/84: "Mary doesn't like to complain to anyone about any-

---

[9] This was possibly another self-fulfilling prophecy by someone else who'd been sucked in as part of the problem.

[10] In retrospect, it seems I missed a chance here to tell her how damned frustrating she was, and to explore with her why this was so. The difference in being frustrated and *saying* you feel frustrated is that in the first case the patient knows you're angry but thinks you can't talk about it, and therefore she can't talk about her part in it, either; in the second case the whole interaction is on the table to discuss, *together*.

[11] Of course.

[12] This was actually a good thing to do. I was making an effort to disentangle myself from the processs, since I seemed unable to cope with it adequately. I was inviting another professional to come in and help. The way I conceived of it, though, was not that the counselor would help me get disentangled, but rather that he would take Mary M off my hands. Because the referral was essentially riddance behavior on my part, it was probably perceived as a rejection by Mary M, and was doomed. The act had potential, but the process undercut it.

[13] Actually, an impressive number of visits, given all that went on before.

thing. She is in the middle of coming to terms with her husband's and her own mortality."

9/5/84: "Mary has a surfeit of anger and expresses only some of it directly. The rest comes out through obsessive ruminations about her health, etc. The more she tries to talk to people (through complaining), the more she turns them off, and the more anger she stores up."[14]

9/21/84: "Connection between nerves, fear of her own or husband's demise, and physical pains."

9/28/84: "Pains are all worse when she is nervous. She mentioned fear of her husband John's eventual need for a nursing home and her own physical deterioration as primary among her worries. At the end of the hour, Mary agreed that she was stressed, and that she would probably do better if she talked more about her life with someone, but she has decided to consult with Dr. Glenn (to question physical rather than psychological etiology) before making another appointment."

There were no further sessions with Dr. Cohen. After each session with him, she found her way to my office during the ensuing week with some physical complaint. After the fourth session, she came in with her same old complaints, saying "I'm not sure anything helps."[15] Two weeks later, she (cheerily!) complained of "having those lousy old pains again—cold feet, I had to lie down, my head was heavy, I'm awful nervous; it's hard caring for John, and the health aide doesn't help."

I planned to keep seeing her every 2 weeks for "supportive care,"[16] since I felt she needed to present her physical complaints to me and would not deal with the emotional side of things separately.[17] Yet this

---

[14]This could have been something to pursue, to link up to my own feelings about this patient. Clearly, we were both furious, but neither of us was talking about it. I have often noticed that the patient somehow manages to create *in the physician* the very same distressing feelings from which he or she is suffering. We call this "mirroring," and it has a rich tradition in the literature on transference and countertransference. The point to bringing this up is, that when a physician starts noticing feelings like this, the time is ripe for using those feelings as a guide to understanding what is happening between physician and patient, and how this reflects the patient's basic predicament in the world.

[15]Rather than pick up on this invitation to discuss the *process*, I seem to have been overwhelmed with having her back on my hands again. I said nothing. My behavior, in retrospect, was an exact mirror for her own. The "problem-system" had been reestablished.

[16]Compare note 8.

[17]Here, I am unintentionally fostering a mind–body split organized around a biomedical physician and a feelings-oriented therapist.

plan would not work. She insisted on coming in more and more frequently. I almost had to push her out of the office to get her to leave. Finally, I confronted her with this fact, but I did it so angrily that all she could do was apologize, and there was no chance of discussing what was happening. She phoned more and more frequently, went to the emergency room more and more. Dr. Cohen and I discussed the situation. as we had during the weeks of her therapy. I refused the idea of a joint session. I was against the idea of "paradoxing" her by demanding that she come in more and more often, or insisting on daily visits or phone calls, because—to tell the truth—I did not want her to be more dependent on the practice.[18]

Mary's sister left to return to Ireland. Her neighbor, who often came in with her, told me she felt as helpless as I did. Dr. Cohen was willing to see her, but she did not want to see him. All I wanted was for her to stop annoying me; I had become like the doctor she'd left before, thereby fulfilling Dr. Cohen's observation about how Mary drove

[18]I wanted to get rid of her. Perhaps at this point it might have worked if I'd asked her to come in more and more frequently, or at least to phone daily. The problem was I felt I didn't want her to become more and more dependent on me. But I didn't really want her to be independent: I wanted her to leave. And yet, here she was, constantly wanting to come in. If I didn't see her, she would come or call anyway. I felt I was in a power struggle. It was unthinkable to "paradox" her by telling her to come in more frequently, because that felt like "letting her win." I was locked into a power struggle with her, and had to reassert my control, rationalizing it by saying she "shouldn't" abuse the medical services. The better move would have been to comment on how wretched a relationship we had developed, on how angry we were at one another, and on how helpless both of us felt. Yet this did not occur to me, because I was so involved in the process. I was so angry, I couldn't look at Mary M objectively any more.

It strikes me how I clung to the dimension of *power* and avoided that of *affect*. In a way, as Marty has pointed out to me, both Mary M and I were collaboratively using our power tussles to keep us both from dealing with affect—her anger at the strokes of fate, her fear of dying, her grief for her husband's situation, her guilt; my anger at her insistent clinging, my feelings around death and loss, and so on.

I was now dreading her visits. Each one seemed to be a victory for her and a defeat for me. I was by now so much a "part of the problem" that I was unable to help or see that I could not help. Instead of trying to solve the problem and "cut the knot," I was myself obsessed with the power struggle. If she refused to see Dr. Cohen, then I would refuse to see her more frequently than once every 2 weeks. If she refused to take antidepressants, then I would refuse to take her somatic complaints seriously. Step by step, I was abandoning my commitment to provide care, which was the only basis for her coming to see me. The more ferociously she clung to the patient role (helpless, dependent, demanding), the more ferociously I refused to relinquish my doctor role (setting limits, prescribing treatment, making myself comply with her entreaties and demands). I could not get beyond this to grasp the next order of change.

people away. In spite of my training, I hadn't been able to get beyond my anger.

Nor did I consider a consultation with a therapist—for myself.[19] This might actually have been reasonable, as I was locked into the situation. A therapist might have helped me get a handle on what was happening. Instead, I told myself this was "her" problem, not mine. If Mary insisted on bringing up physical complaints, refusing to see Dr. Cohen, take medication, and so on, and kept asking about physical illness, then I would ask for a consultation with a gastroenterologist. I then referred her to the local gastrointestinal (GI) man. He, of course, said she was healthy, and he told her that I was doing whatever should be done. He didn't want to take her on. I instructed my secretaries not to give her any more emergency appointments, as they did no good. Taking the hint, Mary M left my practice.[20]

Writing this up proved to be an educational experience. I was amazed at how overinvolved I'd become with this patient, to the point of losing my own perspective. I was struck by Dr. Cohen's correct appraisal of the situation, and by my failure to take it to heart. After reflecting on this write-up, I did several things.

First, I contacted Mary M and asked her how she was doing. She said she was as bad as ever. I offered to see her again, and she came in. So I have another chance to help her deal with her unhappiness and somatic distress.

Next, I talked to Dr. Cohen about our own interaction. I felt he had seen the problem clearly, but hadn't been able to confront me about my own behavior. We discussed this. He said some of his hesitation came from feeling like a newcomer working in "my" practice. Some came from his feelings about doctors being on a pedestal. Some had to do with his feelings about his father of whom I reminded him, and also with difficulties he had in confronting people.

This discussion led to a critique about how we were working together collaboratively. Collaboration is not always rosy. It opens each of us up to criticism, and we have to be ready to deal with this. In Dr. Cohen's case, he had to be ready to stand up to a physician 15 years his senior. In my case, I had to be open to exploring my own countertransferential issues. Our discussion led us to redefine our working

[19]This idea came from Nellie Grose from Houston.
[20]The circle was complete.

relationship, open it up to mutual criticism, and relabel such criticism as valuable communication.

One final thought. While I now have another chance to approach this woman's problems, my partner has pointed out to me that "not all problems have a solution." That is, we may try as hard as we can, but the problem may persist in spite of our best efforts. This understanding is a sober antidote for the wish to solve all problems, cure all ills. Sometimes, with some patients, this is just not possible.

EDITORS' COMMENTS

Dr. Glenn has provided us with a painful look into the complex web of the doctor-patient relationship. It is a rare form of risky self-disclosure to discuss a painful case in this detail; we are grateful to Dr. Glenn for his courage and honesty. Our comments are made in the context of respect for a friend and colleague who has shared a torturous relationship that is painfully familiar to practicing physicians. In writing about his relationship with Mrs. M, Dr. Glenn has begun the process of healing the doctor-patient relationship. Stepping back and writing about the case has made apparent to him alternatives that were previously invisible. As commenting editors we shall do the same.

A final introductory note: This was a hard case to put into our levels of involvement, since operationally the case was managed at an information level but now in Dr. Glenn's retrospective analysis it is written in level five systems terms. We chose to view the case as an example of a level two intervention that was doomed because level five was necessary.

Our focus from a more distant perspective is not on the individuals involved in this conflict, but on their relationship. In the midst of the conflict between Dr. Glenn and Mrs. M, a key decision was made to avoid a joint session with a therapist. If these collaborative sessions had been held, physical complaints, emotional discomfort, and potentially manipulative behavior by the patient and the physician might have been available to the therapist for observation and comment. The major therapeutic intervention would not have had to be directed solely toward the patient but more broadly toward the doctor-patient relationship. A systems view of the conflict suggests that the physician could modify his role in the dysfunctional interaction. In this case, it may have been counterproductive for the physician to try alone to be helpful. The issue is not whether to use a paradoxical suggestion toward the patient but what could both the physician and the patient do differently to reduce the pain in their relationship.

Mrs. M had a history of unsatisfactory relationships with doctors. These physicians had become her metaphorical family and were locked into repeatedly destructive interactions. The individual skills of the physician were unlikely to change the pattern of these interactions unless the physician specifically invited the therapist to intervene: The patient's "family" needed therapy. Without the presence of a third party to destabilize the process, few changes were likely to be created even by the most skilled physician.

An underlying lesson in this poignant case is that when the doctor-patient relationship is out of order, both the doctor and the patient need to meet with the therapist. This unconventional approach assumes that the physician is unwittingly contributing to maintaining the presenting problem. Simply separating the conflicting coreactors (physician and patient) by an attempted referral maintains the status quo and is antithetical to a systems, contextual approach to patient care. Selvini-Palazzoli, Boscolo, Cecchin, and Prata (1980) have described how referrals to therapists are sabotaged when the physician-patient-family relationship is enmeshed and dysfunctional.

Every physician with a busy practice is prone to have several such deadlocked relationships with patients and families. In these cases, the unconventional and risky step of inviting a trusted therapist to help with the doctor-patient relationship offers, in our view, the best hope of breaking the deadlock. The benefits of change will accrue to both the patient and the physician.

Readers who are intrigued by Dr. Glenn's case report are referred to his book *On Diagnosis* (Glenn, 1985).

CRITICAL ILLNESS WHILE ON VACATION

JOHN J. DALLMAN
Wayne State University

This case involves a family who, while on vacation a long distance from home, had a family member become critically ill. To handle this difficult situation, several specialists, a Lear jet, and a family physician were involved.

Mrs. K, a 55-year-old white female, came to our hospital's emergency room one evening in respiratory failure. She was from a midwestern state traveling to Florida on vacation with her family, which included a husband and two children. She required immediate intubation and respiratory support by a mechanical ventilator, and admission to the intensive care unit. This woman was on no medications and had been thought to be in good health prior to her admission. She did not smoke, had had no symptoms except for a minor amount of shortness of breath with mild lethargy for only a few days prior to admission. She had visited a tourist attraction and handled a parrot just a few days prior to her onset of symptoms.

Physical examination revealed a healthy female who appeared to be her stated age with mildly diminished breath sounds in her left midlung field, dullness to percussion in the left lung base, and rales throughout the left lung. Within a few hours, her condition deteriorated, and she developed frank congestive heart failure and pulmonary edema.

The laboratory tests and initial x-rays indicated no significant changes in her complete blood count or electrolytes, but an opaque, poorly defined density was noted in her midleft lung field. Frank pulmonary edema was evident in the subsequent x-rays.

Aggressive therapy was instituted with diuretics, digoxin, and positive end-expiratory pressure ventilation. Appropriate antibiotics were added to cover psittocosis, or an underlying pneumonia from other causes. Blood, sputum, and urine cultures were obtained. Both pulmonary and infectious disease consults were obtained.

Mrs. K responded to the aggressive therapy within 24 hours, but remained dependent on the respirator. Meanwhile, her family was very anxious about her condition and wanted to know what had happened. As the family physician on call, I attempted to reassure the family that all the expertise available was being brought to bear for Mrs. K, but that so far, no known cause for her respiratory failure had been identified. Three days went by; Mrs. K's condition improved, but she could not be successfully weaned from the ventilator. The mass remained in her left lung, and she remained afebrile.

Thoracic surgery was consulted, in concert with the pulmonary and infectious disease specialists, to discuss the most efficacious procedure for obtaining more data on the left lung mass. Bronchoscopy or needle biopsy by fluoroscopy was finally ruled out because Mrs. K could not ventilate herself during the procedure. On the fourth day of her hospital stay, Mrs. K was taken to the operating room and an open lung biopsy was performed. A day later, the pathology reports were unequivocal—Mrs. K had adenocarcinoma of the lung. An oncologist was consulted; his recommendations were for immediate chemotherapy by protocol, but he indicated a poor prognosis for survival.

Meanwhile, the family had spent a very anxious week awaiting the test results. They were staying in a local motel and accumulating large bills just to be near their wife and mother. A decision now had to be made: Should chemotherapy start now, in this hospital, many hundred miles from home, even though we all knew that an even longer hospital stay would be necessary? Since the prognosis for recovery was doubtful even with chemotherapy, the family was counseled that even with excellent medical care, Mrs. K might not survive the rigors of the therapy. She could die in this strange hospital, in a town a long way from home with no opportunity to interact with any of her many other relatives and friends.

Since the patient was able to breath only minimally without ventilator assistance, conventional transportation to their home in the Midwest was out of the question. I finally suggested that she could be airlifted by jet air ambulance directly to her hometown, where personnel from her local hospital could transport her via ambulance to a waiting bed in the intensive care unit.

The K family agreed that they should risk the trip by jet even though there was a possibility Mrs. K would die on the trip. They felt it would be better for her to be in her home hospital where friends and relatives could visit her.

Consequently, a jet was summoned. The hospital furnished a respiratory therapist to go with the patient, and she was successfully airlifted home. She lived only a few more weeks, but at least was able to visit with her friends and relatives, and prepare for her death in familiar surroundings.

The K family was extremely grateful to me for intervening at each step along the way. Convening the specialists, assisting them with the diagnostic decision making, and eventually managing the patient's transport home were all integral parts of this case. Involving the family in the process aided their ability to cope with the disastrous outcome to their vacation.

EDITORS' COMMENTS

Unexpected medical disaster often leaves patients and families with very few meaningful choices. In this case, a family physician became coordinator for the larger medical team and an advocate for the family. The only worthwhile option available was to allow the patient to return home for her final days. The physician translated that request into action by directing a definitive diagnostic effort, addressing family frustrations during aggressive medical treatment, and securing an unusual resource (an air-jet ambulance). Ultimately, the care plan was modified in a reasonable fashion to meet the family's unique needs. The decision to move a critically ill patient was done with the family sharing the responsibility for the action. To have followed the usual medical protocol may have been technically defensible, but would have been insensitive to the context in which the patient presented for care while far from home. This family needed compassionate and collaborative administrative decisions, not therapy, to help them at a time of crisis. And Dr. Dallman provided what they needed.

LEVEL THREE CASES

FEELINGS AND SUPPORT

KNOWLEDGE BASE

Normal family development and reactions to stress.

PERSONAL DEVELOPMENT

Awareness of one's own feelings in relationship to the patient and family.

SKILLS

1. Asking questions that elicit family members' expressions of concerns and feelings related to the patient's condition and its effect on the family.
2. Empathically listening to family members' concerns and feelings, and normalizing them where appropriate.
3. Forming a preliminary assessment of the family's level of functioning as it relates to the patient's problem.
4. Encouraging family members in their efforts to cope as a family with their situation.
5. Tailoring medical advice to the unique needs, concerns, and feelings of the family.
6. Identifying family dysfunction and fitting a referral recommendation to the unique situation of the family.

COMPLICATIONS OF DIABETES

DENNIS M. McCULLOUGH
Wingra Family Medical Center
University of Wisconsin Medical School

Margaret had been a patient of mine for over 6 years when I returned from a Christmas holiday to find her hospitalized under the care of my partner. She had severe cellulitis of the foot, and she was depressed at the thought of losing her leg and her independence to surgical amputation.

She was 71 years old, widowed, and the mother of a true gang of 13 children, nearly all of whom lived in the region. Her diabetes and its multiple, severe, vascular and neurological complications confined her to an existence that would have forced most people into a nursing home. She managed on her own, living alone in her little rural cottage, slowed by her congestive heart failure, angina, and near blindness, but still capable of taking daily walks with her dog on her country road when the weather permitted. Now, a nail puncture wound in her foot, compromised by the diabetes, had brought on a crisis. I had seen her nearly monthly over the past 6 years, caring for minor infections of her nails and bladder, once diagnosing an occult pyometra, and forever recalling the night of her severe pulmonary edema in our little hospital's emergency room. We had quite a bond, she and I, for both of us knew that she had taught me a great deal about medicine and caring for patients.

When I walked into the ward to see her, I knew that this was to be a crisis of major proportion and perhaps her last. She was ill with fever, pale, short of breath, and perhaps most important of all, she had lost her spirit. Despite the intravenous antibiotics and aggressive local care, she had been deteriorating for several days, and she knew it. She wore a look I had never seen on her before. After her myocardial infarction and consequent bout of pulmonary edema, we had talked about the very real possibility of her losing her independence, and about death.

As we talked, the cause of her low spirits became obvious. Not only was the immediate threat of ascending gangrene and an overwhelming sepsis worrying her, but, with her usual insight, she saw the issue of her independent life on the line.

It was an old Yankee's greatest fear—the loss of self-reliance—the same issue I had encountered with so many of my older rural patients. It was an issue of wood pile and scything, of bread baking, and honoring grandchildren's birthdays. So many older folks are tucked into little quarters on seldom traveled roads, supported by a quiet and near invisible network of relatives and friends. I had been to Margaret's home and others like it before, seen the beds in the living room, encircled by useful and familiar paraphernalia spread on tables and chairs, beaten paths in the rugs showing the well-traveled routes to kitchen, bathroom, and front porch door.

Margaret's foot was swollen and angry, skin reddened and peeling to the knee. She seemed to be barely holding her own. She had already talked to my partner and the general surgeon who had helped her with many problems in the past. The issue of amputation had arisen, and recommendations, although not final, were hinted at during their visits with her. After my examination and talk with her, I felt that she was doomed either way.

Returning to the nursing station, I found the usual series of telephone messages from her family attached to the chart. Her family was always mobilized whenever Margaret was ill, although often in a very angry and dysfunctional way. Most of Margaret's 13 children were involved with problems related to alcohol, poverty, illness, and the law. My usual approach was to try to establish who among the 13 had their life under control at the moment. I chose one, and opened up the first of many discussions. This discussion centered on my being unavailable when they needed me, and contained threats about the hospital and comments on the quality of care Margaret was receiving. The conversation was further complicated by some feelings I had of guilt and remorse for my old patient and friend.

During the first 3 or 4 days, Margaret held her own while I tried to get a sense of the progression of her illness and her feelings. Pressure was mounting from our surgical consultant for an immediate amputation. I kept the family at bay with frequent telephone calls, and short conversations in the hospital during their visits, slowly introducing the options available to their mother (which they already had determined through group thinking, and by talking within their own family spheres).

When I spoke with individual family members, it was difficult for me to sense where the whole family stood on the subject of their mother's immediate and long-term care. Margaret, her family, the hospital staff, her consultants, my partner, and I all knew the issue— how long could we postpone making a decision about amputating Margaret's leg. Although I urged Margaret to at least consider amputation, she saw the operation as self-destructive, a virtually final act. Her adamancy on that issue, and her depression continued. I was certain that the end was near, with or without the amputation. Without a family consensus developing, I faced a personal dilemma. I chose to talk again to Margaret, together with as many members of her family as could attend—drunk or sober. Seven relatives appeared, and sweaty in our winter dress and aromatic as a logging camp, we all crowded into the small hospital room. I outlined the issues we faced.

I spent an hour talking with them, trying to find out why they could not unite in support of their mother. A single item stood out— the nail, which was described in profane epithets inspired by alcohol. I had heard some gory details already: ". . . stepped on a rusty nail when she was in the dirt-floored cellar of her house"; ". . . walked with it in her diabetes-anesthetized foot for roughly an hour without sensing its presence"; ". . . finally saw the blood coming into her stocking and shoe."

I previously had not spent much time over the details of the nail because the incident had occurred while I was away, and the injury was already being treated when I entered the case. The family's concern over the nail was so intense that I urged them to tell me more about it. What emerged was that guilt and blame over who was responsible for leaving the nail in Margaret's cellar was crippling the family's ability to function.

Margaret listened patiently as the discussion went back and forth among her children. Then, she intervened with a tone of voice suggesting the Margaret of old and laid to rest the issue of responsibility with the matriarchal command they all recognized: "Put a stop to that bickering." That did it. A few tears flowed, but more importantly, a new sense of will appeared now that the previously unspoken issue was out in the open.

It was the turning point in a long and difficult illness. Her depression lifted, and her body and foot responded. She still didn't want the amputation, and I agreed to support her choice now that the immediate risk of death from sepsis seemed less likely. With nearly continuous attendance at her bedside by her children and grandchildren, her condition improved. They fed and cared for her during the following months in a nursing home, and eventually helped to change the dressings on her chronically draining foot. When she returned home, the family stayed on around-the-clock for awhile, then just nights, eventually bowing to Margaret's insistence that she be left alone. Visiting nurses and I continued to visit.

Before Margaret got out on her first walk that spring, the injury to her foot flared up again. A bone scan revealed a small focus of osteomyelitis. This came as a cruel blow to me, after all the hours spent working with Margaret and her family, teaching nearly everyone except the dog how to change the dressing. Margaret took it more stoically. She had regained her sense of independence, and now was more able to accept the idea of amputation. The issue of the nail and the guilt surrounding it had been healed by time. The decision to go ahead with the operation was made with surprising ease by Margaret and her family.

Her hospitalization and the amputation went extremely well, and no problems were associated with her acceptance of the prosthesis.

That was 4 years ago. Even now at least half of the children will telephone my office to talk to me when she gets a bladder infection or a cold, and their complaints are always the same: "Why weren't you available when . . . ?" However, we have an understanding now, which makes it easier for me, and when we need to, there is never a problem getting them together to talk with and about their mother.

EDITORS' COMMENTS

Who helped whom through this medical and family crisis? Dr. McCullough convened the family at their mother's bedside in order to resolve the physician's "personal dilemma" about amputation. Longitudinal contact with this patient and her family had set the stage for a potent interaction. In that conference, did the proud mother's will to live and her functional role in the family really return in a manner that significantly augmented her existing, but previously failing, medical therapy? If yes, then by what biopsychosocial mechanism?

As a case study, this does not represent a controlled trial for demonstrating the efficacy of convening the family. However, it can move us to encourage such interactions rather than prevent them. In the future, we may move toward more clear understanding of the interactional process represented in this case. For the moment, we feel joy in knowing that physicians, patients, and families are capable of such interaction.

ACUTE VERTIGO IN A HOMEMAKER

GODFREY D. RIPLEY
Texas Tech University Health Science Center

I suddenly became very dizzy this morning. It was directly after breakfast, and quite suddenly I felt very dizzy as I walked out of the kitchen. I had to hold on to the wall to steady myself, and the feeling passed but has come back again a few times since. No, I have never felt this way before, and I do not feel nauseous or sick in any other way. As I drove over to see you, I had some feeling of dizziness again—not very bad but a little troublesome.

Virginia was a 33-year-old homemaker. Since coming into our town about 4 years previously, I had seen her perhaps twice for a checkup, Pap smear, and renewal of her contraceptive prescription. She had no significant past medical history and had always appeared to be healthy, active, and in good touch with her two children and husband. I had seen the family together a few times each year when the children had come in for camp physicals and occasional minor illnesses. A warm, well-nurtured unit, all members appeared to have good contact with one another, and were all able to communicate with me. Intelligent, perceptive, neat; the ideal unit for the family physician.

I felt some concern with her presentation: I do not enjoy diagnosing a subarachnoid bleed, hypertension, or intercranial tumor. Her physical examination was entirely normal—a supple neck, blood pressure of 120/80, optic disks clear. Her differential blood count showed a slight leukopenia.

> Virginia, I am happy to tell you that I can find no signs of sinister conditions causing your vertigo. The most probable cause is a viral infection of the balance tubes next to the ears—a labyrinthitis. This is the time of year when many people have flu or other viral upper respiratory infections, and although you have no signs of a cold, I think it is most likely that this is what you have. It will probably take a few days to get better, and perhaps your husband and children might develop flu-like symptoms. I shall prescribe some tablets for you that will probably reduce the dizziness. I would like you to call me at the end of the week and tell me how you are.

Virginia left the office with a smile and a "thank you." She had a prescription for 12 dimenhydrinate (Dramamine), 50 mg, together with my precautionary advice regarding alcohol and driving. I went in to see my next patient.

Two days later John, Virginia's husband, was on the phone to me early in the morning. "I am not satisfied with Virginia," he told me in what sounded very much like an angry voice. "Her dizziness has become worse since she saw you, and she can now barely walk. Your pills have done her no good at all." I asked him to bring her into the office. As he entered with Virginia, he looked as angry as he sounded. "I have stayed home from work to bring her over to you. Things are not right with her."

Virginia did not look well now; she looked disturbed. Her dizziness prevented her from walking normally, and it was not surprising that she looked somewhat apprehensive or anxious. John sat down with the obvious intention of staying in the room as I examined his wife. Clinically, she was as normal now as when I had seen her 2 days earlier. There was not one objective sign of pathology. I wondered what was going on here. Virginia did not appear in the least neurotic. Her symptoms were obviously both real and disabling. She sat, looking apprehensive, while John looked angry.

I am aware that you are both concerned about this dizziness; more so since it has become worse in spite of the tablets. There are no signs of any organic disease process causing the vertigo [they both looked a little calmer], and the fact that the tablets were of no use suggests that my earlier diagnosis that Virginia has labyrinthitis is wrong. [Now she looked puzzled, and he showed—could it be—justification?] Dizziness can also be the result of many processes that are not diseases—emotions and feelings—and when these are strong, then the dizziness can also be powerful. [Did they both look angry now?] Virginia, is there anything that has happened to you recently that could have contributed to you becoming more tense than usual, putting you under some strain or causing you to feel upset?

John answered for her. This, together with the sharpness of his tone, was not surprising considering this day's presentation. "There is nothing upsetting Virginia aside from the fact that she is not well now." Virginia looked at him, listened to his short disclaimer, looked a bit puzzled, and turned to me. "No, just as John says, I have no worries. The kids are well, and John and I get along very well with each other. I just don't like feeling ill, and this dizziness is just impossible to take."

They both looked at me accusingly. What was I missing? What sort of a doctor was I when I could not even diagnose a pretty common condition, let alone relieve it? The disappointment, the frustration, and the anger showed in their faces. "You have no family problems with your own parents; no money problems?" "Certainly not," John replied, before I had even finished. "In fact, we are enlarging our house, doubling the size of our kitchen, and adding a couple of rooms." A half-hearted smile, together with something else, passed over Virginia's face. "Just as soon as they get on with it."

As he heard his wife's comment and saw the flitting change in her demeanor, John suddenly sat forward, his face lighting up, and the angry tone vanished from his voice. "Could it be; could that be it, Virginia?"

They had finalized the plans with the contractor the previous month, the home extension being based around the remodeled kitchen. The new kitchen equipment was chosen with pride and had already been delivered to their home so that there would be no delay when the contractor was ready to install the units in the enlarged kitchen. This, he had said, would be 4 or 5 days after he started work on the present structure. Their garage was filled with cartons containing countertops and cabinets, a new oven and cooking top, the sink, floor tiles, lumber, and assorted hardware. He had been due to start the following week, and Virginia and John had decided that they could easily accept the inconvenience of their garage filled with boxes for perhaps 1 week, and the kitchen being upside down for up to another week. That was 8 weeks ago.

The contractor had not appeared on the promised day. Phone calls to his office had produced his apologies for a little delay, but two of his key workers had failed to appear. The days progressed; no workers appeared; the contractor said he would be over any time now. The days moved into weeks. Other excuses were given; the Chamber of Commerce, and the Better Business Bureau were contacted. Still, Virginia had to thread her way past the various cartons in the garage every time she went out to the car and returned home. She did not like the untidiness; she didn't even like leaving the cars out in the yard. It was not surprising that she felt frustrated and angry. If it had been too much for the contractor, why had he agreed to take on the job? If he had found that he had underquoted on the price, why hadn't he told them that he needed to renegotiate? Why couldn't John get in touch with him? As the weeks progressed, they realized that they would have to find another contractor. During the past week they had been visited by some promising people. However, nothing had yet been finalized.

As the story came out, partly from Virginia and partly from John, she cried every now and then, and he put his hand on hers. The tension within her was eased. She shared her physiologic response with John in an appropriate fashion, and, as she stood up, her face brightened. "I don't feel the dizziness now!" she said.

A new contractor started work on her kitchen the following Monday. By the end of that week, her garage was clear of cartons and again housing the cars. Virginia's dizziness did not return, and she was able to continue with her task of being a homemaker.

EDITORS' COMMENTS

Bravo, Dr. Ripley! In the face of an angry husband, this family physician stood his ground, did not offer double talk about needing more tests or other opinions, and honestly offered his best medical judgment. Avoiding a defensive posture and persevering in a potentially unpleasant encounter, he quietly asked if there were any recent stresses that could have contributed to the patient's feeling more tense than usual. After a brief flash of anger, the diagnosis was confirmed and the problem resolved.

Why is this type of physician behavior not praised just as we praise sound decision making and technical skill during surgical procedures? Physicians should be rewarded for demonstrating the courage to state a reasonable, though unpopular, diagnosis based on a medical history, physical examination, the patient's nonverbal communication, and an understanding of family dynamics. This case points to what is possible when a medically competent physician practices family-centered care with courage and sensitivity.

THE DELIVERY OF AN ABNORMAL BABY

PETER ROBERT GRANTHAM
University of British Columbia

Ellen, a 33-year-old woman, and Sam, her 34-year-old husband had three healthy children: 6-year-old Sarah, 3-year-old John, both delivered by cesarean section (cephalo-pelvic disproportion, failure to progress), and 15-year-old Dan, their foster child. Ellen and Sam decided that they wanted another natural child.

Sam and Ellen were a happy and mutually considerate young couple. Sam was a successful and moderately prosperous businessman with a national franchise. He traveled across the country, and was away from home frequently. Ellen used to be his secretary before they married. Their children had been planned and spaced using oral contraceptives.

Ellen's third pregnancy was essentially uneventful. Ultrasound examination at 16 and 36 weeks confirmed the due date, and 4 weeks from term, Ellen made an appointment with the obstetrician who had delivered her first two children. He booked an elective repeat cesarean section and tubal ligation for 39 weeks. Ellen was admitted to the hospital the afternoon before.

Although there was much demand for togetherness during labor and delivery in our community, Sam had never been keen on this. He was of the group of fathers who are content to wait outside the delivery suite in the old-fashioned way, and wait for the doctor or nurse to appear with the news regarding the new baby and report on his wife's welfare. He did not wish to be present for the cesarean, and Ellen was happy with this decision. Moreover, she requested some general anesthetic or sedation in addition to the usual epidural. The anesthetist who visited her the night before the surgery agreed.

On the day of the cesarean, there were some annoying last-minute alterations in the operating room scheduling that resulted in my not being present when anesthesia was administered and surgery begun. Sam was waiting outside. A routine cesarean section delivered a largish, unmistakably and unattractively abnormal baby girl. She had a large head resulting from extensive craniosynostosis, exophthalmos, and complete syndactyly of all digits on all four extremities. The baby had poor tone, but was active and had good color; APGARs 7 and 9. The initial reaction of the operating room was relief that Ellen was asleep. It provided us with a bit of time to think, organize our own emotions, and plan. Ellen was kept asleep perhaps slightly longer than usual, and did not effectively regain consciousness until she had been in the recovery room for about one-half hour.

Our first decision was to defer the planned sterilization procedure. A laparoscopic sterilization is readily available as an outpatient procedure. We felt Sam and Ellen might want a chance to reconsider this decision.

Next, I had to inform Sam, and I was not really sure how to tell him. We brought him in to see his baby, and I was completely taken aback by his first comment: "Is there some way we can get rid of it before Ellen wakes up?" Even with the advice of the nurses, the obstetrician, and the pediatrician, I was perplexed as to how best to proceed.

The major support we all needed came unexpectedly from Ellen's parents, who were waiting in her room. Before visiting Ellen, I spent some time talking with them. Their response was, in effect, "Well, she's ours and we'll love her just as much as any other baby." I admit to being obviously grateful for their making this major and firm decision so early. With more confidence, I was then able to return to Ellen in the recovery room where she was now conscious, holding Sam's hand, and awaiting answers to some questions. He'd told her only the sex and weight of the baby. It was not an easy hour and a half.

The next day, a marvelous consultant from the Department of Genetics arrived and provided support, information, and assistance. The baby, Sheila, had Apert's syndrome and a large ventricular septal defect. Treatment was available, but it involved years of multiple surgical procedures.

The next week, while Ellen and Sheila were still in the hospital, we spent hours reviewing what we knew, and what we thought we should do. Should they take the baby east or to Europe to a famous medical center? How do they explain the craniofacial, hand, and toe deformities to the other children? One gut-wrenching question after another. Ellen's parents provided the major support for Ellen. Sam was rational in his questions, and practical in his solutions, but the major burden clearly fell on Ellen. She grew visibly more composed and confident as time progressed, and she emerged as the central figure in the family, a reversal of my previous perception.

Four weeks postpartum, after a series of consultations with a neurosurgeon, a plastic surgeon, an orthopedic surgeon, a hand surgeon, a cardiologist, and an ophthalmologist, a clear plan of management emerged.

A new source of support and assistance appeared—a family 150 miles away with a little girl with the same congenital syndrome. The girl was now 5 years old, and had already undergone a long series of facial and hand operations. Sam and Ellen visited the family, and discussed their adaptation to and acceptance of their daughter's various physical problems. They provided the third major source of strength and support for this threatened young family.

As the months went by, Sheila's hospitalizations, and endless outpatient and office visits took their toll on Sam and Ellen. Sam left more and more to Ellen, and she grew to meet the challenges. For the first 2 months, Ellen didn't take Sheila out very often, but eventually Ellen accepted the stares and unthinking questions of curious children. Recently, she told me a delightful story about her 6 year old, Sarah. Ellen had taken Sheila to Sarah's school one day. After that, Sarah was plagued with questions from the other children about her "funny-looking" sister. A few days later, Sarah said, "You know, there's a little girl at school something like Sheila, so I went over today and sat with her 'cause nobody else wants to."

What I've learned from this family is that my physician's knowledge, experience, or opinion are not necessarily major determinants of how things will go. My role is to provide information, discuss options and priorities, and give an informed opinion. But, most importantly, I must be prepared to adapt to the changes in family members as they grow, and support the decisions they make. I feel I have played a small but significant role in supporting this family through a crisis. Ellen assures me that I provided a thread of continuity throughout the multitude of specialist interviews, visits, and procedures. More difficulties undoubtedly lie ahead, but I feel confident about my relationship with this family.

EDITORS' COMMENTS

"Minor but significant role"—this ironic phrase nicely captures the physician's work with this family. "Minor" because the family, blessed with considerable internal and external resources, did most of the work on their own. "Significant" because Dr. Grantham's presence provided the continuity and served as the linchpin in this family's complex journey from devastating diagnosis to complex negotiations with the health care system. He was with them for information and emotional support. He learned, suffered, and rejoiced alongside them. In fact, at a critical moment early in the case, Dr. Grantham unabashedly relied on the emotional support of the baby's grandparents. The primary medical treatment for this child will be highly specialized, but the family physician's "minor but significant" role with the family has rewards that run deep.

A PATIENT WITH CHRONIC HEADACHE

DANIEL P. RAINS
Private practice, New Castle, Indiana

Ms. E, a 21-year-old woman, came to my office for help with her headaches. She said it was time for her to have a complete physical examination. Her symptoms were very typical of tension headaches, which were occurring on a nearly daily basis. Upon examining her, I did not find any signs of increased intracerebral pressure, or similar problems. During her complete physical, she mentioned that she didn't like having pelvic exams, they always hurt her, and that she also had painful intercourse. Anatomically, her pelvic examination was also normal, although she expressed some discomfort. (I take a lot of interest in seeing that my patients are comfortable during examination, going slowly, explaining all the steps involved, and not even proceeding if I feel that they are not yet ready for examination. Discomfort during an otherwise normal examination is therefore unusual and I suspect a sexual/emotional problem as well as the possibility of an occult pathologic cause.) After she had dressed, we spent more time talking about her background. She had left home at age 15, and gotten married about 1 year later. She had one child, age 3. She was the oldest child in her family of origin. Her father was an alcoholic, and she recalled many episodes of her mother being beaten so badly that she would be in bed for several days. Ms. E would then be left in charge of the younger children, cooking, cleaning, and so on. In fact, this combination—her mother's abuse and her excessive parenting responsibilities—were the reasons she left her home at a young age. She denied any personal abuse or knowledge of any of the other children being abused. Her mother and father subsequently divorced, and the father lived some distance away.

Her choice of words amazed me; they sounded straight from a text of behavioral medicine. She said that in the family, "I was the one always in control," and "I have a great deal of trouble handling my anger." With the above information in hand, I went out on a limb and said, "Based on what you have told me so far about your family I would think you would have a lot of anger toward your father." She immediately replied, "Yes, and he is coming to visit next week." Another sibling was getting married, and she was very concerned that both her father and mother would be at the wedding. She was fearful that she would once again be the one in control and would have to deal with the anger she held toward her father.

She also expressed happiness in her involvement over the last year in a fairly fundamentalist church that seemed to be a source of many of her friends and social supports. (In fact, she later sought counseling with the pastor of this church, to which I did not object. However, it did not seem to solve her problems, and she was unwilling to follow through with a family therapist as I had suggested.)

We talked about her pain with intercourse and her sexual experiences. In spite of the pain and tension she displayed during my examination, and the anger she felt toward her father, she said she was orgasmic. I had trouble believing this, faced with the mentioned incongruities, but she did not stray from this position on subsequent visits either.

She responded dramatically to some heat and massage applied on an outpatient basis, but seemed unable to follow up on this treatment on a long-term basis. She, as mentioned, did not follow up with the family therapist as I recommended. She would not arrange for her husband and son to come in for a family interview, and she was not receptive to the idea of a home visit. She continues to come in periodically, usually with the same kind of problems. The visit with her father at the wedding went well.

Ms. E has already, to me, accomplished quite a bit, given her family background, but chooses to maintain a large blind spot instead of coping in more depth with her feelings about her parents, her headaches, her siblings, and her body in general. My main goal with her was to try to create a positive framework for everyday functioning so that she would not waste a lot of money on remedies or tests. By doing this, I hoped to help her maintain or improve her current level of functioning. At the same time, I was aware that a crisis would come up sooner or later in her marriage, social life, parenting, or other aspect of her life. Meanwhile, I continued to listen for an opportunity to give her permission to find new ways to deal with her feelings, especially her anger.

EDITORS' COMMENTS

We admired this case at two levels: the physician's skill in evaluating the family context of the patient's headaches, and his patience in supporting the patient while waiting for the nearly inevitable crisis forming in her life. Once having uncovered the psychosocial origins of a problem such as headaches, it can be difficult for the physician to accept the patient's pace in working on these issues. This patient was not even willing to have a family conference or a home visit. Rather than rejecting her for not allowing him to use his psychosocial skills, Dr. Rains wisely accepted his powerlessness to compel her to deal with her family problems. Instead, he supported her surprisingly high level of functioning, helped her to avoid unnecessary medical workups and treatments, and waited patiently for another time when she might be ready to confront the dark side of her life.

DEATH AS A PART OF FAMILY LIFE

PETER A. GOODWIN
with ROBERT B. TAYLOR
Oregon Health Sciences University

A 76-year-old active married male, Mr. X, who owned and operated his own business, was seen with a 4-month history of progressive exertional dyspnea and fatigue. He was frequently light-headed, and suspected an "obstruction of the blood flow to his brain" because he was unable to concentrate or think as clearly as before. He complained of much flatulence but no loss of appetite, no weight loss, and no change of bowel habit. Apart from severe pallor and a positive test for occult blood in the feces, the examination was normal. The blood count showed a profound iron deficiency anemia. A barium enema x-ray examination revealed a carcinoma of the ascending colon. A right hemicolectomy was performed, and a solitary nodule of the liver removed, which subsequently confirmed metastatic cancer.

Mr. X initially attempted to deny the implications of the operative findings. At first, he brushed aside the recommendation by a surgical oncologist that liver perfusion with anticancer agents be performed, as he feared it would affect his sexual functioning. After a delay of several months, however, he agreed. The treatment was performed over several weeks with no complications.

I had cared for Mr. X's wife for several years for hypertension, severe coronary artery disease, and angina pectoris, but had seen him only on rare occasions prior to the onset of this illness. He had impressed me as a stubborn, demanding man. The couple had three children, a son and two daughters. I had seen each as patients on occasion, but was not their primary physician. The children seldom visited their parents. Two of them had expressed resentment of their father's overbearing attitude to them, and the third was timid and self-effacing.

I saw Mr. X 1 year later; he had been followed by the surgeon in the interim. His primary complaint was of back pain, which he blamed on surgery done many years before for a lumbar disc. He had lost weight, which he ascribed to a conscious effort to eat less, and he had much abdominal cramping. He was superficially jovial, denied the likelihood of any serious problem, but was obviously fearful. A CT scan confirmed the clinical diagnosis of carcinomatosis of the abdomen. In addition, metastases were widespread in both lungs.

The oncologist and surgeon were consulted, and agreed that chemotherapy would not be helpful. Mr. X was informed of the diagnosis and prognosis. His denial was obvious, and he wanted "something done." After discussing the issues privately with his wife, and with her concurrence, I prescribed a small daily dose of oral cyclophosphamide (Cytoxan), telling him that it was "worth a try," and would not be unduly toxic. A month later a friend recommended to him a South American herb tea reputed to have produced miraculous cures. It appeared to have no ill effects on him, and I supported him in its use.

Two months later, Mr. X had an episode of persistent vomiting and abdominal pain. When I saw him at home, his wife and one daughter were present. After the acute symptoms subsided, I arranged a conference with his wife and children to ascertain their ideas about the appropriate management of his terminal illness. They agreed that his interests would best be served by their attempting to care for him at home as long as possible, and the children agreed to share the load with their mother. The local hospice organization was alerted to his condition and agreed to respond to whatever nursing help the family needed. (They were actively involved only in the final 10 days or so.)

I visited Mr. X at least weekly, to evaluate his progress physically and emotionally. He was fully accepting of my medical care, but my attempts to gently draw him out about unmet psychological needs were met by remarks such as "I am satisfied" and "I have led a full life."

In passing, I must mention that grandchildren, and one greatgrandchild had been free to come and go as they pleased, and on more than one occasion were ushered out of the room only when I commenced my examination.

Mr. X remained demanding of his family to the end, requiring them to turn him, prop him up, get him closer to or further from the window, and so on. The children bathed him, cleansed him, fed him, and for the last three days, under the supervision of the hospice staff, managed his intravenuous fluids and medication. His wife, too, was intimately involved in his care, but was spared those tasks involving unusual physical effort on her part. I was impressed by, and wondered at, their willingness and good humor in the face of his unyielding gruffness.

Mr. X died at home the day after my last visit.

Three days later, I visited the family and found them in good spirits. They had agreed with their father during his illness that the son would run the business physically, and one daughter would manage it. They explained to me that the business had been his "life," and they wished it to remain in the family. As we talked about him, they joked lovingly about his behavior during the time they had cared for him, following each story of his crabbiness with another one even more outrageous. Their admiration for his fortitude was unspoken, but deeply felt. There was a closeness and a sharing that I had not perceived before, and I commented on it. His wife talked about their support for each other, and their shared perception that he had been sustained to the end by their presence. One daughter said that she understood her father much better, and with that understanding had come a renewal of love.

Comments by Robert B. Taylor

In the case reported, Dr. Goodwin faced a classic ethical dilemma: the conflict between beneficence and autonomy. Dr. Goodwin, like all good physicians, felt a strong urge to provide the best medical care possible for his patients. He wished to "do good" for Mr. X, who had come to him for care and who, as it developed, suffered a terminal disease.

On the other hand, Mr. X obviously placed a high value on autonomy, as evidenced by his wanting "something done," and his willingness to try several remedies unlikely to yield benefit. I suspect that avoiding Dr. Goodwin and failure to seek medical care for a year reflected Mr. X's desire to treat his body as a machine that he could control and repair, and to deny any emotional needs that Dr. Goodwin might try to help him meet.

Nevertheless, as so often happens in family practice, Mr. X came back to Dr. Goodwin when symptoms became worse, and perhaps when he was willing to face the inevitability of his prognosis. Dr. Goodwin wisely called a family conference to plan care, and, more important, to allow other family members to express their feelings about events that had transpired, and about what was likely to occur in the future. Parenthetically, I wonder if the patient should have been included in the family conference.

It is significant that the family elected to support the patient's autonomy in preference to medical beneficence. That is, they agreed to care for their father at home rather than admitting him to the hospital, where high-technology care, intensive therapy, and resuscitation would be available.

It becomes apparent from the narrative that during the last days of the patient's illness, the family and patient alike came to realize that dying and death are a phase of life. There seems to have been a realistic acceptance, and to the patient's credit, he maintained his independent character and gruff exterior until the very end.

The call made by Dr. Goodwin 3 days after his patient's death was perhaps the most important visit of all. This allowed the family to talk about their father and his death, to discuss how they will move forward in the future, and their joint recognition that caring for their father had been a growth experience for all concerned.

EDITORS' COMMENTS

Dr. Goodwin's case came with insightful comments from Dr. Taylor, a colleague of his at the Oregon Health Sciences University School of Medicine, and well-known author and textbook editor in family medicine. We are pleased to pass on these comments, and have nothing to add.

A FAMILY WITH ALZHEIMER'S DISEASE

HARLEY J. RACER
Hennepin County Medical Center, Minneapolis, Minnesota

Hilda, a 47-year-old patient, showed me her aching left heel. It had bothered her on and off for years, but in the past several weeks it had become almost unbearable.

Her left heel looked very normal, as did her right, although she did have marked bunions and rather flat longitudinal arches. The aching heel was reproduced reliably by pressure at the insertion of the plantar fascia on the talus, the typical site for a heel spur. X-ray confirmed it. I offered her a local steroid injection if she would agree to the faithful use of a tapered foam heel wedge for the next several weeks.

It was after the steroid injection, and while I was cutting out a model foam wedge for her heel, that she suddenly said, "I've been wanting to ask you something about Al [her husband] ever since we've moved back to Bloomington last year. Is it common for a man of 50 to get a little forgetful?"

She went on to describe a series of really quite alarming events: Al got lost on the freeway while driving home from work; on a long familiar drive to visit relatives in Michigan, he asked, "Where are we supposed to be going?"; he was unable to master the installation of a new washer and dryer a few days before (mechanical work and tinkering of all kinds had been his forte and his career).

As I finished the foam heel wedge and tucked it into her shoe, she stood up on the anesthetized trigger point and said, "Boy, that's the first relief of pain I've had in a month!" But our pain as Al's family and family doctor due to his Alzheimer's disease had only just begun.

I urged Hilda to make a prompt appointment for Al to see me. I was actually expecting that a recent major job change had precipitated an emotional crisis in this quiet, gentle man.

Al's disorder was promptly recognized by our consulting neurologist. He and I sat down with Hilda and Al and two of their three children, 20-year-old Mark and 13-year-old Ryan, and talked about Alzheimer's disease. But it was 1973, and there wasn't much to tell. Our diagnosis was based on a painstaking normal neurological evaluation and electroencephalogram. A pneumoencephalogram suggested borderline cerebral atrophy. Psychometrics revealed marked deficits in memory, reasoning, and performance, while verbal skills were still superior. A new study called computerized tomographic scanning (the second or third one I had seen!) was done. The neurologist and the radiologist were then fairly sure of the results suggested by the pneumonencephalogram.

This strong, intelligent family vigorously sought answers to their turbulent questions. Their oldest child, 22-year-old Marsha, was teaching school in Illinois, and needed as much explanation and detail as we could provide through Hilda and the two boys. I met Ryan and Mark (a good friend of my own son) as they visited their dad in the hospital, during follow-up office visits, and through frequent contacts at church and in the community.

I saw the family reaching hungrily for information, baffled by a disease that had a name but no known cause, and that threatened steady, progressive loss of the role and function of their strong leader.

They needed an independent, second opinion, and I referred them to the nearby Mayo Clinic where the diagnosis and prognosis were confirmed, but without new hope for recovery or specific treatment.

So the family struggled for the next 6 years with the problems that arose as they now consciously became a "family with Alzheimer's disease," as they described themselves.

Hilda constructed a careful genogram of Al's genetic inheritance, and researched rumors and reports of senility among more than 130 relatives. She and the children asked for a referral for genetic counseling, and were much reassured by clear and direct sessions with our consultants.

Family finances were the next order of business. Al had walked out of his 25-year career when he had been passed over for the last promotion (unwittingly, because of his disease!). It was my role as family doctor to correspond with his employer and the insurance carrier in order to get his retirement and disability benefits reinstated. Their generous responses set precedents for other employers and the insurance industry.

Family leadership had been shifting to Hilda over the prodromal years. Now, she needed to fully assume that role willingly and creatively. She worked full time, got her bachelor's degree within little more than a year, and became the breadwinner in a productive job.

Taking care of Al, the disabled father and husband, was a major issue. Ryan, then 14 years old, became the primary caregiver, because Hilda was busy, first with schooling and work, and then with a career. Day care and daytime occupational and recreational therapy for Al was necessary (Mace & Rabins, 1981), and would be available for a short time, as long as I could justify treating his reactive depression by those methods.

The family's church support was remarkable. Their pastor found Al a job running a freight elevator at a construction project for a year (until he couldn't remember which floors to stop on).

More than that, the church provided a constant network of support for Hilda and Ryan (and for Mark and Marsha on their visits home). Hilda met another woman whose husband had advanced Alzheimer's disease and with three others they began a support group that exploded into the national Alzheimer's Disease and Related Disorders Association (ADRDA)[1] during the next 2 years. Hilda asked for and got a year of social service leave from her employer, Control Data, to serve as the founding executive secretary of the national organization.

Ryan, the primary caregiver, experienced the stresses common to

[1] 360 Michigan Avenue, Chicago, Illinois, 60601.

family members who get locked into the "keeper syndrome" (Banahan & Abbott, 1983). He developed migraine headaches, and, after several months of medications, had three automobile accidents in 1 month (no serious injuries!). After a year, Al's sister became available to move in from a distant state and help with his supervision. Mark got a transfer to live and work in the Minneapolis–St. Paul area, and has been nearby ever since.

By the 6th year after Al's diagnosis, his mental status required him to have constant supervision, and his moods no longer responded to milieu therapy or to antidepressant or tranquilizing medications. It was clear that he needed institutional care. The family made that difficult decision firmly and confidently, seeking only affirmation from me as their family doctor.

The most reliable institutional care for Al was found in a Veteran's Administration hospital 200 miles from the family. His deterioration has continued. He no longer remembers them or me (or *is* there a deep recognition in his vacant eyes?), but the family is strongly linked together in respectful love for him and for each other.

Alzheimer's disease in this father, husband, and leader of his family literally shifted the focus and activity of my care to his family. I saw them mostly during office visits for minor complaints and illnesses, never in conjoint family sessions (after those first agonizing days of diagnosis and incomplete explanations of what we knew and what might be ahead). Most of the business of dealing with family issues was done in dozens of contacts at church, in the neighborhood, by brief phone calls, with one or another, occasionally two or three together, and fees for those services were not requested. But the family and I always have known throughout this 10 years where each of us were all of the time, and I have learned in depth what "family-centered" patient care must mean.

Postscript: Hilda had her third bunion operation 6 months ago, and her feet are hurting less.

EDITORS' COMMENTS

What can we say? The family physician supported this family at the time of a devastating diagnosis, encouraged them as they mobilized their considerable family and community resources, advocated for them with employers and insurance companies, and continued to care for their physical and emotional "bunions" over 10 years. One outcome of this extraordinary collaboration was the birth of a self-help organization that has helped thousands of families.

PATIENT–PHYSICIAN BONDING DURING LONG-TERM CHRONIC HEMATOLOGIC ILLNESS

CHARLES E. SHIELDS
CLARK A. JOHNSON
Texas Tech University Health Science Center

Mr. B, an 86-year-old white male was found to have an anemia when he was hospitalized 5 years ago for cholecystectomy. A previous history of peptic ulcer disease was not associated with blood loss. Preoperative laboratory findings included hemoglobin of 11.2 g, hematocrit 35%. After surgery, his hemoglobin was 8.2 g, and his hematocrit, 25%. After being given a unit of packed red blood cells, his hemoglobin was 10 g, and his hematocrit, 31%.

A return visit 4 weeks later indicated a continuing anemia, and another transfusion was given. The anemia persisted over the following months, and additional studies revealed that iron stores were adequate; folate and vitamin B_{12} levels were in the normal range; there were no signs of bleeding, hemolysis, or clotting difficulty. Bone marrow studies showed moderate erythroid and granulocytic hyperplasia, and thrombocytosis. The findings were suggestive of myeloid metaplasia and myelofibrosis.

At this time, he came to ask us to supervise the transfusions he required, since the Veteran's Administration clinic was not able to provide this supervision.

When medical judgment and responsibility for continuing management of the same chronic medical condition is divided between two different groups, sometimes there can be honest differences of opinion, and the patient's care may suffer. This was discussed by our staff. We then discussed the possible problems with Mr. B and his family.

His wife said, "You have been seeing Papa in the emergency room and giving him his transfusions. We like the way you have taken care of him, and we would like to have you do this for him regularly. That way, we'll know who to call."

Since there was a genuine medical need that we could meet, we agreed to supervise the transfusion therapy.

At this time, he was requiring transfusions of two units of packed red cells every 6–8 weeks. His hemoglobin would fall to 6.6–7.5 g, with hematocrit, 18–21%. After replacement therapy, these values would rise to hemoglobin, 9.5–10.0 g, and hematocrit, 29–30%.

Our initial contacts with Mr. B and his family were mostly on an as-needed basis. He would either call, or would appear at the emergency room with the results of his blood count. He would be seen there, be admitted for the few hours required for him to receive the packed red cells, and would be discharged. Gradually, Mr. B's visits became more frequent, until he required a transfusion every 4 weeks or less, and our contacts with the family became more frequent.

The immediate family unit consisted of Mr. B and his wife. His two daughters lived in nearby communities, and provided both emotional and care-giving support. All family members were personable, agreeable, and pleasant to work with. The couple spent most of their day leisurely on their farm. Mr. B was capable of taking care of himself, but he relied on his wife for most household tasks. Few physical demands were placed on Mr. B, except for a few light tasks around the house and some social activities. He was able to maintain about the same level of activity over the 5 years of his illness.

The increased frequency of our contacts with Mr. B and his family led us to appreciate their warmth, concern, and pleasant attitude. Mr. B was not a demanding person. His family were not particularly verbal in expressing their feelings and emotions. They were concerned, and his wife and at least one of the daughters were always with him while the transfusions were given. Their genuine love and concern for Mr. B was expressed by their presence, rather than by words.

He would occasionally have a mild febrile reaction near the end of a transfusion, and would have to remain in the hospital overnight.

"What caused the fever?" his wife would ask.

"It is probably due to a mild reaction to some of the white blood cells," we would reply.

"Is it serious?"

"No, the temperature has already returned to normal and there are no other side effects."

"I am so glad. We appreciate having him stay here and having you check him," a family member would say.

All of the house staff remarked how gratifying it was to care for Mr. B and see his family. It was a buoyant experience for them.

We began to spend more time with him, and began to assume more and more responsibility for his care. We shared with him and his family his joys and triumphs, such as his small successful and productive garden. He told us, "I really didn't do any work in my garden. Other people did that. But I enjoyed watching it grow, and enjoyed eating the fresh vegetables."

We also came to appreciate the help and support of his daughters, one of whom brought him to the hospital for therapy on a day when the roads were covered with snow and ice.

"This is not a good day for you to be on the highway," we told her.

"I know that! But Papa was beginning to feel weak and didn't sleep well last night. So I thought I should bring him in," she replied.

As time went on, his course proceeded downward with continued anemia, and he also developed thrombocytopenia. The transfusion cycle shortened to a biweekly basis, and at times he required platelet transfusions. Symptom relief was clearly evident after the red cell replacement. Mr. B developed problems with dyspnea, ankle edema, and cardiomegaly. This congestive failure responded to sodium restriction, diuretics, and digoxin.

During the last year of his illness, Mr. B was readmitted to the hospital for a complete reevaluation of his hematological problem. A diagnosis of myelofibrosis was confirmed by bone marrow biopsy.

We told the patient and his family, "Mr. B, your bone marrow is not able to make the blood your body needs because it is being replaced by fibrous tissue."

"Is it cancer?" he asked.

"No, not in the usual sense."

"Can it be cured?" a daughter asked.

"No, not at this time," we replied.

"Is there any medicine that will help?" the daughter asked.

"None that is known at present."

"Will the transfusions continue to help?" Mrs. B asked.

"Yes," we responded.

"Well, then we must continue and do the best we can," Mr. B said.

"We thank you for telling us what you found," Mrs. B said. "We appreciate all you have done in taking care of Papa, and know you will continue to do your best."

In the final month, a rash appeared on Mr. B's legs and lower trunk that appeared infectious in origin and was not related to prior transfusions. The platelet count was in the 14,000–20,000 range, and the white blood cell count well below 2,000. We began Mr. B on antimicrobial therapy. The rash spread and became somewhat purpuric. Mr. B became more dyspneic. He began to cough blood, lapsed into coma, and expired a few hours later.

A few weeks after Mr. B's death, one of his daughters wrote a very kind letter to the president of our institution, expressing the thanks and appreciation of the family for the care and support we had provided Mr. B and his family.

The caring for patients with a progressive condition can be trying for the patient, family, and physician. In this case, Mr. B was seen originally for a specific procedure. In the course of meeting his needs, a true patient–physician bonding occurred, and a very satisfactory relationship developed. In part, this was from the increasing responsibility we assumed for this patient. But, the attitude of the patient and his family was the primary factor in developing this close harmonic connection.

A strong family support system was shown not just by words, but by the actions of the family. They were genuinely and appropriately concerned for the health and well-being of their husband and father. The family also understood and accepted the medical situation. They appreciated the care and concern we felt as physicians. In turn, we responded in a very positive manner to the feelings the family projected. The pleasant and appreciative attitude of this family unit made a difficult situation much easier.

EDITORS' COMMENTS

The evolution of the doctor–patient–family relationship in this poignant case developed over several months. Depth was not forced to occur at the first visit but grew gracefully as it seemed appropriate. An initial task was clarifying the physician's role, which left fewer chances for confusion as the patient grew more ill. By providing continuity, Dr. Shields and his colleagues reduced family and patient anxiety. Simple and direct communication about the treatment and expected course of the illness communicated respect toward a family that was soon to experience loss.

Warm friendship carried this team through the individual interactions toward the inevitable death of Mr. B. Ultimately, he was "Papa" to family and physicians alike. In this case, sound medical care was integrated with straightforward interactions between family, physicians, and the patient to produce simple elegance in the midst of pain and death.

PHYSICIAN HOME VISITS WITH A TERMINALLY ILL PATIENT AND HER FAMILY

STEPHEN J. SPANN
University of Oklahoma Health Sciences Center

I was called to the rural home of Mrs. M, a 73-year-old widow, mother of 14, who was chronically bedridden. As I drove the 15 winding miles to her hillside home, I remembered her past history.

I had first met Mrs. M some 2 years ago when she was admitted through the emergency room with an acute myocardial infarction. At that time she gave a 5-year history of being confined to bed, secondary to diffuse osteoarthritis and morbid obesity. Her hospital course was stormy; she kept going in and out of multifocal atrial tachycardia, and remained on the verge of respiratory failure secondary to restrictive and obstructive lung disease. She was discharged home, to the care of a loving extended family. Most of her children lived close by, and took turns staying with her, providing her with the best of home care. I made periodic house calls to follow her progress; she did well for some 3 months. She suddenly became acutely ill, and was readmitted to the hospital with pneumonia and respiratory failure. Endotracheal intubation and mechanical ventilatory support were required, but the patient survived. During a family meeting prior to discharge, she requested never to be intubated again. The family and I agreed, and I sent her back home; she had done well until now, almost 2 years later.

Upon arriving at Mrs. M's home, I found her to be alert but in moderate respiratory distress. My diagnosis was pneumonia with acute respiratory failure. I reviewed our previous contract with Mrs. M and her family, and offered the option of hospital readmission. Mrs. M requested admission for symptomatic relief, insisting that I promise that she would not be intubated for mechanical ventilation. She improved minimally with antibiotics. What initially appeared to be pneumonia proved to be metastatic renal cell carcinoma. The patient was begun on hormonal chemotherapy and sent home on chronic oxygen therapy. In a family meeting prior to discharge, the patient requested to be allowed to die at home and never to return to the hospital. Her family was supportive, and continued their usual excellent constant home care.

I sensed that the patient did not have long to live. I visited Mrs. M and her family as often as I could, although I had little in my curative armamentarium to offer. I directed my efforts toward ensuring her comfort and supporting the family. My visits became longer. Sometimes I stayed long enough for a piece of homemade pie and a cup of tea, taking the time to get to know my patient and her family better. I learned that she had been born nearby, married young, and delivered 10 of her 14 children right there, on the side of the hill where she now lay dying. I came to know all of her children who lived in the area, and to feel almost like a member of the family myself. Strong, close, and cohesive, the family seemed to be dealing very well with the stress of their mother's terminal illness.

Around 2:00 a.m., on a cold winter night, I received a call from one of Mrs. M's daughters, who seemed to be in a state of panic. The entire family was assembled, and Mrs. M appeared to be dying. "Shouldn't we transfer Mother to the hospital to see if we can do something to save her?" I offered to come to the house immediately. When I arrived, I found Mrs. M to be uncomfortable, in moderate respiratory distress. She was lethargic, but squeezed my hand in recognition. I increased her oxygen flow and gave her a narcotic injection. She responded quickly, and began to rest and breathe easier. All of her children were present. I stayed some 2 hours, reassuring them of the correctness of her dying at home, supporting them, and reminiscing with them about her long and full life. Mrs. M died quietly the next afternoon. I attended her wake a few days later and was welcomed by the family as an esteemed friend.

Terminal illness is a major stress for the patient, the family, and the physician. Many patients want to die in the familiar surroundings of their own home. While there are many resources, such as hospices, to assist in this process, the patient's family plays a major role in the care process.

In this case, meeting with Mrs. M and her family helped all of us understand the patient's desires, and we were able to make a contract to allow Mrs. M to die at home. The family was anxious to comply with their mother's wishes. Physician home visits, though logistically difficult, helped support and encourage the family in the time and energy-consuming efforts of home care. Toward the end of the patient's life, while there wasn't much that could be done for the patient medically, there was much in the way of support that could be done for the family. The panic surrounding the terminal event and the questioning of the decision to allow the patient to remain at home are common in my experience. As in this case, the family usually responds positively to gentle reassurance that they are doing the right thing. Though physically and emotionally taxing, it is my experience that physician home visits to the patient and family during a time of crisis pay rich dividends by decreasing family anxiety and overall family demands, and by helping the physician feel that he or she has contributed to a therapeutic intervention in the family.

EDITORS' COMMENTS

We were emotionally touched by this case report. It tells of beautiful nurturance among patient, family, and physician. The patient's resolve to die naturally made the family and the physician stronger; the family's sharing of their lives, and their pie, with the doctor made him stronger; and his firm, quiet support for the family allowed them to work through their fears just before their mother died. This process demonstrates an important aspect of family medicine that has both humanistic and economic rewards, that is, the process of caring for seriously ill and dying patients at home, with the physician in a primarily supportive rather than curative role.

FAMILY SUPPORT IN TERMINAL ILLNESS

PETER ROBERT GRANTHAM
University of British Columbia

Mr. and Mrs. J had three sons. The oldest, George, a married lawyer with a history of hospitalization for depressive psychosis, had two children. His wife, Christine, was a retired head nurse from a surgical ward of my hospital. The middle son, Fred, was single, lived alone, and worked sporadically as a carpenter. The youngest, Barry, was married with three children, and was anxious and mildly depressed over a nonsexual, extramarital personal relationship, and unemployment in his engineering firm. He had intrinsic asthma, and was seen frequently and regularly in my office for desensitization shots, and to monitor his emotional status.

Mr. and Mrs. J had been "neighborhood parents" to dozens of my friends and acquaintances, as well as many of my patients, who had been active in an athletic club, along with myself and the J sons, for over 20 years.

Mr. J had essential hypertension and asthma. In November, at age 74, he collapsed at home, and was repeatedly resuscitated by the paramedics and later by the emergency room staff. On admission to the intensive care unit (ICU) he was found to be essentially decerebrate, but was placed on monitors and ventilated. It became clear he would soon die; our ICU routinely ceases total life support after 48 hours in such instances. There was little time for the sons to adjust to the forthcoming death of their father. A major request was that Grandpa not die on the birthday of Barry's oldest son. This took some explanation to the ICU director, who eventually was very cooperative. All three sons and the two daughters-in-law spent many consecutive hours at the bedside of their unresponsive father.

Mrs. J intensely disliked hospitals. She "knew he'd really died at home," and never did visit her husband. Life support systems were turned off after 4 days, and death was pronounced immediately. I was uncomfortable about the short duration of life support provided by the hospital. Whatever happened to the Karen Ann Quinlan ethic?

Mrs. J adapted well to her husband's death, and she continued to live in their family home. The sons and grandchildren visited far more often than before Mr. J's death. After her husband's death, I saw Mrs. J a few times in my office to monitor her mild arthritis-associated iron deficiency anemia, for which she was taking oral ferrous gluconate, which regularly made her stools black. In March, 4 months after her husband's death, she complained of lower abdominal pain in addition to mild arthralgia. Physical examination revealed a palpable right lower quadrant mass. Hemoccult was positive. (Six years earlier, she had had a barium enema and colonoscopy for removal of a benign rectal polyp.)

She was sent for abdominal ultrasound, which revealed a solid mass in the right lower quadrant, minimal ascites, and two hepatic masses. Barium enema suggested a nonobstructing 6-cm carcinoma of the cecum. Laparotomy 1 week later confirmed an infiltrating adenocarcinoma of cecum with ascites and extensive peritoneal, lymphatic, and hepatic metastases. No bowel surgery was performed. She was not happy in the hospital, and was discharged 5 days after surgery. She refused referral to the regional cancer clinic; we did not push it, and no specific treatment was undertaken. Her son, Fred, essentially moved in with his mother, and together they painted the house inside and out during April.

Four weeks after discharge from the hospital, Mrs. J was seen at home with severe abdominal pain and vomiting. It appeared that intestinal obstruction might be imminent. To make her more comfortable, I gave her intramuscular meperidine for the pain, and trifluoperazine to calm her stomach. Christine, her daughter-in-law, attended to her needs, and administered the parenteral medication for the 2 or 3 days it was needed.

Fred needed to be able to leave the house more often, so a housekeeper was arranged for through Provincial Long Term Care Services 3½ days per week, to act essentially as a babysitter.

During May, Mrs. J required no medication and no real nursing care other than superficial dressing for a small third-degree burn she received from a heating pad in the hospital. In June, however, she began to complain of abdominal distress. The mass in her lower abdomen was melon-sized by this time. Her discomfort was controlled easily with oral codeine phosphate, 30 mg two to three times per day, but she obviously expected someone to be in constant attendance. Fred and Christine provided most of their mother's care. Occasionally, a home-care nurse was hired for the midnight shift. Fred became tearful whenever we discussed his mother's impending death, and his brothers expressed concern about how difficult this was for him. Yet we all agreed, Mrs. J, her sons and their wives, and myself, that hospitalization was undesirable at this time, and that dying at home was preferable.

By late June, we had to increase the analgesia to morphine sulfate solution, 5–10 mg every 3 hours around the clock. Mrs. J became incontinent of stool, and she could eat very little food, only a chocolate-flavored liquid nutritional supplement.

Fred was unable to handle the soiled disposable diapers, so Christine and the home-care nurses assumed that responsibility. I visited two or three times a week, and received almost daily phone calls, at home and at the office, from one family member or another.

Finally, George and Barry both phoned me to say they were really worried about Fred. Fred came over to the office, cried a bit, said they couldn't manage at home anymore, and that his mom said that she was now ready to go to the hospital. She was transported by ambulance to the hospital's palliative care unit (PCU), accompanied by one of her sons.

The boys and I did not expect Mrs. J to live much longer. Her sons and their families had given her 3 extra good months of quality company, caring, and life at home. We all agreed they should be proud of their mother, and proud of themselves for all the help they had given her, especially at the end of her full and happy life. We were all able to confidently look to the staff of the PCU to provide additional psychological support for this family over the next few days. After that, I expected that their own resources would enable them to cope, and eventually adjust.

It is impossible to imagine attempting to medically manage a situation such as this at home for so long without a willing, supportive, and resourceful family. By comparison, the physician has relatively little to offer.

Mrs. J became comatose after only 3 days in the PCU, and she died the next day. Fred was still with her when they called me to pronounce death at 2:00 a.m. We were both pleased we had managed so long at home, and that Mrs. J had only a very short stay in the hospital.

Four days later, I was invited to a wake held in the garden at Barry's home—three generations of families and friends were there. It rained a little, and much beer and wine were consumed. It is always a little uncomfortable for a physician to attend the funeral ceremonies for a former patient. You can't help but wonder if some of the people blame you for the event.

Fred subsequently moved into the family home with his girlfriend (a relationship I never knew existed), and did well. The other sons and their families were pleased with his adjustment, and proceeded on with their lives. I will remember how this family coped with parental demise, and probably will recount the experience during future counseling with other patients, and perhaps even in my own personal life. Contact with this family has been essentially a reassuring and uplifting experience for me, even though we have had to deal with the death of two respected and beloved parents, friends, and patients within a very short period of time. Families confer great strength onto individuals.

EDITORS' COMMENTS

This case touchingly shows the benefits for everyone, including the physician, of close collaboration during terminal illness. Sudden, unpredictable events did not create chaos. Through shared decision making and demonstration of mutual respect, the physician–patient–family triangle grew stronger and remained functional during a time of great stress. The weakening patient was offered maximum influence in a setting where she would usually experience powerlessness. The family remained as primary caretakers for as long as they and the patient wished. When no curative treatment was possible, the physician and the medical institution responded with flexibility and worked to preserve the patient's dignity when nothing else was left. In attending the wake, Dr. Grantham demonstrated that he too has strong feelings surrounding death, and that he too needs to bring things to closure. Facing certain death and a grieving family was an act of courage with benefits for all.

THE STOIC CARETAKING SISTER WITH CONGESTIVE HEART FAILURE

JOHN J. DALLMAN
Wayne State University, Detroit

I first met Annie P, a 70-year-old widow, when she came into the emergency room complaining of shortness of breath. Initial examination revealed that she was in congestive heart failure and borderline pulmonary edema. Accompanying Annie was her 65-year-old sister, Mary, who explained that Annie had just moved into town and did not yet have a doctor. Annie was transferred to the intensive care unit (ICU) and was treated with diuretics and digoxin for her congestive heart failure. Over the next few days, Annie told me some of her medical and social history, and began to reveal some of the dynamics of her interaction with her sister.

Annie had lived in the country with her husband, who was a farmer, until his death 6 months earlier, at which time she moved into town to live with her sister. Her sister was also recently widowed and neither of them had had children. Since their financial resources were meager, they decided it would be more economical for them to live together.

Mrs. P had severe health problems including adult onset diabetes mellitus requiring large doses of insulin twice a day. She had been diagnosed with congestive heart failure several years earlier but had been successfully treated with digoxin and diuretics in the past. She had visited her physician infrequently in the past, preferring to "tough it out" if she developed any symptoms.

Her sister Mary, on the other hand, was quite healthy but had many psychosomatic complaints. These complaints often required trips to the emergency room, where no one could find any organic disease. Annie could drive a car while Mary could not. Consequently, Annie needed to help her sister with shopping and trips to the doctor by acting as her chauffeur. After 6 months of this activity, Annie's physical condition worsened, probably as a result of moving into her sister's home and the demands placed on her by her sister. These events probably led to the current admission for congestive heart failure.

After appropriate therapy in the ICU, I discharged Annie and saw her several times in my office for continuing care. Over the next few months, while Annie's diabetes and congestive heart failure were being stabilized, I learned more about Annie's relationship with Mary. Mary's dependency on Annie was a chronic problem, yet one that Annie felt compelled to endure without complaint. I wanted to meet with both sisters together to discuss their relationship, but Annie refused. She said she had made the choice to live with Mary and would just have to cope with it. Her major worry was what would happen when she died and Mary was left alone.

After 3 years of seeing this patient on a regular basis and watching her diabetes and congestive heart failure become increasingly intractable to medical management, the inevitable happened. Annie was brought in by ambulance to the hospital in florid pulmonary edema. She was admitted to the ICU and treated aggressively. She developed renal failure and renal dialysis was started. After a few days, she recovered but was faced with the need for chronic hemodialysis for the rest of her life, due to renal failure. A MUGA scan revealed that she had less than 30% left ventricular function remaining. Because of her diabetes and poor cardiovascular function, the nephrologists were less than optimistic about Annie's chances for trouble-free long-term hemodialysis.

Throughout this hospitalization, Annie maintained her stoic attitude. She often told me that she wanted to die but had to find a caretaker for her sister first. When faced with the inevitability of chronic hemodialysis, she was forced to finally choose which was more important—her life, or that of her sister. When I told her the alternatives that she had, namely to undergo chronic hemodialysis or die from uremia, her answer was that she wanted to die, but first had to go home and "settle things" with her sister. She was released on a pass on Thursday, went home to her sister, and died of unknown causes the next day. I found out later that she had been able to convince a neighbor to look after her sister.

In this case, a family interview might have been helpful in prolonging Annie's life, yet I was unable to accomplish that task. Although I learned the dynamics of Mary and Annie's relationship, I was unable to effectively intervene. Perhaps it would have been helpful to both parties if I could have done so. On the other hand, perhaps because of Annie's stoic nature, she ultimately dealt with the family problem better by sticking to her commitment to her sister and ignoring her own problems.

EDITORS' COMMENTS

This stunning case shows the value of trusting the patient's own sense of which burdens she wants to endure, and which she wants to shed. Annie P, in her last years, preferred to end her life's drama with her and her sister playing the same roles they had played all their lives—Annie as the caretaker, and Mary the one cared for. For Annie P to act otherwise would have felt to her like a betrayal. The physician wisely accepted this decision, just as he also accepted her decision to die after she had made arrangements for her sister. We disagree with Dr. Dallman when he says that he was not able to effectively intervene. His intervention was to respect the patient's decision not to change her lifelong relationship pattern with her sister. Because of this, we suspect that Annie P died at peace.

IT'S HOW YOU LISTEN: A BOY WITH DIPLOPIA

JEFFREY GRABENSTEIN
Private practice
Rogers Park Family Practice Center, Chicago, Illinois

An 11-year-old boy (we'll call him Johnny) was admitted to the pediatric department of the hospital with a 2-week history of diplopia. His attending physician had been unable to determine its cause. Being the senior family practice resident on the pediatric unit, I saw him soon after admission to the unit. He was a pleasant boy who wore a black patch over his right eye, as if he were a pirate. During our initial meeting, he was evasive in the typically teenage manner. Results of Johnny's physical and neurological examination at that time were remarkably unremarkable, except that he saw double images of everything. This diplopia was most severe when he had to use both eyes, but was present when he looked through either eye. Johnny was told that the cause of his diplopia was a mystery, but that we would try to find a cure. I asked him to help me treat his eyes by switching the patch to cover the right eye to exercise the weaker one.

Further history, obtained the next morning, did not provide any insight into the problem. Results of all admission blood work were appropriate for a healthy, prepubescent male. The neurologist arrived later that day and confirmed my impression that there did not seem to be an organic etiology to the problem.

I spent more time with Johnny later in the day, and he proved to be a bright child who did very well in school. His favorite hobby was reading science fiction novels. He aspired to become a computer whiz like those he read about in the sci-fi books. His father was Hispanic and a member of the local Teamsters Union. His mother was of Polish descent. The maternal grandmother, who lived with them, had been born in Poland. As both parents worked, the grandmother was entrusted with many of the caretaking responsibilities for Johnny.

I asked Johnny to tell me exactly what had happened right before he developed the double vision. He said that he was talking with his grandmother, who told him very sternly that she would no longer tolerate his wasting his time reading all those stupid science fiction books. Computers were also a waste of time, she said. The only meaningful activity for him was to study to become a priest. This was his duty to the family. No member of the family had joined the Church since she left Poland, many decades ago. The salvation of family members depended upon having a member in the Church. Some moments after this encounter the diplopia developed. I told Johnny that it did not appear that his diplopia was caused by any life-threatening condition, and that there was hope that this problem could be resolved.

The following afternoon both of his parents were visiting. I told them the progress of the evaluation thus far. I then asked the boy if I could tell his parents what we had talked about the day before. He nodded his head up and down. He was quiet as I told his parents the story of his discussion with his grandmother prior to the double vision. Occasionally, he would glance furtively at either his mother or father. When I finished relating the story, Johnny's father gave his son a very puzzled look, and appeared about to speak when the boy blurted out, "You told me that I have to listen to my grandmother!" After hearing this, and pausing a moment to let it register, his father replied, "When we told you to listen to your grandmother, we meant to listen to her, but don't listen to her." Johnny stared right at his father during the silence that followed his father's words. Then I stated that nothing life threatening had been uncovered, and that as the problem had evolved over time, it might resolve itself in a few days.

The next morning, Johnny's vision was not quite as double as it had been the previous day. By the afternoon, he could see clearly enough that he was able to watch television. By that evening, when his parents came to visit, he was no longer seeing double and was discharged.

This case was an important event in my training for many reasons. Of major importance is the concept of the family life cycle. The different members of this family were all struggling with the issues of their respective stages. In response to the pressures of financially supporting their children, as well as their parents, the second generation in this family had given up part of their authority as parents to the preceding generation. This grandmother, who was struggling with the issues of her inevitable death, made an attempt to alleviate that anxiety by coercing her grandson into becoming a priest. The parents were able to reestablish the appropriate boundaries and power structure with a powerful paradox.

EDITORS' COMMENTS

This encounter changed the physician's vision just as clearly as it changed the boy's vision. The doctor's probing allowed the boy to open up about the bind that he felt Grandma and his parents had put him in. Then, a low-key presentation of this disclosure to the parents enabled them to break the bind in a masterful way. Significantly, Dr. Grabenstein did not blame the grandmother for victimizing the boy; he understood how the developmental trajectories of all the family members led to this impasse. Since this was a hospital case on a pediatric service, Dr. Grabenstein probably had no opportunity to follow up with this family. In a family pratice setting, one follow-up discussion with the family, including Grandma, would have been helpful to ensure that she was not scapegoated by the parents after this worrisome episode with diplopia. As it stands, however, this case is the kind that can change the world view of the physician who was fortunate enough and courageous enough to get involved with the mysterious workings of family relations.

AN OVERWEIGHT ADOLESCENT

MILTON H. SEIFERT, JR.
Private practice, Excelsior, Minnesota

Rachel J was a 14-year-old second child whose main health concern was that of being overweight. She very much wanted to lose weight, but was gaining instead.

Approximately 5 months earlier, Rachel had been seen because of lower urinary tract symptoms. She had a previous history of severe meatal stricture, which had required urethral dilation. Subsequent urine culture showed no growth, but Rachel had a second item she wanted to discuss—she weighed 152 pounds, and she wanted to lose weight. At that time, the examining physician provided some health education directed at a weight-loss program and prescribed a 1,000-calorie diet and a program of physical exercise. However, when Rachel and her mother came to see me 5 months later, she had gained 3 pounds. Rachel was quite intense about her body-weight management problem.

On examination, Rachel's blood pressure was 110/70, and her weight 155 pounds. Otherwise, results of her physical examination were all within normal limits. Laboratory examination revealed a normal hemogram. Her blood lipids were normal, as were the other items of the chemistry profile. At this point, I entered into a process of negotiation with Rachel and her mother to develop, first a more complete problem list, and then a consensus treatment plan. This process and its results are described below.

Rachel was a very nice young lady who was shy, compulsive, sensitive, and very concerned about her body weight of 155 pounds. She exhibited symptoms of sleep disturbance, fatigue, irritable colon, and occasional dyspnea. We all agreed that Rachel had difficulty assuming the patient role, mostly because she was shy and sensitive. We decided that Rachel did not get enough physical exercise, and that she did not wear her seat belt.

Rachel's mother had other concerns of her own, which she had expressed to me in the course of an employment physical examination a few weeks earlier. These earlier concerns now surfaced during this process of negotiation. She identified the stress of parenting as one of her important health concerns.

Rachel's mother, a registered nurse, is a very caring and family-oriented person. She agreed that Rachel had difficulty assuming the patient role, and at the same time she was very concerned about what would happen if Rachel could not be helped. She felt somewhat helpless, as well as anxious and guilty.

At this point in the process, the negotiation of diagnostic understandings began to blend into the negotiation of a treatment plan. We talked about the need for stress management as it applies to the management of compulsive eating. We agreed that stress management skills would be useful, and I suggested that we use our health educator to aid in achieving these skills. Finally, we decided that Rachel's difficulty in assuming the patient role could potentially reduce the effectiveness of the health educator.

As a family physician, I am often faced with my own helplessness and this was one such instance. Adolescence is a time when help may be desired, but it is also a time when the help of parents or other adults can feel threatening and may be avoided. Thinking about the possibility of an eating disorder and its long-term consequences is stressful for me. The intensity of Rachel's feelings, my personal concern for this family, who are long-time friends, and the knowledge that one treatment plan had already failed, acted to increase my own personal stress level. Clearly, we all needed help. As we talked, we developed a plan to help one another while at the same time dealing with our own concerns.

Therefore, we negotiated that Rachel's mother would join Rachel in learning stress management skills together. This would have the affect of providing adequate support for Rachel while she learned how to manage everyday stresses. Rachel's mother would then have a direct way to help Rachel, while at the same time she would be learning methods to deal with her own guilt, fear, and anxiety. Other aspects of the treatment plan negotiated with Rachel were: She would wear her automobile seat belt regularly; she would do some type of aerobic exercise, such as using an exercise bicycle daily; she would consider joining a small support group, and consider joining Weight Watchers.

Our health educator saw Rachel and her mother for five 1-hour sessions. The health educator and I both evaluated the results of the therapy after Rachel and her mother completed the prescribed health education. Both of them reported symptom improvement, some positive life changes, and an overall improvement in quality of life. Both expressed their willingness to maintain this therapeutic gain, and to schedule periodic appointments with our health educator. Rachel and her mother felt that they had both given and received support from one another. At future appointments, we will consider dividing up a session to provide some time together, and some time alone with the health educator for each of them.

I don't know which of Rachel's presenting complaints, dysuria or overweight, was the most important, but I suspect it was the latter. Perhaps family practice is a discipline wherein we make it a point to look for the "other complaint." The annual or routine physical examination can serve as a vehicle for prevention of incipient problems and promotion and maintenance of both personal and family health, as it did here for Rachel's mother.

There were several factors that worked against a successful outcome. Rachel had difficulty assuming the patient role; Rachel's mother was hampered by the nature of adolescence; and, I had no particular treatment that I knew would be successful. The breakthrough came when we realized that we were all in this together and that we would have to create our own solutions in a collaborative manner. As a physician, it was natural for me to be thinking about how I could solve the problem, but it was more productive when I let the patient and the family help me in both the diagnostic and treatment processes. By using a negotiated approach, we were able to be creative and to find workable solutions.

The stresses I experienced were significant, and our long-term relationship magnified this discomfort. While I had been taught in medical school to avoid becoming emotionally involved, I don't believe this is either helpful or desirable for a family physician. In this case, the emotional pain may well have pulled us (physician, patient, and family) together so that we were able to develop creative solutions to the problems at hand.

EDITORS' COMMENTS

This case demonstrates one family physician's approach to a patient's problem of being overweight. Dr. Seifert had an already established relationship with the family, especially with the patient's mother. The clinical problem of obesity in adolescence provoked powerful feelings in this physician. His awareness of the low probability of meaningful weight loss and of the dynamics of adolescent autonomy made the initial problem seem hopeless. Setting up a treatment plan that would help all members of this complex team, including the physician, reduced the "casualty rate" from 100% to something less than that.

Experts in special centers for obesity might have chosen different treatment approaches that offer more powerful interventions but that also involve rare professional skills and risks that are greater than most primary care physicians can tolerate. In the unique context of this physician–patient–family interaction, this treatment approach had greater merit than doing nothing (which is sometimes a wise choice), or then suggesting intervention resources that were not available. This resourceful physician incorporated family and allied health support into a plan of action that made everyone hopeful—whether or not weight loss was achieved. Ultimately, it may be less important for this adolescent to surrender to the "patient role" than to find a way to become personally responsible for her own health in a manner that is more satisfying to her. The mother and the physician can then deal with individual and interactive issues between them without involving the daughter.

A FAMILY COPING WITH DEATH

DAVID TANNENBAUM
Mount Sinai Hospital, Toronto, Ontario, Canada

Mr. C was a 58-year-old grounds maintenance worker at the local school. He was a reserved, stoic man, rarely willing to see a physician. I only saw him periodically when he accompanied his 30-year-old mentally handicapped son to medical checkups. Mrs. C was a demanding, difficult, somewhat bothersome patient toward whom I had developed a dislike. I had seen her episodically for problems ranging from back pain to sexual dysfunction. She called late one afternoon saying that her husband had a red left eye that had not responded to a few days treatment with steroid–antibiotic drops. These had been prescribed over the telephone by an ophthalmologist who had recently seen Mrs. C for conjunctivitis.

Since I knew of Mr. C's general reluctance to see a physician, I was impressed by his wife's call and saw him at the end of office hours. Apart from conjunctival infection, his eye examination revealed an opacified pupil, the cause of which I could not determine. Only at that point did he admit to being unable to see out of the eye.

That evening, I sent Mr. C to an ophthalmologist who suggested referral to a major medical center, where a diagnosis of melanoma was made. He underwent enucleation and subsequent extirpation of the orbit. He was fitted with a prosthesis, but he found it uncomfortable and rarely wore it, making his appearance bizarre, with a normal right eye and an empty left orbital cavity.

My attitude toward Mrs. C was changing. She rarely presented with complaints of her own at this point, and was very supportive of her husband during the treatment period. I had previously been concerned with problems in their relationship, but clearly these problems did not interfere with Mrs. C's dedication to her husband.

One year later, Mr. C developed epigastric pain. He was admitted to hospital with marked hepatomegaly. Workup revealed metastatic disease. Chemotherapy was unsuccessful in slowing the extraordinary rapid growth of the metastatic liver masses, which quadrupled in size over the next month. He and his wife decided that further care would be carried out at home.

As Mr. C became more cachectic, Mrs. C continued nursing him. She titrated his pain medication, provided oral feedings, and walked him about. She rejected the assistance of hospice workers and visiting nurses, but accepted help from other family members. Mrs. C was one of the few patients whom I allowed to telephone me directly at home in time of need, and she never abused the privilege. I visited periodically, and generally found her to be doing a better job than I had seen in many health care facilities. I would find Mr. C content, lying prone and unclothed in their modest home. Family members were often visiting, and there was no difficulty discussing plans and preparations for Mr. C's death. Mrs. C's frankness with her husband allowed a smooth transition through the stages of dying. When I came to the house to pronounce his death, I was surprised by the few tears shed by Mrs. C. Stolid throughout, she showed no later signs of delayed grief, which I had expected to see.

In retrospect, I felt somewhat guilty about originally disliking Mrs. C, and by my sensitivity only to the negative aspects of her character. I was concerned about how her behavior affected me, rather than looking for those positive aspects in her behavior that were important for her family. It took a major family crisis for me to realize her many positive attributes, and the significance these could have in guiding her family through difficult times.

This family taught me a considerable amount about death and dying by the way they dealt with Mr. C's dying. Here, it seemed appropriate for me to avoid intervening, so I served as a resource, assisting with medical concerns and providing other input when asked. By not interfering with the family's decisions, I could maintain a beneficial working relationship with Mrs. C. This allowed her the independence and control she merited.

EDITORS' COMMENTS

Here a serious medical problem resulted in more intimate contacts with this family. Even though a previous longitudinal relationship with Mrs. C had created a negative image of her, Dr. Tannenbaum was open to changing that image. Mrs. C became a major resource for her dying husband, her children, and for the physician. The circumstances demanded more than the usual level of contact between the family and the physician, so the physician responded by permitting phone calls directly to his home, and making house calls. The family's decision for home care was supported and led to excellent patient care. The physician cooperated with the treatment needs and desires of the family. In moving from the role of direct medical care provider to that of medical consultant for a family that provided most of the care, Dr. Tannenbaum preserved the family's autonomy and dignity, and in the process learned more about living and dying.

A FAMILY WITH A DYING SON

LISA C. BAKER
University of Oklahoma Health Sciences Center

Stephen H was a 27-year-old white male with cerebral palsy and mental retardation occurring as a result of anoxia at birth. He had been in a nursing home since age 10. Stephen was admitted to the hospital after vomiting blood and was found to have a small Mallory–Weiss tear of the esophagus. Over the next 2 to 3 days, his condition deteriorated, and he underwent exploratory laparotomy, which revealed an infarction of a large segment of small bowel due to arterial thrombosis. His course was further complicated by an infarction of his stomach, necessitating gastrectomy and esophagostomy. Fistula formation required a third operation.

Further history obtained from Stephen's father after the first surgery revealed a familial tendency toward thrombophlebitis and clot formation over three generations on the paternal side of the family. Clotting studies on Stephen's blood showed him to have a deficiency of antithrombin III, an autosomal dominant inherited trait.

At this point, a family conference was arranged with the following goals: (1) to provide information to the family; (2) to explore the father's expressed guilt about having passed on the inherited trait; (3) to be supportive of the family's grief process regarding Stephen's impending death; (4) to find out more about the family's needs and resources. Attending the conference were the family medicine faculty physician, a 4th-year medical student who had been involved with the case, the patient's parents, and a behavioral scientist who observed behind a one-way mirror with the permission of the family.

The conference began with the physician bringing the family up to date on Stephen's condition, and inviting questions from Mr. and Mrs. H. The family was calm, interested, and appreciative of the opportunity to talk. After some discussion of Stephen's condition and the recent information about the inherited trait discovered through the clotting studies, Mrs. H broached a new topic. "Is cancer hereditary?" she asked.

The physician answered her question with a few comments, and then said, "Why do you ask?"

"Because my brother and I had a disagreement about it last month at my mother's funeral. She died of bone cancer, and he said it was hereditary."

The doctor reassured Mrs. H with facts about the etiology of cancer. The meeting ended with plans to convene at the hospital the next day, and the family was reminded of the availability and support of the health care team.

In the discussion following the family conference among the faculty physician, the medical student, and the behavioral scientist, we all commented on the remarkable strength of this family. This case seemed to be one in which a family had "risen to the occasion" and had handled inordinate amounts of stress and pain in extraordinary ways. In addition to the death of Mr. and Mrs. H's parents, the family had also suffered the loss of a 10-year-old child to kidney failure, possibly related to the same bleeding disorder that Stephen had.

It became clear that the whole family was the patient in this case and that our interventions, though now limited in what we could do to help Stephen, could be meaningful and helpful to other family members. As we discussed the needs of the family, it was easy to identify Mr. H as a person needing special support. But, as we looked at the genogram and reflected on Mrs. H's questions about cancer, we realized that she might be a "hidden patient."

Mrs. H had recently lost her mother and was about to lose her son. From a standpoint of the family life cycle, the family was experiencing a "changing of the guard" with the death of the last person in the grandparent generation. Mrs. H was moving from being the generation in-between to being the oldest generation. From her question about cancer, we guessed that she might be concerned about her own vulnerability and the potential of passing on that vulnerability to her children. We believed that we had allayed some of her fears by providing medical information, but we also realized that we could do more to help by talking about her feelings also. We planned that the next time we saw the family, we would ask Mrs. H how she was feeling, in light of the severe losses she was experiencing in her life. We would make a point of focusing on those feelings and communicating understanding and support. We planned to ask her and her husband how they dealt with such feelings as a family, and we decided to offer follow-up clinic visits for further discussion.

A few days after this encounter, Stephen was transferred to the surgery service, and after a short time, he died. The family physician contacted the family several times by phone and saw the family when they came in to have blood levels drawn. He observed that the family was not feeling overly guilty and that they were working through the mourning process without suppressed or pathological grief. In one conversation, the mother said, "Stephen had such a long illness. We hated to see him die, but we are glad that he is not suffering anymore." The family did not express anger at the health care team, and the father commented, "We are confident that you did everything that could be done. There was nothing else the family could have done since we did not know about the genetic problem." The other sign of healthy coping was that the family was taking appropriate and realistic steps to test for the Antithrombin III deficiency in other family members. Our eyes had been opened to some of the particular needs of this family as a result of the physician's careful attention to the more basic request for information.

EDITORS' COMMENTS

In this case, the surviving family members needed to (1) process important new medical information (was their son's fatal illness inherited?), (2) question whether another recent death was also genetically linked and therefore a threat to others in the family, and (3) adjust to new generational leadership roles for the patient's parents. It appears that this large agenda was reasonably satisfied in one family conference. As a healthy family, they rose to the occasion following respectful but minimal help from professionals. This is what Gerard Zuk (1975) has called the "celebrant role" in family therapy. It is a brief interaction that serves as a formal recognition of life events and signals the time for change. It marks a rite of passage for the family. With the crisis past and the new reality accepted, the family's longitudinal relationship with the primary medical team returned to a less intense mode. This process occurs commonly between healthy families and medical teams who are attuned to family issues.

CLYDE AND BETTY: PROBLEMS OF THE HEART

A. PATRICK SCHNEIDER II
Private practice, Burlington, Iowa

My most vivid recollection of Betty is of her standing at her husband's side as he lay in bed 6 of the cardiac care unit. It was February 8, 1981. The frozen Mississippi could be seen as I looked over rooftops. Her tall good looks contrasted with those of her husband, Clyde. She seemed calm and strong. He appeared to be dying.

Forty-five-year-old Clyde weighed 200 pounds and was being treated for a Class IV inferior myocardial infarction with posterior and lateral extension. Prior to admission, he had been smoking three packs of cigarettes a day. He was also obese. He presented 3 days ago with classical symptoms of an acute myocardial infarction. All had gone well until yesterday, when he developed more chest pain and extended his infarction. A Swan–Ganz line was in place, but today, atrial fibrillation had compounded Clyde's troubles—and mine. Clyde was in cardiogenic shock. I suggested helicopter transfer to the University of Iowa.

A month later (March 9), Clyde was at my office. He had done well after transfer. He was walking one-half mile per day, but still smoking at least one pack of cigarettes a day. He had made it, but the major precipitating risk factor was still there.

That November, his wife, Betty, was seen in my office by a locum tenens doctor for depression. Elavil was prescribed. On the next visit, sexual antipathy was discussed. Through the winter and first half of 1982, regular visits continued.

I saw Betty on June 30, 1982, after returning from a year's educational leave in Boston. It had been a year and a half since the encounter at Clyde's bedside. What a change. She was unkempt, almost dirty. She was raising goats. Their odor was unforgettably pungent. Betty was depressed and I was shocked.

I began to probe into the etiology of the depression, although I know that current dogma disparages of such an inquiry. I sketched for Betty the three steps necessary to cure depression: (1) What's wrong? (diagnosis); (2) Why is something wrong? (insight); (3) How can future episodes of depression be prevented? (action).

I obtained the following information: No family history of depression. No past treatment of depression. Psychological stresses included her mother's death 3 years ago and Clyde's myocardial infarction. He is back at work and doing well.

More about Clyde poured forth. In 1973, he went overseas and became entangled with a woman who became pregnant. A few tears now. Clyde and Betty nearly divorced. "I don't love him anymore," she confessed.

Things waxed and waned through the fall and winter. I increased her dosage of Elavil to 250 mg. Marriage counseling was suggested from time to time, but Betty saw no use in it.

October 31, 1983, Clyde was back in the local emergency room. New heart damage in the inferior lateral area was present. Heart failure did not occur as before. Smoking was back up to one and one-half to two packs per day. By mid-December, a university noninvasive cardiac evaluation was completed that showed "organic heart disease, atherosclerotic coronary artery disease, status post myocardial infarction, ejection fraction 48%, Functional Class I . . . 1 week ago a treadmill stress test positive at 14½ minutes. . . . We recommended that he totally abstain from cigarette smoking."

In December 1982 Betty had more ruminations over the "hurt" of 10 years ago. Marriage counseling was suggested multiple times. In March, a university psychiatric evaluation of Betty was obtained that stated: "major depression disorder. . . . Appears to have problems and ruminations about an affair. . . . There are suggestions of marital discord and there appears to be an inability of the two to talk together about problems. . . . The best thing now in her life are the animals in their small farmstead, which includes 17 goats, 9 kid goats, 1 horse, 8 dogs, and 26 cats. . . ."

A switch to Desyrel was suggested.

Early 1984 brought no significant changes for Betty. A switch was made back to Elavil, but at a more moderate 125-mg dosage at bedtime. In May, Betty's hygiene was better. With a laugh, she said her energy was "one-tenth."

Clyde was last seen August 21, 1984. He was pain free. He was working. He was smoking. Things were "better." We did not discuss marriage. We never had.

August 30, 1984—9 days after Clyde—was Betty's most recent office visit. The chart read: "Patient is doing better than ever before. They have had no sex for 6 months. She readily admitted that she really does not want to [have intercourse]. She has never really forgiven him." Betty looked squarely at me and leveled, "The man I loved died 15 years ago." She was more receptive to the suggestion of marriage counseling. I left the room overwhelmed by her admission, but faintly hopeful.

Who knows what will happen to Betty and Clyde? In 1628, William Harvey said, "Every affection of the mind that is attended with either pain or pleasure, hope or fear, is the cause of an agitation whose influence extends to the heart." A recent report substantiates the notion of a causal role for biobehavioral stress in cardiac death (Ruberman, Weinblatt, Goldberg, & Chandhary, 1984). Ruberman and coworkers have observed that high indexes of life stress and social isolation are significantly associated with a high risk of cardiac death. The hypothesis is not new. The strength of the evidence is.

Clyde has been repeatedly advised that smoking is his primary risk factor for coronary artery disease. I remain suspicious that Betty's depression is not endogenous, but rather chronic reactive (heretical, noncurrent nomenclature). I doubt that either Clyde will conquer his smoking or Betty her depression without a reconciliation. Fundamentally, I believe that their problem is one of isolation. Two hearts are troubled, each in its own way.

EDITORS' COMMENTS

Along with sensitivity to family context comes the pain of our impotence. Individuals and families adapt and change at their own discretion. In this case, Dr. Schneider offered his compassion, technically competent medical care, access to consultants and tertiary level care, and still the patient was unable to change critically important behavior (smoking). His wife was in emotional pain with depression, and declined to deal directly with the marital relationship that was giving her pain. Perhaps she felt that therapy would bring the issues into focus and result in divorce. For her, the status quo may have been the least uncomfortable option.

The final burden may rest with the compassionate physician who feels compelled to influence a couple who have chosen their own path, no matter how painful and irrational it may appear to others. Respect for a family's autonomy may offer some comfort to physicians who care deeply and also realize that they cannot command obedience. In this case, the interactions between the physician, patient, and family were honest; the family's dignity and autonomy were still intact. To ask for more than this would be unwise, disrespectful to this family, and a possible source of iatrogenic illness for the physician.

DIGNITY IN DEATH

RUSSELL J. SAWA
University of Calgary

I was working in the intensive care unit on a weekend, when I was called to a code arrest. The patient, John, an elderly, very emaciated gentleman, had arrested. I was informed that his physician had left clear instructions that John was to be resuscitated, despite the fact that he had recently had operations for cancer of the tongue, larynx, and prostate. John had been resuscitated successfully 1 year previously. I complied with the physician's orders, and continued resuscitation, which succeeded, and John was admitted to the intensive care unit.

While John was in intensive care, I had the opportunity to talk to his wife and his sister. They were both very relieved to talk about John's illness. His wife in particular was distressed by the amount of pain her husband was in. She said John had told her that he did not want to be resuscitated. She wondered when the doctor was going to discuss this with her.

Both women seemed to appreciate the opportunity to be able to disclose their feelings about John's illness and impending death and were relieved to discover that they could allow him to die in dignity. They very much appreciated an opportunity to give input, and requested, for their part, that he not be resuscitated in the future.

That morning John's endotracheal tube was removed, as he was able to breathe on his own. Everyone, including the head of the department, agreed that John would not be resuscitated in the future. He returned to the ward, and died peacefully later that day.

From this case, I learned how easy it is to forget to take into account the meaning of illness and death in a family. The patient's personal physician had adopted the attitude of life at all costs. Yet, for the family, living with the illness had become too painful for everyone, including the patient. By taking into account the meaning of the illness in the family system, the patient and his family were allowed to receive compassionate, sensitive, and dignified health care.

EDITORS' COMMENTS

Family-centered care was clearly contrasted with traditional physician-centered care in this case. Even without prior contact with the patient or his family, Dr. Sawa perceived the need to involve the family in the critically important decisions of whether or not to resuscitate the patient. From the family-centered perspective, that was an obvious way to resolve a delicate issue. No lawyers, no courts. Just a concerned family and a respectful physician who came to a serious decision together.

PAIN IN A TERMINALLY ILL PATIENT

S. LAWRENCE LIBRACH
University of Toronto

I knew at a glance that Mrs. D was in trouble. Although she had metastatic breast cancer, she normally walked with ease. Today, as I escorted her to the examining room, she moved very slowly and with what appeared to be considerable pain.

To backtrack a little, Mrs. D was a 43-year-old married woman. Four years ago, she developed a small mass in her left breast, which on biopsy proved to be an anaplastic adenocarcinoma. One year later, she developed back and chest pain which, unfortunately, was found to be due to bony metastases. Initial treatment with chemotherapy and antiestrogen drugs relieved most of her pain. However, after 1 more year, she developed increasingly severe pain unresponsive to antineoplastic therapy. As a family physician with an interest in palliative care, I saw her at that time on referral from her oncologist because of her pain problem. Treatment with oral morphine and appropriate antiinflammatory agents quickly relieved her pain. I followed her regularly over the ensuing months. Her family, consisting of her husband, 15-year-old daughter Amy, and 19-year-old son Sean joined my practice as well.

On this visit, she complained of a dull, severe, aching low back pain that seemed to be different from her previous pain. She was sleeping poorly and felt weak and easily fatigued. She was tearful and sad. I interpreted this initially to be a reaction to her severe pain and her progressing malignancy. Physical examination did not seem to be any different than previous ones except for her obvious distress. I decided that her pain was due to her cancer, and I increased her morphine dose. I sent her home to rest, promising that I would visit her at home in 3 or 4 days. It was on this home visit that the possibility of another factor in Mrs. D's pain became evident to me.

Three days later, in the early evening, I made that house call. Mrs. D's pain had not improved much, despite a 50% increase in her morphine dose. If anything, she looked to me to be in even more distress and seemed to be more depressed as well. I was sitting in the living room discussing with Mr. and Mrs. D the possibility of hospitalization when Amy walked into the house carrying her school books. She quickly surveyed the living room scene and walked away. With a troubled look on his face, Mr. D excused himself and followed his daughter. Almost immediately, from the back of the house, came the sounds of an argument between Mr. D and Amy. I caught snatches of it as I continued to talk to Mrs. D. "Home late again!" "You're not pulling your weight." "Don't you think your mother is worried enough?" My first inclination was not to interfere. But, Mrs. D's tears told me something. Could some family problem be a factor in her pain? While the argument continued to rage in the background, I gently questioned Mrs. D. What was happening at home? Mrs. D seemed visibly relieved to talk. Yes, her daughter seemed to be having problems and causing problems. She was angry, irritable, and argumentative; her school grades were slipping. I asked her if she thought that it would be a good idea for the family to sit down with me and talk about the situation. She agreed that something had to be done, adding the words "for my comfort."

I gathered the family for our impromptu conference. This turned out to be easier than expected since Mr. D and Amy seemed relieved to be able to discuss their difficulties. After fetching Sean from the television room, we began the family session.

As part of my initial palliative care consultation, I had assessed this family's function as being quite good. I therefore thought that to begin the conference I would tell them that, indicating that even the best of families could begin having problems when facing such a serious illness in one of their members. I asked Amy to lead off the discussion. She feared that her mother would die soon, but she was afraid to talk about it with any other family member because they all seemed so stressed. She felt that her father was expecting too much from her, expecting her to carry out too many extra household chores that her mother normally did. She felt overwhelmed. She also felt "different" from her friends and was socializing less. Her grades were slipping, and her late arrivals at home were, in fact, due to her trying to study in the library at school, without much success because she had problems concentrating. Her mother had been her closest confidante, but now Amy felt unwilling to burden her with other concerns. Both Mr. D and Sean shared Amy's fears about Mrs. D's illness. Mr. D had not realized that the extra burden he had placed on Amy was too much for her.

Mrs. D then spoke up. She had also not been able to speak about her fears of dying with anyone other than her physician. She felt ashamed and somewhat useless in that she could not fulfill her usual role within the family. She had withdrawn from her major role as the facilitator of communications within the family. She also felt that soon the family would have to do without her, and that it was best to see now how they could do on their own.

I did little but listen during the initial part of the session. This previously very functional family seemed to have the resources necessary to make changes to accommodate to Mrs. D's illness. My remarks to them were brief and revolved around the need for more communication between them, the need to recognize some of the role changes that were occurring, and the fact that Mrs. D still had a vital role to play in the family. I left them alone then with instructions to arrange a follow-up appointment the next week.

The effect of this one family session was dramatic on both family functioning and Mrs. D's pain. Within 3 days, her pain problem resolved, and she returned to her previous dose of morphine. At the next family session, considerable progress had been made in all areas. Mrs. D died at home about 8 months later, cared for by her family even though she had become paraplegic. At follow-up, the family was handling the grieving process quite well.

I learned a number of things from the D family. Pain problems require continuing assessment of psychosocial factors that may affect pain control. This has been further supported by encounters with other similar patients and families since that time. Even very healthy families can become dysfunctional when facing serious illness of a key member. Regular family conferences with such patients and their families are needed to assess their functioning and to mobilize their resources to help them cope. Also, such interventions can help the family during the period of their bereavement.

EDITORS' COMMENTS

Using the home visit and an impromptu family conference, this family physician with special interest in palliative care helped a normal family face an overwhelming stress, the impending death of a young mother. Dr. Librach convened the family in their own home and then sat back and allowed them to adapt to a serious problem. In so doing, he came to understand how to treat his primary patient's recent exacerbation of metastatic pain.

A therapist may have interacted in a similar fashion with this family but would not have been called in until the family dysfunction was worse. A family-centered physician achieved effective medical management of the patient's problem while also addressing other family members' significant needs. This led to more satisfaction for everyone in the therapeutic triangle.

MISSING DATA: A BOY WITH GASTROINTESTINAL PROBLEMS AND HYPERVENTILATION

JAMES W. MOLD
University of Oklahoma Health Sciences Center

WG was a 16-year-old young man who came by himself to my office with complaints of frequent paroxysmal episodes of belching followed by vomiting. Symptoms had first started 2 years earlier, but had increased significantly in the past 6 months. The episodes occurred usually after eating, but could occur at other times as well; once they started they would last for approximately an hour before they spontaneously resolved. The episodes were occurring at a frequency of at least three times a week and were causing WG to miss a fair amount of school (enough that he was in danger of failing a grade). This was the first time I had seen WG, but I had taken care of his father several years earlier for a variety of medical problems, including systemic lupus erythematosus. WG's father had died in a motor vehicle accident 3 years before.

WG had been seeing another physician in town for about 5 months for the same problem of belching and nausea, and had had a series of blood tests and x-rays including upper gastrointestinal series, barium enema, and gall bladder series, all of which were normal except for the presence of significant osteoporosis with multiple compression fractures of the spine, a slightly decreased total globulin concentration, a slightly increased phosphate, a slightly elevated alkaline phosphatase, and elevated triglycerides. He had been tried on multiple medications including cimetidine, antacids, metoclopramide, and simethicone without any significant improvement in his symptoms. When the other physician suggested that he see a dietician, he decided he should seek another medical opinion and, at the insistence of his mother, came to see me.

He seemed to be a very mature young man who was able to give a detailed and comprehensive medical history, including proper names of tests and medications. When asked about specific stressors in his life, he denied any significant ones and denied any knowledge of factors that could have contributed to the development of his symptoms. I mentioned his father's death 3 years earlier, and he indicated that it had been difficult for him but that he had recovered from that long before the symptoms began.

The observations made during WG's physical examination were interesting in that he had an unusual body habitus with truncal obesity and a fairly short trunk, shortened fourth metacarpals bilateral, and Tanner stage 3+ pubertal development. I requested his records from the other physician, reviewed his x-rays with one of the radiologists in town, and scheduled another appointment 4 days later. I learned that he had had a previous endocrine workup at age 14 for evaluation of delayed sexual development and elevated cholesterol and triglycerides, and also for metabolic bone disease. The workup was never completed however, because of a miscommunication between the patient's mother and the consultant.

On the second visit, I spent more time taking a history but did not make any significant progress toward understanding the cause of WG's difficulties. I had run out of ideas and was feeling lost and anxious. I decided to schedule a meeting with him and his mother together, mainly to bring her up to date on what I felt was going on, but also to gather some more information from her that might be helpful in deciding what to do next. At this point, I had pretty much decided that the osteoporosis and the belching and vomiting were two separate problems, and that the former required referral to an endocrinologist and the latter was probably psychosomatic, although I couldn't decide exactly what was contributing to it. I was also a little bit uneasy dealing solely with a 16-year-old without some interaction with his mother, even though WG obviously preferred to be treated as an adult.

My first conference with the patient and his mother was quite interesting. WG seemed anxious and was having some adventitious movements of his neck and facial muscles. This problem seemed to become worse and worse as the session went on, and eventually we had to stop the session. I tried some Serax by mouth (thinking that he was simply anxious), and then a shot of Benadryl when the Serax didn't work after half an hour (thinking that this might be an extrapyramidal reaction from his Reglan). When that didn't work, I gave him a rebreathing bag, and he got immediate relief.

Before his symptoms became too severe to continue with the conference, I was able to present my concerns to his mother, and I asked her if anything had happened at about the time of the onset of the symptoms 2 years earlier that could have contributed to a stress reaction. She told me that indeed his father had died 3 years ago, but that his grandmother, who had lived with them and had been quite close to her son, had died 10 months later (2 months before the onset of the symptoms). She also related that another relative had died several months after the onset of the symptoms, and a very close friend and father figure who lived in the neighborhood died 6 months ago at the time when the symptoms became much worse. She had not previously made the association, and when she remembered these things her son was quick to agree with the information.

After the hyperventilation symptoms had subsided, we talked briefly about the likelihood that WG's symptoms were anxiety-related. I started WG on Tranxene three times a day, and told him to return in several days for further discussions with me and a psychiatric consultant who visited our office every other week. WG was referred to an endocrinology clinic at the medical center for a workup of his bone disease. By the time of our next meeting several days later, he reported no further gastrointestinal symptoms and satisfaction that I was right about the etiology of his symptoms. He and his mother decided it would be best for him to go ahead and drop out of school for the rest of that school year and start back in the following school year. The psychiatrist's recommendation was that he have continued outpatient counseling, which was arranged through the local mental health center. His Tranxene dosage was changed to once a day at bedtime.

WG has had no further episodes of belching or vomiting in the 6 months following the above visits. He did not continue with the outpatient counseling and chose to continue on the Tranxene instead. His endocrine workup was inconclusive as to the etiology of the osteopenia and the bone biopsy is pending. I have encouraged him to reconsider counseling and to consider trying to taper the Tranxene after he makes the initial adjustment to the new school year. This is a situation where information provided by a family member was quite important in understanding the problem that the patient was having. He had seen the previous physician for a period of 5 months, and apparently during that time the mother was never consulted.

EDITORS' COMMENTS

Dr. Mold did something different from the patient's first physician when he directly involved this young man's mother in the discussion. In doing so, Dr. Mold obtained a more complete history and a better understanding of the problem by observing the patient's actual symptoms exacerbate in the presence of the mother. The presenting symptoms soon abated.

As for the follow-up care, we would like to second-guess our colleague. It is possible that the symptoms would have abated once the patient and his mother understood the nature of the son's discomfort. Once the patient's progress was attributed to medication, it proved difficult to move the family into ongoing nonmedical therapy. It was also difficult for the physician to convincingly stop the medication without seeming to be withholding the most efficacious therapy. On the other hand, by not immediately prescribing medication, the physician could have demonstrated that (1) the patient and not the physician is in charge of these symptoms, (2) the symptoms are not medically serious, although they are uncomfortable and disrupt the patient's life, (3) the problem will not be solved chemically, and therefore there should be little need for future use of any medication, and (4) the symptoms are more likely to be resolved through some type of talking therapy rather than through medical treatment.

For these reasons, we believe that medication in this type of case is generally counterproductive. It's use is understandable, and it is still commonly accepted medical practice. It may even have been the best choice in this specific case (we were not there and do not know the nuances of the case). However, if the physician's anxiety is under control enough to allow the patient's symptoms to resolve more slowly, medication often is not necessary. Subsequently, medication use would not be an ongoing issue, the family would be less dependent on physicians, and nonpharmacologic therapy would be more easily accessed if the problem recurs.

A WOMAN LEARNING TO LIVE WITH OSTEOPOROSIS: MAKING LEMONS INTO LEMONADE

STEPHEN A. BRUNTON
Memorial Medical Center of Long Beach

Mrs. W was a 60-year-old white female who first presented to my office in May 1980 with a 2-month history of low back pain. She stated that she had been in her usual state of good health up until March, when her mother had been readmitted to a hospital in Florida with terminal carcinoma of the uterus. Mrs. W had driven by herself across the country from California in order to help care for her ailing mother. During the 6 weeks before her mother's death, Mrs. W had spent the majority of time caring for her, which involved a considerable amount of lifting. This resulted in the acute onset and persistence of back pain. In Florida she went to a chiropractor who on at least a dozen occasions manipulated her back and treated her several times with short-term traction. She stated that this therapy, although providing some transient relief, did not result in any major improvement.

The patient returned home by car from Florida, taking aspirin almost constantly in an attempt to relieve her persistent low back pain. On arrival back in Southern California, she felt that the time had come for medical consultation and thus presented for the first time in my office.

The examination showed a young-looking 60-year-old woman in apparently good health, but in some discomfort. Major findings were in her back, which revealed several lower thoracic and midlumbar vertebrae that were tender to palpation and percussion. There was marked paravertebral muscle spasm, and a mild kyphosis was noted. Straight leg raising was negative. X-rays revealed severely osteopenic bones with compression fractures of T_6, T_{12}, L_2, L_3, and L_4.

I was concerned about the patient's severe osteoporosis and the possibility that I was witnessing pathological fractures secondary to either multiple myeloma or metastatic disease. Appropriate laboratory tests revealed that this was not the case, but confirmed that the patient was suffering from severe postmenopausal osteoporosis.

With the history of cancer in this patient's family, particularly the most recent episode involving Mrs. W's mother, she was of course extremely concerned that she had also succumbed to a malignant process. She was relieved to know that this was not the case. Being an extremely active woman, she was very worried about the limitations that might be imposed upon her by her pain, and ultimately by the fragility of her bones. A woman who lived alone and managed her own business, she was now being forced to consider restrictions imposed on her by her illness.

Mrs. W had been divorced 10 years earlier and lived alone. She had five children and six grandchildren. Most of her relatives were living in other states; however, she did have a daughter and a 15-year-old grandson who were living in relatively close proximity. I received several calls from some of her other children who were concerned about their mother as well as about the change they had noted in her attitude. She had been an important, positive, and motivating force within the family. It was now their impression that she had become depressed and fatalistic. This was exacerbated by a second hospitalization resulting from an aggravation of the T_{12} compression fracture, and the need for further acute pain relief. She was started on cyclic estrogen and progesterone therapy, calcium, vitamin D, and fluoride to try to diminish the ongoing demineralization of her skeleton. Nonsteroidal antiinflammatory medications, and transcutaneous electrical nerve stimulation (TENS) were also prescribed, which provided significant pain relief.

The second hospitalization provided me with an opportunity to meet with other members of her family who had flown in to see their mother. A family conference was organized to discuss future issues. Mrs. W was extremely troubled by the thought of being a burden to her children and was insistent that she maintain her independent lifestyle. It was apparent that her children loved and respected her greatly and were concerned about her future. One daughter felt that this illness might provide Mrs. W with the opportunity to explore other interests. Picking up on this idea, while recognizing their mother's need to be involved in projects and to continue a high level of activity, the family made many positive suggestions. Those that were particularly appealing included the proposition of retirement and enrollment in college courses in areas of her interest—most notably, American history. Additional suggestions involved writing a book, performing volunteer work, and the loving invitation that she consider adopting the role of "mother-in-residence," traveling the country to spend time with her children.

Home health services were organized to help her with routine household maintenance and two daughters offered to take turns staying with her at least for the following month.

The opportunity to undertake a lifestyle change appealed to Mrs. W, and the chance to indulge her lifelong interest in American history seemed to turn the tide in her declining morale. She was discharged to her home several days later with ongoing physical and occupational therapy, and was able to maintain relative pain control using the TENS.

After overcoming her initial depression, she decided to muster her energy and resolved to "take charge of her situation." She did a literature search on different aspects of her condition and its therapy. She often arrived at my office with a bundle of clinical articles and a plethora of relevant and challenging questions. She stopped smoking and started a vigorous walking program. She read widely on other health-promoting activities in an effort to develop an optimal level of health.

Over the ensuing months, Mrs. W directed some of her seemingly boundless energy toward helping those in similar physical circumstances. She contacted various physicians in the area, notified them of her intention to start a self-help group for people with osteoporosis, and invited them to send along their patients.

Mrs. W has proved to be an excellent resource for other osteoporosis sufferers. She continues to maintain a positive attitude despite a subsequent hospitalization for exacerbation of her T_{12} crush fracture.

She is progressing in her studies and maintains her independence, which she guards fiercely. I continue to receive Christmas cards from Mrs. W and from those of her children whom I met during that family conference.

Mrs. W is a source of inspiration to her family and to patients with similar afflictions.

The effects that an illness can have in a previously healthy and fiercely independent woman were apparent in this case. I was impressed with my patient's intelligence and with how her independence translated into taking great self-responsibility within the patient–physician encounter. Her need for autonomy initially caused some difficulty in developing effective communication and support from the family because of her desire not to "bother them with her problems." The family's concern, however, resulted in them rallying to offer support. A personal tragedy resulted in a positive outcome, with the patient developing alternative interests and using her energies to help others. It is enlightening and gratifying to me as a physician to see how illness can be a turning point in a patient's life. In this situation, I was able to witness how personal resources can be mustered to make "lemons into lemonade."

EDITORS' COMMENTS

This inspirational patient was becoming overwhelmed by life events. At a critical time, when she could have spiraled downward, she benefited from Dr. Brunton's respect for her independent spirit and his eagerness to meet with her loving family. Together, the physician and patient recruited powerful family resources—creativity, love, optimism, respect for the patient. They projected their belief that she would meet her problems with the same spirit that she had met other challenges in life. Once energized, this woman became a source of hope for others.

This secure family physician did not become irritated with her as she demonstrated newly found expertise in her medical problems, even though each office visit probably took some extra time. Technically excellent medical care, a family-centered approach, a competent responsive family, and a determined patient came together to create a positive force when disability could have remained the major theme. Sometimes, the chemistry is just right!

PARKINSON'S DISEASE AND THE AGING PATIENT

EDWARD T. BOPE
Riverside Methodist Hospital, Columbus, Ohio

Sixty-nine-year-old Miss Alice S was brought to my office by her older sister and brother-in-law, Mr. and Mrs. F, who had been patients of mine for just short of a decade, and patients of my father's for 3 decades before. This form of continuity of care intensifies the meaning of family practice. Miss S had been living alone in Illinois where she was a retired beautician. In that profession, she had grown accustomed to a hectic day and totally peaceful night. Now her days and nights were spent alone. Her long-time physician had retired and she had visited a new doctor several times. "I like him," she said, "but I just don't trust him yet and really hate to bother him." His diagnosis for her gradual onset of stiffness, stooped posture, and tremor was Parkinson's disease. Artane and Sinemet were started, but resulted in anorexia, nausea, and her seeing blue halos around everything. Each time she called the doctor, he added a new medicine. She would not go to his office. Her list now included Dilantin, Parlodel, Artane, and Larodopa. "I am lonely and afraid that someone will break in," she told me.

Her sister, Mrs. F, was not in good health. In fact, Mrs. F's physical activity was limited by a fractured hip that did not heal well. Mr. F had emphysema. Together, they ran a rural grocery store before retiring to the city. "I want Alice to move to this city to be closer to us. I don't think she can live with us, but if her health doesn't improve she cannot live alone. I can deal with her physical ailments, but I can't accept this mind stuff. I mean this idea that someone is after her is ridiculous, and she has to get over that. If not, she'll have to go into a nursing home." Alice sat without expression, a result of her disease and her perplexity as to how to change her lifestyle and thoughts. I felt strange having this conversation in front of someone I had just met. I felt allegiance to this family I had known for many years, and also to this person with whom I had now entered a doctor-patient relationship.

The best solution for all was one that was satisfactory to both parties. Decreasing her toxic symptoms was a successful first step, and within 1 week of stopping the medications, her nausea was gone. I gave them an assignment as a group: to tour two retirement centers. One week later, Miss S returned to Illinois, having been put on the waiting list for an apartment close to her sister. Two weeks later, the F family anxiously called to report that they were going to get Alice, as she was ill again. Off her medications, she again became stiff and paranoid, and by telephone she got her other doctor to renew her medications. Again she suffered from anorexia and blue lights. She was to stay with Mr. and Mrs. F until her apartment was ready, 1-2 months away.

Visits from the home health nurse and my housecalls made this temporary situation workable. Artane was restarted in small doses, and increased gradually. Her stiffness and tremors improved. Her paranoia seemed gone without the responsibility of her home. She saw Mr. F as her protector, and he accepted that position. I could see that Mrs. F gradually had begun to tire, and was growing more and more ill and fretful.

Finally, the apartment was available, and a nephew and the family helped Aunt Alice become settled. She loved the apartment and did well for weeks. Suddenly, however, she became very paranoid and would not even take her medicine. Haldol did not help and caused sedation. Another family conference in my office brought the problem to direct focus. "Either she has to quit the paranoid stuff or go into a nursing home," said a stern and resolved sister. Both Miss S and I were stunned by that reality. I felt a need to defend her, but we all understood the fairness and necessity of this resolve.

I elected to admit Miss S for medical evaluation, medication trial, and possible nursing home placement. I had as much trouble accepting this solution as the family did. We had all seen her living independently and happy. Physical therapy, stopping all medications, and the slow introduction of Sinemet proved successful. After 1 week, she was ready to leave the hospital. I knew that her sister could not stand another live-in visit and presented that option as undesirable. All parties seemed relieved. I arranged a trial 4-week stay in a convalescent center for further physical therapy and medication adjustment. If, at the end of this time she could care for herself and walk to meals, she could go back to her apartment; if not, she would stay indefinitely. This was agreeable to all. At the 2-week visit, Miss S walked to greet me. An increase in Sinemet further decreased her tremor and rigidity, and at 4 weeks she was beginning to pack her belongings. She now lives in her apartment where visiting family and nurses watch over her. The two sisters and Mr. F visit me in the office every 2–3 months. Together we support each other.

EDITORS' COMMENTS

This case could not have worked without a long-term trusting relationship between Dr. Bope and Mr. and Mrs. F. Indeed, here the relationship went back to Dr. Bope's father. Such a solid bond, where "together we support each other," allowed the doctor to take risks in the care of a troubled patient who was dropped on his doorstep. The medical, psychiatric, functional, and psychosocial aspects of this case were quite complex. Arriving at a satisfying solution took several attempts and as many false starts. What may have sustained Dr. Bope through all this was his conviction that "the best solution for all was one that was satisfactory to both parties." Neither an authoritarian posture ("here's what you should do") nor a passive posture ("let me know when you've made a decision") would have worked here. And coming up with one that is right down the middle between these extremes—active involvement that supports the patient's and family's needs and wishes—is no easy task. It requires a trusting physician–patient–family triangle.

BIRTH OF A DOWN'S SYNDROME BABY

KARL B. FIELDS
Nantahala Health Services, Andrews, North Carolina

An extremely challenging clinical case taught me a great deal about myself and about the role of the family in supporting medical illness. It reemphasized that the family means a group that extends well beyond consanguine boundaries.

Baby Girl W was born after an uncomplicated pregnancy to a 30-year-old, white, mother of one, who was in excellent health. Both parents were outstanding athletes and leaders of outdoor expeditions. They were extremely conscious of health concerns and took every precaution to ensure a healthy prenatal period. Ms. W had such a good knowledge of prepared childbirth and such an outstanding library of books concerning obstetrical topics that I often used her as a resource person to talk with other prospective mothers.

As the W family physician for 4 years, I attended the normal delivery of their first child. They experienced the true exhilaration that should accompany first childbirth. With the onset of Mrs. W's second labor, I shared the sense of excitement felt by the parents. A short first stage led to an uncomplicated birthing room delivery of a female infant, with a 1-minute APGAR score of 8. However, immediately on delivery of the infant, I had a sinking feeling that the child had Down's syndrome. Shortly after I gave the baby to her mother, the infant experienced a spontaneous respiratory arrest. Resuscitation was easily accomplished, and a 7-minute APGAR score returned to a level of 7. With this additional complication, my initial dejection about a less-than-perfect infant changed to strong feelings of despair.

A pediatric consultant and I sat down with the parents in the birthing room area. We discussed frankly that we felt the child had

Down's syndrome but was currently doing well. We gave the family a chance to express their concerns and relieve some of their emotions. I found my personal reactions to be very similar to those that I have experienced when I counsel families about the death of a loved one.

Unfortunately, the child did not do well and the respiratory arrest became a repetitive problem. After the first 24 hours, it was obvious this child had choanal atresia in addition to Down's syndrome, and was an obligate mouth-breather. Thus, after stabilization, the infant required transfer from our small hospital to a tertiary care facility, where a procedure was performed to open a nasal airway and place silastic tubing to ensure patency of the nose.

This situation was highly stressful for both parents. Parent–infant bonding was a potential casualty, as were marital harmony and a normal home life. Fortunately, the family withstood these initial stresses, stayed involved in the care of this child, and, over subsequent months, the child has done well. Undoubtedly, the medical course will wax and wane and will require extensive physician involvement but, at present, the parents have managed to learn to manipulate the nasal airway and ensure airway patency. They have become astute observers of their daughter's status, so that when she becomes fatigued with feedings or other problems, they adjust her schedule.

Surprisingly, at her 6-month evaluation this Down's syndrome infant was meeting most physical and developmental milestones. She had developed significant muscle tone and had done very well with home physical therapy. Both parents have managed to learn unique child-care skills that enable them to share the burden and relieve each other so that each can pursue personal interests.

The family's role in this child's care emphasized to me the tremendous need for family interaction in illness. As physicians, our healthcare team often struggled with the complicated medical management of this child. On numerous occasions, parent observations changed our plans for management of the respiratory complications, feeding difficulties, and physical therapy activities. Many of their observations were augmented by help from friends who would come to their home and assist them with the care of their daughter. A number of these friends had some professional training, either as physical therapists, nurses, or nutritionists. While these people were not initially a part of the care team that we physicians had organized, their insights have been helpful and have steadily expanded our therapeutic options in the management of this case. This couple lives in a unique environment in which they have not only their immediate families to rely on but a large peer group who have worked with them at their outdoor recreation center. These friends have served as extended family, and have provided strong psychological support for the W family. All have viewed this child as a special person and are helping her reach her full potential.

Each practitioner's experience with rare congenital defects like choanal atresia was obviously limited. Thus, in many ways the W family, because of their "hands-on" experience, has become more knowledgeable about this condition than any of their attending physicians. The positive attitude of family and friends buoyed our confidence and helped overcome the negative feelings that initially affected our medical care team. We have regained our enthusiasm about the challenge of assisting this family in any way that we can with their ongoing medical and personal needs. The W family, too, have made adjustments that have allowed them to pursue their outdoor interests and to take extended trips. They have not allowed themselves to become victims of the congenital misfortune that befell their daughter.

In family medicine, we are fortunate to be taught the importance that the family plays in every patient's care. We sometimes forget that our best teachers are often our patients. The W family taught me a great deal about dealing with despair, relying on one's resourcefulness to overcome major handicaps, and learning to listen to parents. Humbling as it is, physicians must also be comfortable with the awareness that families often become more expert and competent at dealing with the medical concerns of uncommon illnesses then we medical experts do.

EDITORS' COMMENTS

Dr. Fields began by sharing in the pain and confusion of a family facing despair. He then wisely accepted the family's leadership and became a supportive consultant to a parental team that soon became more expert on their daughter's rare medical condition than the physician was. This courageous and resourceful family outpaced the medical team in organizing assistance for their newly complicated daily lives. The family became the medical experts. The patient benefited from everyone's effort, as demonstrated by her satisfying level of growth and development.

Consider the complexity and changing nature of the physician's tasks with this family: provide primary prenatal care; competently deliver and resuscitate the baby; communicate the initial diagnosis (Down's syndrome), recognize a more acutely dangerous medical problem (choanal atresia); stabilize this potentially life-threatening problem; arrange for transfer of the baby to a tertiary level care setting to manage this complex medical emergency; be aware of the complications of this intervention in reference to parent–child relationships and to the parental dyad; offer support to the parents while their child is in the larger medical center; recover from his own sense of loss; and, finally, gracefully accept leadership from the family and their newly organized medical support network.

We never believed that family-centered care was easy. However, Dr. Fields's case demonstrates that this approach is achievable, practical, satisfying for the physician, and adaptive to the patient's and the family's unique needs.

LEVEL FOUR CASES

SYSTEMATIC ASSESSMENT AND PLANNED INTERVENTION

KNOWLEDGE BASE

Family systems.

PERSONAL DEVELOPMENT

Awareness of one's participation in systems including the therapeutic triangle, the medical system, one's own family system, and larger community systems.

SKILLS

1. Engaging family members, including reluctant ones, in a planned family conference or a series of conferences.
2. Structuring a conference with even a poorly communicating family in such a way that all members have a chance to express themselves.
3. Systematically assessing the family's level of functioning.
4. Supporting individual members while avoiding coalitions.
5. Reframing the family's definition of their problem in a way that makes problem solving more achievable.
6. Helping the family members view their difficulty as one that requires new forms of collaborative efforts.
7. Helping family members generate alternative, mutually acceptable ways to cope with their difficulty.
8. Helping the family balance their coping efforts by calibrating their various roles in a way that allows support without sacrificing anyone's autonomy.
9. Identifying family dysfunction that lies beyond primary care treatment and orchestrating a referral by educating the family and the therapist about what to expect from one another.

BEHIND THE MASK: "UNNECESSARY" PEDIATRIC VISITS

WILLIAM L. MILLER
University of Connecticut

It had seemed just a routine pediatric prenatal consultation. Admittedly, it was the end of the day, we were running unusually late in our schedule, and my partner was able to spend only 10 minutes for the visit. Nonetheless, the clues forewarning the future were all revealed and recorded; for a few months, we merely forgot to remember them. Three months after this visit, Mrs. B gave birth to a delightful 6-pound, 9½-ounce baby girl, Glee.

Everyone seemed to do well for 3 months. The 2-week and 2-month well-child visits were a pleasure, with Mrs. B and Glee smiling and charming throughout. Then, Mrs. B returned to work, and the tapestry world of princess Glee began unraveling. Over the next 6 months, we saw Mrs. B five times, we saw Glee 13 times, and we talked with Mrs. B on the telephone 16 times. All except 3 of these 34 interactions concerned suspected illness. The chief complaint was always nasal stuffiness and dry cough. Glee's presenting problems were the same, except for one self-limited bout of diarrhea. Only twice did physical examination reveal any actual abnormalities. At every visit, Glee appeared exquisitely dressed, playful, and pleased with herself. Mom always sounded confident, denied problems at home, and beamed her disarming smile. Everyone in our office knew Glee and Mrs. B.

At Glee's 9-month well visit, I finally noticed edematous turbinates, and, suspecting possible allergy, recommended a 1-week trial off dairy products and a few small changes in Glee's bedroom. Mrs. B, who had been remarkably patient with our past inability to make a diagnosis, bubbled with enthusiasm as I explained my suggestions. Her excitement was contagious, and after the visit, I shared my triumph (or was it relief?) with our head nurse. I was stunned when she commented, "They'll call back. You know, we still haven't seen or talked to Dad." My exuberance collapsed. We had trained our nurse well; she had seen behind the mask that had so successfully deceived my partner and me. Three hours later, the nurse's words throbbed in my ears as I answered the phone to speak with Mr. B for the first time. He was furious. He demanded to know what was wrong with his daughter and what gave me the right to tell his wife to completely refurbish their house. Evidently, Mrs. B had gone home and taken all the curtains down, thrown out many of Glee's toys, cleaned out Mr. B's closet, and was about to remove the sofa covers when Mr. B arrived home.

With the mask removed and the disarming smile no longer mesmerizing me, I remembered all the forgotten clues. Mrs. B suffered nausea for all 9 months of pregnancy; Mr. B was taking Valium chronically before coming to our office; Mr. B never called or appeared in our office; Mr. B remained silent throughout the prenatal consult; and, most obviously, Glee came for frequent office visits for illness though her exams showed her to be healthy. I almost felt as angry (embarrassed?) as Mr. B, who continued to demand an explanation.

After reassuring Mr. B that I had not prescribed redecorating their home, I began probing into Mr. and Mrs. B's marital relationship. I hit the jackpot! Their marriage had been struggling prior to the pregnancy, but the conflicts were overshadowed by Mrs. B's constant nausea, and then, after birth, by Glee's continuous "need for attention" because of her repeated illnesses that we unwittingly acknowledged by agreeing to see her (and getting paid). Mr. B admitted his anger toward us had been mounting steadily with each new bill from our office because he never thought Glee was sick. I accepted his anger, and asked that Mrs. B also join our phone conversation. We all finally agreed that the entire B family would come for the next visit.

The family session reinforced the information obtained by telephone. After 20 minutes, Mrs. B agreed to make appointments at our office only at times her husband could also come. She also agreed to argue with her husband instead of immediately going to check on Glee when conflict arose. Mr. B then agreed to listen to his wife when they did argue. In addition to these instructions for improving communication, they were also advised to spend 15 minutes touching each other daily. The smiles were gone when they left the office.

The B's medical bill has been much less over the last 6 months. Glee's nasal congestion has apparently resolved, and the need for telephone advice diminished. Glee even seemed less of a princess at her last well exam. I suspect problems will reemerge and more intensive marital therapy will be needed, but I am optimistic. I no longer have to peer behind the mask.

Family system disturbances usually present to the physician behind the mask of an individual illness complaint. In this case, that occurred over and over again before I unmasked the family problem. There were many pressures, all common in private fee-for-service practices, that operated to keep the mask in place. The demands of full schedules, fatigue, economics, and emotional stress combined with the B family's superficial acceptance and contentedness with our minimal efforts all conspired to keep the marital conflict hidden. This case also reconfirmed the value of training the entire office staff in family systems thinking and then paying attention to their observations. Their differing pressures and perspectives often allow them to see behind the mask sooner than the physician.

EDITORS' COMMENTS

Dr. Miller's own comments capture most of our thoughts about this case report. We would add the observation that a brief, primary care family intervention can be helpful without necessarily being definitive. The clearest outcome emerging from the family conference reported here was a healthier relationship between the family and the health care team that was no longer serving as an intermediary for the couple. The physicians in particular were no longer collaborating in a dysfunctional triangle with the spouses: "When I'm angry at you, I take baby to the doctor; the doctor understands my needs." Everyone's masks were off, and Dr. Miller's relief was palpable.

THE DEATH OF A TEENAGER

G. GAYLE STEPHENS
University of Alabama

Four members of the B family, representing three generations, have been in my practice for 4 years. Collectively, they have made 53 office visits and experienced an unusual number of life-threatening and serious illnesses. However, many of the visits arose out of the death of the 17-year-old daughter, whom I never met. She died from a massive intracerebral hemorrhage under circumstances that threatened the integrity of the family in an extraordinary way, influenced their attitudes toward physicians, and made my role as family physician difficult. Even now I am uncertain about what they expect of me.

My whole experience with this family was colored by the first visit with Mrs. B. She made an appointment for a physical examination, and I was completely surprised by her outburst of uncontrollable crying that began almost as soon as I entered the room and introduced myself. Slowly and painfully she recounted the death of her daughter, Caroline, 2 months previously, and said that she wanted to find a family physician. She told me that Caroline died because they did not have a family physician. This cryptic statement reflected her anger at an emergency department physician who had not recognized the serious nature of Caroline's illness 24 hours before her death, as well as at the on-call family physician, one of a group to whom she was referred by the emergency room. Mrs. B spoke to that physician by phone the next morning and was reassured that Caroline's symptoms did not seem serious.

This is what happened to Caroline. One evening, Caroline returned home in the company of friends complaining of headache and weakness in her legs. In the course of deciding what to do, Caroline's father made a fateful remark that, in retrospect, he said was in jest, but the remark probably reflected his style of parenting, his suspiciousness, and his fears about teenage behavior. He said, "What's the matter, did you smoke some 'funny cigarettes'?" Although Caroline was not known to use marijuana, the remark, tragically, was transmitted to emergency room personnel where Caroline was later taken. Drug use appeared on the medical record as the reason for the visit and influenced the treatment decision of the physician on duty. The hospital's policy of not allowing anyone but the patient in the examination room probably prevented the physician from getting a more appropriate history, and probably contributed to the parents' belief that a proper medical evaluation was not done.

Caroline was given an injection of prochlorperazine for the headache, and sent home. She spent a restless night, vomited several times, and had to be helped in and out of bed. She remained at home for about 24 hours, and her condition continued to worsen. Caroline was taken back to the emergency room the next evening where she was found to be *in extremis*. She died while being transferred to a university hospital. An autopsy disclosed massive intracerebral bleeding, probably from an arteriovenous malformation.

Mrs. B was grief-stricken, guilty, and angry. It was apparent that family members were not talking to each other about their feelings, denying their grief, anger, and guilt, escaping into work and social activities, and suffering in individual isolation. I recommended a joint visit with Mr. and Mrs. B, which took place a week later.

At the meeting, Mr. B talked while Mrs. B sobbed, and the whole sequence of events was reviewed in detail. Their focus was on medicolegal issues. They had retained an attorney, with whom they were also dissatisfied because he had been unsuccessful in obtaining the autopsy report. They seemed less interested in revenge or monetary gain than in understanding how this tragedy could have occurred and why the medical care system had failed them. They were so obsessed with questions that they could not begin to deal with their grief. Although they seemed eager to accept my offer of more joint visits, they did not return together.

Mrs. B seemed in good spirits when I saw her a week later, and chose to use the visit for a physical examination instead of counseling. I had obtained a copy of the autopsy report and urged Mr. B to talk directly with the emergency room doctor or the hospital administrator. He spoke with the doctor and seemed satisfied that the doctor appeared heartbroken about Caroline.

During the next 4 years, I saw four members of this family for a variety of medical problems, some quite serious. The problems were dominated by Mrs. B's unresolved grief, which manifested as anniversary depressions. I have summarized my experiences with the B family in a genogram (Figure 1), which also indicates how they have utilized the medical care system. I believe that they consider me and my colleagues their family physicians, but we have not provided all of their care. In spite of Mrs. B's initial statement to me that she wanted a family physician, it appears that they feel "burned" by Caroline's death, and they frequently refer themselves to other specialists.

This is the complex story of a devout, stable, closed but not close, middle-class, urban family of traditional patriarchal structure that suffered the [probably] unpreventable death of a teenage daughter. Their grief remains unresolved in spite of repeated attempts to deal

FIGURE 1. Genogram of the B family.

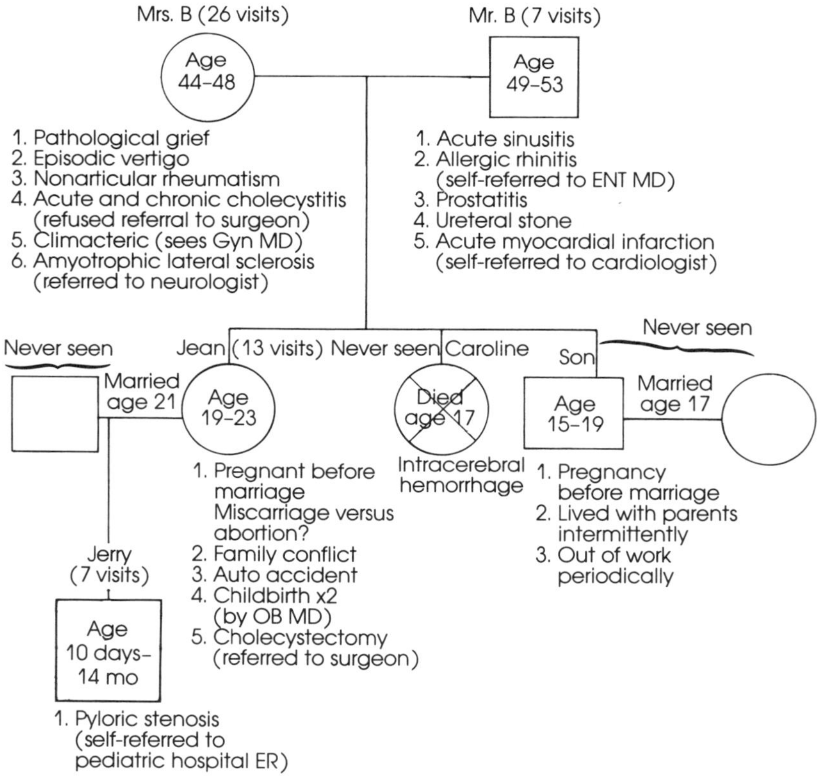

Mrs. B (26 visits) — Age 44–48
1. Pathological grief
2. Episodic vertigo
3. Nonarticular rheumatism
4. Acute and chronic cholecystitis (refused referral to surgeon)
5. Climacteric (sees Gyn MD)
6. Amyotrophic lateral sclerosis (referred to neurologist)

Mr. B (7 visits) — Age 49–53
1. Acute sinusitis
2. Allergic rhinitis (self-referred to ENT MD)
3. Prostatitis
4. Ureteral stone
5. Acute myocardial infarction (self-referred to cardiologist)

Never seen — Married age 21

Jean (13 visits) — Age 19–23
1. Pregnant before marriage Miscarriage versus abortion?
2. Family conflict
3. Auto accident
4. Childbirth x2 (by OB MD)
5. Cholecystectomy (referred to surgeon)

Never seen — **Caroline** — Died age 17
Intracerebral hemorrhage

Son — Age 15–19
1. Pregnancy before marriage
2. Lived with parents intermittently
3. Out of work periodically

Never seen — Married age 17

Jerry (7 visits) — Age 10 days–14 mo
1. Pyloric stenosis (self-referred to pediatric hospital ER)

with it. I counseled them, as their family physician. They were referred to a priest (this was unsuccessful) and to Compassionate Friends (this was partially successful as Mrs. B attended a few meetings).

I believe their grief has contributed to the poor health of all of the remaining members of the nuclear family, including a grandson with pyloric stenosis, though it probably is not sufficient to cause the remarkable sequence of medical problems that have plagued this family during my 4 years of observation.

There were three teenage children in the B family when Caroline died. Since then, the parents have been preoccupied with issues of control surrounding choice of friends, sexuality, and drug use. There is unremitting remorse, guilt, and blame that has never been discussed between the parents, or between the parents and the other children, and that has been displaced onto physicians and hospitals. It has resulted in attempts at tighter parental control over the two remaining teenagers, which may have contributed to unplanned pregnancies, forced marriages, and unprepared independence. It undoubtedly contributed to Mr. B's untimely heart attack, and may also be responsible for Mrs. B's fatal neurological disorder. They are now faced with her progressive disability and her death possibly in the next 2–5 years.

This family's strength, a traditional internal structure based on the father's authority, is also their weakness. It keeps them together through adversity, but it also prevents them, as a family unit, from expressing their feelings and coping with situations that threaten their family's integrity. They suffer alone, in silence, and keep up a strong front at all costs.

Their medical sophistication, perhaps pseudosophistication, is also a problem for me as their family physician. They believe in the science of medicine. Yet in a paradoxical way, medicine has let them down. They believe that medical problems can be fixed, and I often feel pressured not to make the same "mistake" that happened with Caroline. In spite of my best efforts, I did not prevent Mr. B's heart attack; I did not recognize the early onset of pyloric stenosis in the 10-day-old grandson; I took several months to diagnose amyotrophic lateral sclerosis in Mrs. B. I do not know whether or not they consider these to be derelictions, but the circumstances feed my fantasies of shattered omnipotence. Perhaps in my own way, I am grieving for them the way they are grieving for Caroline, through helplessness, guilt, and fear.

This story has no end, for the worst may be yet to come—Mrs. B's disability and death. I can only hope that what I have learned about this family can be used to help them cope better with another tragic loss.

EDITORS' COMMENTS

The author discussed many interesting facets to this case. We shall explore two more points. First, Dr. Stephens's case demonstrates that skilled, compassionate, family-sensitive care cannot overcome every barrier to a mutually satisfying doctor–patient–family relationship. He brought them together to discuss their tragedy and demonstrated open and direct communication. This was reinforced by encouraging the grieving parent to talk directly to the villainized emergency physician. (Did this action prevent a painful and expensive lawsuit?) However, further progress toward acceptance and healing was not forthcoming. Can anyone expect more from this family under these circumstances? In the future, someone in the family may allow more open discussion of painful feelings, perhaps around the care of the slowly dying mother. Until then, the physician can only struggle to limit the sense of becoming a "casualty" by respecting the family's autonomy.

This case study includes an impressive genogram outlining 4 years of the family's health problems. This longitudinal observation suggests that there may be a meaningful relationship between the death of their daughter and subsequent health problems for the surviving members of this family. Huygen's (1982) long-term observations of families suggested similar patterns. The association of these health events with family events does not prove an etiologic link, but case studies such as this one may lead us to more powerful methods of investigating these complex relationships.

LEUKEMIA AND THE RELUCTANT HUSBAND

JAMES J. McCOY
West Suburban Hospital Medical Center, Oak Park, Illinois

I became acquainted with the B family through a series of visits for well child care on behalf of 4-year-old Samantha. The family had recently moved to the Chicago area from North Carolina when Mr. B failed to receive an expected promotion from his employer. The decision to move to an urban area was based on Mr. B's hope of returning to graduate school and eventually making a major career change. Both Mr. and Mrs. B were originally from neighboring towns in Massachusetts where their parents and siblings still reside.

Approximately 2 years after their joining my practice, I treated Mrs. B for a series of infectious diseases: four within a 4-month period (pelvic inflammatory disease [twice], urinary tract infection, and sinusitis). The sinusitis was confirmed by sinus x-ray. A complete blood count (CBC) drawn at the office revealed a low white corpuscle count, relative lymphocytosis, and a dangerously low platelet count. I repeated the CBC 2 days later with the same results.

As before, with antibiotic treatment, Mrs. B recovered from the acute infection but further diagnostic evaluation stimulated by the abnormal peripheral blood findings revealed a diagnosis of hairy cell leukemia. This diagnosis was accomplished in consultation with a hematologist with whom I worked frequently.

Mrs. B was hospitalized and underwent a splenectomy and liver biopsy. During her hospital stay, Mr. B's frequent absence became noteworthy. I learned that he was not visiting daily, and that his sporadic visits were brief. I began to have the feeling that he was avoiding his wife, and me. Based on my knowledge of this family, I felt fairly confident with my hypothesis that Mr. B, as a means of coping with the situation, was distancing himself from the problem and not being supportive toward his wife. That is, I assumed that he was afraid and was protecting himself from experiencing the emotional pain associated with his wife's serious illness.

My awareness of Mr. B's physical and emotional withdrawal from his wife triggered two behavioral responses in me. One was to become more active in involving Mr. B in the health care process, by calling him frequently with the explicit purpose of keeping him informed of his wife's progress. Implicitly, I was making myself available to him if he should decide to discuss his fears and I was subtly encouraging him to be closer to his wife.

My second response was to become more attached to Mrs. B. I made frequent daily visits and we held lengthy discussions, often not related to the health problem. I soon realized that besides being her physician I was beginning to substitute for her husband. Fortunately, I was able to back away from this overly supportive role. As I did, she began to demand more support from her husband. (She insisted that he visit her daily, provide food she enjoyed from home, and get some support for child-rearing from someone other than her. Prior to this confrontation he had been calling her several times a day for routine child-care instructions.)

Following hospital discharge, I suggested, as is my habit, that both Mr. and Mrs. B attend the follow-up visits at my office. Mr. B did not attend any of the initial six biweekly visits. During these brief office visits (15–20 minutes), besides attending to the surgical wound and tracking peripheral blood smears, I inquired about Mr. and Mrs. B's emotional status vis-à-vis Mrs. B's serious illness. Mrs. B's reports led me to conclude that while she was making good progress in coping emotionally with her disease, Mr. B was not. During one visit, I asked how she thought her husband was dealing with this crisis, to which she replied, "Poorly."

I briefly explained my view to Mrs. B that although *she* was sick, her husband was sharing the illness and that he might benefit from a meeting to discuss his thoughts and feelings about his wife's cancer. The next day Mrs. B phoned to schedule a meeting to which Mr. B agreed to come. We met for 1 hour on a Saturday morning.

During this meeting, with his wife's support (she was touching his arm) and my encouragement, Mr. B was able to talk about his fears of losing his wife and of being left alone. He vividly described how he spent his lunch hours praying and crying in a church near his office. He angrily described how he was preparing to refuse an expected promotion because if he could not have what he wanted (a healthy wife) he didn't want anything. He cried openly during the session and gradually was able to speak more freely with his wife about his concerns and feelings.

We held three additional 1-hour joint sessions over a 2-month period and I saw that Mr. and Mrs. B were adjusting as a couple to their crisis. When the couple decided to discontinue our sessions, I felt comfortable with their decision because of their progress in coping with the crisis as a couple and because I still would have diagnostic and therapeutic access to the family through Mrs. B's office visits to manage her leukemia.

Mr. and Mrs. B later sought my advice on whether to have another child. As a team, we discussed the possible consequences of their having another child, including the possibility of Mrs. B dying of her disease, leaving Mr. B with the whole responsibility for parenting.

I consulted a hematologist regarding any effects pregnancy might have on exacerbating hairy cell leukemia and whether the leukemia might pose a threat to a developing fetus. The B's decided to have another child and are currently in the 4th month of a, so far, uncomplicated pregnancy. I see them both for prenatal visits, and occasionally their daughter accompanies them. Although Mrs. B's peripheral blood smears remain abnormal (mild anemia, leukopenia, relative lymphocytosis), there has been no evidence of a worsening of her leukemia.

I became acquainted with this family, like many others, through routine child-care visits. Through these pediatric visits and some others (Pap smears, employment physicals, minor infectious illnesses), I developed an awareness of how their family systems functioned. Only later did I realize how useful these observations were.

When Mrs. B developed leukemia, the family functioned in much the same manner as it had during lesser crises. Mr. B withdrew and isolated himself from the family; Mrs. B increased her role as caretaker (even though in this case it was she who required extra care) and complained of being lonely.

Because I knew this family and they knew me, I feel I was in an excellent strategic position to intervene in their crisis. We already had a good working relationship, and I was confident in my assessment of their family dynamics.

I almost undermined this family's natural coping ability when I allowed myself to get too close to Mrs. B. I was more than ready to replace Mr. B as the primary support person to Mrs. B. Had I done that, I am sure Mr. B would have withdrawn further and become more depressed, and Mrs. B would have become even more lonely. By treating this problem as a "family" crisis, I was able to promote a much more viable support system (the marriage) than I could provide as a person outside the family unit. A good outcome was achieved by the couple with my facilitation and encouragement rather than by me in a rescuer role.

I continue to work with this family (now primarily around prenatal care) and I'll have to admit they have become very special to me. I have a feeling of being a "complete" physician with them. I find myself integrating medical and psychosocial skills to adequately manage the illness process. I find this context of biopsychosocial service very rewarding.

EDITORS' COMMENTS

The key here was Dr. McCoy's awareness that he was replacing Mrs. B's husband, thereby blocking the process of the patient and her husband facing squarely the lack of mutuality in their relationship. Mr. B was an easy setup for the villain role; after all, he was grossly neglecting his seriously ill yet brave and loving wife. Once the doctor withdrew from being overinvolved and instead broached the subject of how Mr. B was coping, Mrs. B prevailed upon her husband to accept couple counseling. Then Mr. B's pained humanity was plainly visible, and the couple used four counseling sessions over a 2-month period to readjust their relationship so that they could each give and receive. They apparently did most of this work on their own after Dr. McCoy showed the wisdom to back away from his patient and the persistence to keep extending a hand to the husband, whom Dr. McCoy refused to regard as a villain. This represents quite skilled Level Four primary care family counseling: the physician managing his or her own role in the therapeutic triangle, patiently working toward getting the relevant characters in the family drama together, and then providing a supportive atmosphere for a basically adaptable family to break an impasse and acquire more satisfying ways of relating.

A THERAPEUTIC FAMILY DISRUPTION AFTER CANCER SURGERY

THOMAS L. SCHWENK
University of Michigan

Mrs. L was a 46-year-old woman who was born in Germany and had been living in the United States for many years. I first saw her when her family physician left the area and suggested she transfer her care to me. Her problem at that time was that she was recovering from a modified radical mastectomy for adenocarcinoma of the right breast, with subsequent chemotherapy. This occurred about 1 year earlier, and there had been no residual cancer or metastases discovered since. Her overall physical health was good, but she continued to be listless, sad, and unconcerned about her appearance and to experience sleep disturbances. A diagnosis of depression was made and psychotherapy and pharmacologic therapy begun. She continued to do poorly, however, and I was besieged by telephone calls from the patient's adult daughter who lived at home and was worried about her mother's seemingly hopeless situation.

Mrs. L's condition was complicated by the fact that, shortly after the breast surgery, she fell and suffered an ankle fracture that required a walking cast for 6 weeks. Subsequent to that, she had a pulmonary embolus from an occult deep vein thrombosis, resulting in hospitalization and anticoagulation. The patient had no other significant medical or psychiatric history.

Mrs. L and her husband were both born in Germany and manifested personality traits of stubborn independence. They had had two daughters, the eldest of whom was described by the patient as the "perfect" daughter—respectful, helpful, and very neat and orderly. This daughter was killed in an auto accident very close to the time of the breast surgery. The remaining daughter felt very keenly the differential feelings of her mother, who described her daughter as unhelpful and untidy. The daughter attempted to do everything in the household—all house care, meal preparation, and nursing care for her mother—which had the result of keeping Mrs. L more or less bedridden, though there was no reason for her to be. The husband was emotionally supportive but distant from the mother–daughter interactions. Only the daughter came with her mother to medical appointments.

In the space of 1 year, Mrs. L had lost a daughter, undergone radical cancer surgery, and suffered an ankle fracture and a pulmonary embolism. She had more than enough reason to be depressed, especially on the anniversary of the surgery and the daughter's death. What was striking about this patient, however, was the marked unresponsiveness to appropriate drug and talk therapy. She was not suicidal, and the depression was not really that severe, but the woman was remarkably more passive, dependent, and listless than she was before her daughter's death. There was also a marked discrepancy between her relatively good physical condition and the description given by her daughter at visits and in telephone conversations. The daughter portrayed the patient as physically disabled and requiring total home nursing care, which the daughter took great pride in providing. The mother seemed almost excessively appreciative of this, and would take great effort to tell me how wonderful her daughter was, "just as good as my other daughter."

My impression was that the mother–daughter relationship was highly dysfunctional and detrimental to the patient's rehabilitation. I felt that Mrs. L was physically capable of complete functional recovery but was blocked from doing so by her daughter, who made and kept her mother a complete invalid. This seemed to fulfill the daughter's need to prove that she was as good a daughter as the one who had died. It also seemed to fill Mrs. L's need to compensate for her differential love of her two daughters by turning control of her life over to her remaining daughter. It also seemed to please Mrs. L that her daughter was so organized and competent at home. This family seemed to demonstrate characteristics of severe enmeshment.

Much to my own amazement, I decided to recommend to the family that the daughter leave home. She had previous plans to enroll in college and live on campus, and I suggested she keep these plans. I did not go into great detail about my rationale for this, but was quite firm. The family, though somewhat confused and angry, complied.

Mrs. L made a quick and complete recovery. Within a few weeks of the daughter's departure, Mrs. L was taking complete care of the household, exercising, becoming involved in community activities in which she had previously been interested, and making plans for reconstructive breast surgery. The antidepressant medication was stopped. The mother maintained contact with me, but revealed in retrospect how confused and angry she had been with my suggestion. The daughter was equally angry. We had a final conference at which I explained my decision, and I was satisfied that they understood and agreed. I have remained on friendly terms with the family ever since (about 3 years).

I tend to think of helpful family interventions as those that bring families together. This intervention did just the opposite, but seemed to work well. This case also demonstrates how appropriate behavioral science care of the *individual* may not be enough, that only when *family* factors are examined can some difficult problems be solved. I continue to be amazed at the complexity of factors involved in medical care and at the importance of the family in these difficult cases.

EDITORS' COMMENTS

This case illustrates an unusual and spontaneous family intervention by the physician. In an effort to move a patient and family from a rigid pattern of interaction, this physician suggested a creative change in family relationships. The risks to the physician were considerable. Had they not trusted him, the family might have called him uncaring and broadcast a negative image to the community. Instead, the family gave him the power to intervene. They were ready for change. Dr. Schwenk trusted his judgment, and offered a surprising intervention. His understanding of family systems was integrated with his understanding of biological systems. The result here was an effective approach to a difficult clinical problem.

Not all physicians would have the combination of knowledge, skill, and courage to interact with a family in this manner. Not all families would have responded favorably. However, this case demonstrates that some families are susceptible to change at times of medical crisis, and that a physician trained to understand common family interaction patterns can intervene successfully.

THE VENTRILOQUIST: FEAR THAT FATHER WILL DIE

YVES R. TALBOT
Mount Sinai Hospital, Toronto, Ontario, Canada

The B family sought service at the Family Practice Unit for their 16-year-old son, Jim, because of progressive fatigue accompanied by an episode of fever. The symptoms had persisted over the last 2 months, resulting in Jim's increased absence from school. Because Jim and his family lived on a small animal farm, I suspected many esoteric infection processes. A thorough investigation was done, requiring a few visits to the hospital, but it failed to reveal an organic source for the fatigue, and the episode of fever was considered as probably fortuitous.

The nurse thought Jim seemed to be depressed, though he was not presenting any other signs or symptoms of depression. I decided to meet the family to share with them the results of our investigation. At the interview, Jim sat close to his mother and father on the other side of the desk. During the interview, Mrs. B (Linda) revealed that her husband (Paul) had suffered a myocardial infarction several months before. A meeting with the family had been conducted at the time by Mr. B's cardiologist to explain the disease to the family, and highlight for Mr. B the importance of stopping cigarette smoking and the need to reduce somewhat the number of heavy activities he performed around the house.

During the interview, I probed Jim's concerns about his father's recent illness:

DR. T: Jim, that must have been a frightening experience to see your dad sick and in the hospital.

(At this moment, Jim's eyes filled with tears and his mother reached for his hand.)

MRS. B: Yes, it was for all of us. Paul had always been such a strong man. It caught us by surprise. We were afraid to lose him.

DR. T: You felt you needed to do something about it.

JIM: *(looking at his mother)* Yeah, because Dad did not seem to want to do anything about it. He does not want to slow down. I even caught him many times smoking behind the barn.
DR. T: Did you know your family cared so much about you?
MR. B: No, I never realized it affected Jim so much.
DR. T: It sounds like both your wife and Jim were concerned.
MRS. B: Yes, and I don't think you want to listen.
DR. T: Paul, I think it must have been difficult for you, too.
MR. B: It came as a surprise. I have always done what I wanted to. It really caught me by surprise.

I had identified a current concern of the family around Mr. B's illness, and had shifted the focus temporarily away from Jim. Detouring of communication through a child is not an unusual way for some families to communicate in a situation of high intensity. In this case, it served to bring the father back to a physician through his son's complaint. It is a way of communicating to protect the father's denial (not uncommon after a heart attack). Unfortunately, such a pattern, if allowed to persist, could have been detrimental to Jim's growth and to his father's recovery.

DR. T: Do you feel, Jim, that by staying home you can keep a close eye on your father?
JIM: Yes, and I have been doing some of his work but he still finds other things to do, and Mom worries a lot about it.
DR. T: Your mom worries?
JIM: Yeah. She keeps talking to me about how her uncle dropped dead on the farm—my Uncle Charles—a few years ago.
DR. T: That is pretty frightening.
JIM: Yeah.
DR. T: Linda, you said your husband does not listen. Your husband must be a very proud and responsible man.

This last exchange indicated to Linda that the physician had heard her concerns, but also addressed her husband's concern—what happens when illness strikes the breadwinner of a household.

DR. T: *(to Mrs. B)* It appears that Jim is doing some of your talking. You are some sort of a ventriloquist. *(Family laughs.)* *(to Jim)* Did you know your mom was a ventriloquist?
JIM: *(laughing)* No.
DR. T: *(to Mr. B)* I think you have a very concerned family.
MR. B: I guess so.

During the rest of the interview, I helped the family to understand that they need not worry about Jim's health; results of the clinical investigation have been negative. I also indicated that it was not unusual, when the father in a family was struck by disease, that everyone try to protect everyone.

In my experience, situations such as the one with the B family are not unusual. I am always suspicious when assessing absenteeism from school following an acute, potentially fatal illness like heart disease in one family member. I have found it very helpful to spend time with the family, in my office or at home, in the weeks following discharge from the hospital. It allows me to assess how the family copes with the situation and, it is to be hoped, prevents a situation like Jim's.

EDITORS' COMMENTS

The family interview was arranged with the goal of sharing information about the young man's medical evaluation. This routine led to improved understanding of the context of his symptoms: family stress over his father's recent heart problems. Quickly, Dr. Talbot explored this important issue in a way that gracefully connected the son's fatigue with his father's illness. The family was treated with respect. No one was identified as specifically "causing" the young man's symptoms. The key decision was to discuss the findings of the medical evaluation with both parents as well as with the primary patient. Having assembled this powerful group, the skilled primary care physician gently led the family to understand the son's complaint. Since everyone discovered the biopsychosocial connections together, the physician did not have to convince a possibly skeptical family member who was not in on the discovery. The family-centered approach offered an efficient method for the physician to approach the patient's complaint. Everyone benefited. No one lost. In the process, everyone involved was given permission to be human.

Dr. Talbot is a trained family therapist and family physician. Some of his writings can be found in Christie-Seely (1984).

OUTPATIENT CARE OF A NEWLY DIAGNOSED ADOLESCENT DIABETIC

DAVID O. HOUGH
Michigan State University

Ms F, a 17-year-old white female high school senior, came into my office complaining of a 2-week history of polyuria, polydipsia, polyphagia, a 7-pound weight loss, fatigue, and nocturia. She told me that she had an upper respiratory infection 2 weeks prior to the onset of these symptoms. Significant family history included an 11-year-old paternal cousin with Type I diabetes mellitus, and hypertension in both her father and paternal grandfather.

She had been completely healthy and, in fact, had taken her health for granted. She was very active physically, captain of her swim team, and involved in aerobic dancing, weight lifting, and daily running. She came from a well-educated family that included her father, a university professor, her mother, a housewife, and two siblings. She was active in many community and high school activities (she had recently been prom queen), and had close relationships with her many friends and family. The rest of her medical history was insignificant at this time.

I immediately became concerned that she had Type I diabetes mellitus. Physical examination revealed a 5-foot, 103-pound, slightly ill and anxious-appearing young female. She had evidence of less than 5% dehydration, her lungs were clear but she had a grade I/VI systolic ejection murmur. The rest of her examination was normal. A random blood glucose obtained in the office was 271 mg%. Urinalysis revealed 2+ glucose and 3+ ketones. Her serum ketone level was negative and routine Smac was within limits. The patient had Type I diabetes mellitus without ketoacidosis.

Ms. F's reaction to her illness was interesting. Her own words, written months after the diagnosis was made, reminded me of how careful I and other physicians should be in making a diagnosis and then presenting it to the patient and family. She wrote:

> No. Not me. It's not possible. Diabetes? What does that mean? Isn't that sort of like having leukemia? This was supposed to be the best year ever—my senior year. It had gotten off to such a good start, too—my trip to France over the summer, captain of the swim team, president of the National Honor Society, on the Homecoming Court (with the date of my choice)—how could this happen to me?! I suddenly felt the ground fall out from under my feet as a lead balloon made a crash landing on my head, leaving my brain in a flurry of unsorted emotions. I couldn't even cry at first, I just felt numb.

These emotions are typical of the newly diagnosed adolescent diabetic, and they made me think carefully about how I was going to help Ms. F manage her disease in a way that would upset her life the least.

Since she had no evidence of ketoacidosis, I elected to treat her as an outpatient, despite the fact that most diabetic education is done in the inpatient setting of our community. Before making this decision, I decided to talk to Ms. F and her parents. During the family interview, I learned that the family worked closely as a unit. They seemed to handle pressure during family crises extremely well. They communicated openly and freely, and obviously trusted each other. Compliance with medical issues appeared to be excellent. The family APGAR scores were within normal limits. I then asked Ms. F about her personal resources. In descending order of importance, she listed: her steady boyfriend, girlfriends, parents, and siblings as those involved with her emotional support. When asked about who should help her manage her physical ailments, she listed her parents, physician, and nurse as resources. With this information, I felt more comfortable treating her in the office setting.

I was confronted with a number of medical issues over the next 2 weeks.

What would be the effect of interrupting her usual daily schedule, which included a very active exercise program and her school work? I found she had very supportive coaches and teachers who, with increased understanding of her problem and a little extra work, were able to keep Ms. F in the swimming pool and up-to-date with her classwork.

How would her exercise program affect diabetic control? I felt that an active exercise program would facilitate improved glycemic control as long as the insulin dose was properly managed and spaced in accordance with proper timing of her meals. Insulin was started after her first visit, and she was given divided doses of regular and lente insulin. I was concerned that she might have a hypoglycemic reaction, so I instructed her on how to manage that problem. She was seen by the office nurse for daily serum glucose testing the first week, and this proved very useful in managing her diabetes and adjusting daily insulin doses.

Ms. F was concerned about her recent weight loss, and she wanted to know how best to maintain her weight during competition. With the nurse's help, a reasonable weight maintenance diet was determined and presented to Ms. F and her family. She eventually sought the help of a nutrition consultant on her own, and this served to reinforce what our office had taught her. Many hours of nursing time were spent educating Ms. F about urine and serum glucose testing, how to use a scale for dietary management, how to manage her swim practice schedule and travel, and how to control hypoglycemic reactions and other illness problems related to her disease.

A number of family issues were discussed during the first several weeks of treatment. Ms. F felt that her family and friends were wonderful, and that they were always there when she needed them. She felt incredible guilt, and wondered what she had done to cause all these problems. She was very upset with her family when they did not understand what was going on inside her. She sometimes found herself unnecessarily short-tempered with her family, saying things like, "If they love me enough they should feel sorry for me and not get mad when I get upset." Of course her parents loved her, but they, too, were becoming increasingly frustrated. Many arguments ensued. The family was becoming more protective and restrictive of their daughter because of their inability to understand not only her new medical problems but also the normal biologic and emotional problems of adolescence.

I used several office visits to discuss these issues with Ms. F and her parents in an attempt to work out a manner in which they could all live more easily with the diabetes. These discussions seemed to work extremely well, but it still took her 6 months to feel more comfortable with her disease and to adapt to the restrictions in her life. The family gradually gave her more responsibility, such as allowing her to drive the family car without an escort. Ms. F was able to manage every aspect of her diabetic condition. Though there are still times when she wants to prove her independence, she is trying to deal with these feelings. Her parents have gained a lot of confidence in her, especially since she went on a recent vacation alone and managed her diabetes extremely well. Six months after initiating treatment, she was confident of her ability to manage most problems common to adolescent diabetics. She is now looking forward to starting her college career away from home.

After seeing Ms. F daily for approximately 2 weeks, we (the nurse or myself) began to see her weekly, and then monthly. Four months after initial diagnosis, she had established a home glucose monitoring program and was able to maintain her glucose between 60–120 mg% while adjusting her own insulin. Her hemoglobin A_{1c} ranged between 4.3%–5.4%, her weight had stabilized, and she was having one of her best years in sports. The majority of her emotional problems have been resolved through her own efforts and with the help of her boyfriend. She still feels some antagonism toward her parents when they are overly protective, but, with more open discussion, they will be able to work things out as a team. She is now taking two insulin injections daily, testing her urine three times daily, and using home glucose monitoring approximately every other day. She sees me every third month and will be leaving for college soon.

Her own comments best summarize how she feels about being managed as an outpatient:

> I think that the most valuable part of having not been hospitalized is the feeling of accomplishment I gained from keeping my independence. That outweighs any of the problems that I have come up against. It feels good to know that I can do it and do it for myself. Diabetes is a long-term disease and the sooner one can come to terms with it and incorporate it into one's daily life, the easier life is. Long-term control is what we have to strive for; one must not focus on the day-to-day problems. One has to learn to deal with the emotions that are part of this problem and use them to one's advantage. Fight for your life; its worth it!

In this case, I felt confident that I could manage the patient's diabetes in the outpatient setting because of a lack of severe complications or ketoacidosis. The pivotal point was the patient's and her family's ability to communicate effectively with one another and to work problems out in the face of uncertainty. I felt that knowing the family as a unit of care and understanding the patient's emotional background helped me to make appropriate decisions, although her outpatient course was not without problems.

The hardest part of this case for me personally was Ms. F's difficulty in accepting her diagnosis and interrelating with her family, though the problems she experienced are common to all newly diagnosed adolescent diabetics. Only after seeing the patient together with her appropriately frustrated family did the picture make any sense to me. I felt the patient, her family, and the medical staff were ultimately pleased with the overall outcome and clinical course of Ms. F's diabetes management in the office setting. I developed a close rapport with both the patient and her family and eventually became her confidant and consultant for other problems relating to adolescent health care.

I learned a great deal from helping Ms. F manage her diabetes in the ambulatory setting. I know it can be done, and I feel confident about using this management process with selected patients in the future.

Successful treatment of any ongoing medical problem involves a health care team that is attuned to the special needs of the patient, and must involve the patient and family in every step of treatment. Management of this patient was both interesting and exciting, especially as I watched her work with the information we gave her and overcome the hurdles in her way. Many of the lessons I have learned from this case can be applied to other cases, especially those involving chronic diseases.

EDITORS' COMMENTS

Initiating the management of Type I diabetes on an outpatient basis is rarely attempted within a patient care model that emphasizes the doctor–patient relationship alone. Working within a family-centered model, Dr. Hough was brave enough to help his adolescent patient and her family to weather the emotional trauma of the diagnosis, the complex informational and dependence-independence issues of diabetes management, and the normal developmental tasks of an adolescent and her parents achieving more autonomy while still being caring and supporting. In facing a disease that takes lifelong control, the patient and her family were able to be in control of their lives from the outset. The experience was clearly a breakthrough for Dr. Hough in his willingness to risk sharing responsibility for patient care with patients and families.

A DETERIORATING FAMILY

RUSSELL J. SAWA
University of Calgary

My introduction to the G family, 35-year-old Bob, 33-year-old Donna, and their sons, 13-year-old Brian and 10-year-old Sheldon, occurred about 5 years ago. At that time, Brian was enuretic. This was helped at the time with Tofranil. A few months later his mother presented with anxiety. A brief inquiry as to how things were going in the family disclosed that she was having trouble communicating with her husband and that she felt that he was not adequately involved with his two sons. I asked for a meeting of the whole family to assess the situation. At this meeting, I learned that Mr. G was not responding to the emotional needs of his wife and children. The elder son was somewhat depressed and was concerned that his parents might divorce. Mrs. G had doubts about her husband's commitment and love for her. There were disagreements about how the children should be disciplined. Also, it was disclosed that Mr. G had had an episode of paranoia several years ago and had been admitted to a psychiatric ward. Mrs. G was considering divorce at that time, a fact that Mr. G continued to resent and hold against her. The family requested family therapy, which was initiated. Mr. G's paranoia increased however, and the family therapy sessions were abandoned after several sessions.

The situation deteriorated over the next half year. Mr. G had a second psychotic break. He was admitted to the hospital, where a diagnosis of paranoid schizophrenia was strongly suspected. Again, Mrs. G made overtures toward marital separation.

For the next several years, things were rather difficult in Mr. and Mrs. G's marriage. Mr. G had difficulty accepting his illness and at times refused to take his medications. He had several more psychotic breaks. Mrs. G developed a reactive depression.

During this period of strife, I met with members of the family at various times. Sometimes I met with just Mr. and Mrs. G; sometimes the entire family met. After years of consideration, Mrs. G decided to separate from her husband and moved out of their house. I continued to meet with family members. I also had group meetings with the children and each parent separately to help each of them work out separation and child-rearing issues. With Mr. G, I focused on coping with the separation. Sheldon was feeling particularly responsible for the separation. I met with him and his father to help his father set the record straight and give Sheldon the support he needed. I also met with Brian and his mother on several occasions to help her deal with the problems he was going through both at home and at school. I met with Brian and his dad to help Mr. G to stop using Brian to get back at Mrs. G.

Mr. and Mrs. G are both working to create new lives for themselves as separate individuals. I have met with them individually on several occasions and worked with them to sort out issues regarding custody of their children.

Each member of the G family seems to be adjusting to the new situation. Mr. G's paranoia is under control and he is coming to grips with his new life. He has even begun a new relationship. I see all four members for various physical problems, and I try to help them with some of the problems created by the family separation (e.g., I talked about the situation with Brian, who had problems at school during periods of conflict at home).

From this involvement, I learned that one need not do sophisticated family therapy to be able to help. By having the trust of the family and by being available to them, I was able to intervene successfully during periods of crisis. I now find that it is a tremendous advantage to know all four members of the family as well as I do. Because of this, I am able to help each one of them individually while taking into account the entire family system, and thus avoid siding with one individual in a manner that could be detrimental to the individual and the rest of the family.

I learned a great deal about helping families in crisis through my experiences with the G family. I found that by getting to know each individual family member I am better able to help the whole family. I discovered that it is possible to help families and individual family members through times of emotional stress and help prevent further emotional damage in a family even when the marriage itself cannot be saved.

Following the separation, I have continued to work with the G's. I helped Mr. G with the traumatic task of arranging visits with his children, and with other issues involving their care and welfare. I have developed a good understanding of Mrs. G's depression and her efforts to establish a nurturing relationship with another man. I am also able to deal with the children and their emotional and school problems because I understand their family situation. Without such an in-depth knowledge of this family, I might have supported Mr. G's bitterness toward his wife and not have been able to see its destructive effect on the children. I might even have treated Mrs. G and her children as emotionally disturbed rather than as people reacting to a difficult situation in their family life cycle. Without adopting a family approach, I could not have helped this family deal with their emotional problems. This approach provided the context for helping each of them as individuals to cope with an exceedingly difficult family crisis. The success of this "untraditional" approach has added depth to the unique role I have as a family doctor helping my patients and their families.

EDITORS' COMMENTS

Dr. Sawa is an experienced family therapist as well as a family physician (see Sawa, 1986). He is able to work at whatever level of family involvement seems appropriate. At first, he began level five family therapy aimed at changing long-standing family problems. Blocked at this point by Mr. G's deteriorating condition, Dr. Sawa shifted into a level four primary care approach for the duration of the case. That is, he focused on helping the family adjust to the painful changes they were experiencing during the peak of marital strife and the subsequent divorce. In a flexible style quite suited to the multiple ways a family physician can engage family members, Dr. Sawa worked with the family in different combinations of individuals, pairs, and triads. Sometimes these contacts were for primarily biomedical reasons, and sometimes for primarily psychosocial reasons. But the blending over time is a hallmark of a biopsychosocial and family systems approach to medical care. Dr. Sawa put a lot of time and work into this family, but his sense of satisfaction is palpable.

DEMENTIA OR ALCOHOL INTOXICATION?: A CASE FOR HOME EVALUATION

J. M. PONTIOUS
Private practice, Madill, Oklahoma

Mr. G, a 72-year-old white male, presented to my practice for chronic care. His complaints were often deceptively simple on the surface, but frequently complicated by the severity of his chronic medical problems. The patient was being followed for hypertension, right cerebrovascular accident with intermittent aphasia, transient ischemic attacks, and prostatic carcinoma, metastatic to bone.

The patient complained mainly about bilateral knee pain from his severe degenerative arthritis. "It seems that with as much medicine as you have me on, my pain ought to be better controlled!"

Meanwhile, I was seeing his 70-year-old wife of 40 years for repeated difficulty with depression. "My husband is getting more and more abusive verbally," she explained, adding that it was getting to the point at home that he would not allow her out of his sight. He would become immediately agitated if she was not available. He was also becoming more difficult to manage in any social gathering; he did not hear well and would speak inappropriately and abusively. Their current social contacts included his sister and her husband and occasionally Mr. and Mrs. G's four children, although they would only be present for short periods of time so as not to risk agitating their father.

Mrs. G was frustrated that she was unable to do any traveling. She felt that retirement was a time to travel, but Mr. G was much too difficult to take on trips, and he would not allow her to go alone. The family and friends were not willing to help out. She felt trapped.

Mr. G required hospitalization over the Thanksgiving holiday for sepsis, which developed from a urinary tract infection. During this hospitalization, he was evaluated for a sudden worsening in his mental status and increase in his aphasia. A CT scan showed multiple old cerebral infarcts. This was explained to the wife and family, who appeared to understand and were appreciative that Mr. G was improving enough to go home. He required a visiting nurse for 2–3 weeks after discharge, but he improved rapidly.

He persisted in his marked agitation, which was becoming more pronounced and frequent. During clinic visits, if he was checked into the examining room and not seen in about 2 minutes, he would become belligerent and use abusive language to the staff and his wife, complaining in a loud voice, "Where is that damn doctor?" His mental status was worsening to the point that he could not recognize me when I entered the examining room.

Over the Christmas holidays, I was visited by Mr. and Mrs. G's youngest daughter, who felt that it was time that something be done with her father. She said that he had always been a mean man, mentally abusing his children and his wife. He never allowed anything or anyone to be good enough. The daughter felt that the current care that he required was causing her mother's health to suffer. She had come as a spokesperson for the family, to let me know that the family would like nursing home placement and would work with Mrs. G and myself to get this done.

At this point, I had markedly ambivalent feelings about the current development. On the one hand, I was not used to getting help from families when it came to the care of my patients. Most families in my practice did not want to make decisions of this kind. On the other hand, I had a feeling that the family was teaming up against Mr. G, and that, no matter what happened, the family was going to make the decision for him and Mrs. G.

I elected to table the nursing home question for a few days, to give myself and the family time to consider the implications of such a move. While contemplating my next move, I received a call at home on a Saturday morning from Mrs. G. She apologized for bothering me, but she had found her husband on the floor, unconscious and incontinent, at about 3:00 a.m. She had gotten him back to bed, but was calling because she had noted weakness in his lower extremities and worsening of his speech. She wanted to know if I would make a house call, to evaluate Mr. G.

When I arrived at the home, which was in my neighborhood, Mr. G was still asleep. On arousing him, he smiled and greeted me as a long lost friend. When I asked if he knew who I was, he replied sheepishly that he did not know my name, but that he had seen me before. I noted marked slurring of his speech and continued my exam, which did not show any additional findings, with the exception of his gait, which was wide-based and staggering.

At the bedside, I noted several partially empty plastic containers that held a dark liquid. I asked Mrs. G what these were for, and she explained that Mr. G liked to pour small amounts of wine and keep them by the bedside. "Our son buys his father a case of wine every 2-3 weeks, and has for years. My husband says it helps him sleep better." When I asked how much he drank daily, she was unable to tell me.

After I quit chastising myself for not thinking of alcohol much earlier in Mr. G's presentation, I decided that all family members, who "enabled" him, would need to help me see if, in fact, the alcohol was causing the behavior changes. We held a meeting that Mrs. G and two of her children attended. I presented my conclusion that Mr. G was suffering from chronic alcohol intoxication. After allowing them to discuss the pros and cons of the problem, it was decided that Mr. G would receive no further alcohol. He would be allowed to use what he currently had in his room, but all further alcohol would be removed from the house.

Mr. G returned to the clinic to see me in 3-4 weeks. He sat peacefully as I walked into the room 10 minutes late (fully expecting a tongue-lashing for my tardiness). He had much less difficulty with his aphasia, no slurring, normal gait, and no signs of his usual agitation. He continued to be angry about his arthritis, but did not complain of other physical problems. Mrs. G was very pleased with the change; she was also pleased to report that there had been no difficulty tapering him off the alcohol and he had not even asked for further alcohol. He would allow her to go shopping without becoming agitated, and she had gone so far as to arrange a 2-week trip to visit relatives, and Mr. G was going to stay with his sister and her husband.

I last saw Mr. G about 6 months after stopping his alcohol intake. He was functionally caring for himself, and his wife had resolved her depression.

EDITORS' COMMENTS

Here we see a good demonstration of an important way in which the family can be a valuable resource to the physician. A diagnostic impasse was resolved and minimally disruptive treatment begun only after the family "secret" was discovered. The diagnostic value of the house call was critical in the face of the family's covert denial of, and the physician's initial inattention to, alcohol use by the primary patient. Retrospectively, many of the patient's "personality" traits and the family members' anger may have been influenced heavily by chronic alcoholism.

Observing the family in their home ultimately led to the proper diagnosis. At this point, the initial treatment plan was simply to control the patient's access to the offending drug—alcohol. If requested by the family or deemed necessary by the physician, education and counseling about the impact of alcoholism on the individual and on families could have been offered through community resources. But at this late stage, such a suggestion might not have been appropriate. Quick and simple intervention was reasonable and effective. We can't help but wonder what would have been possible had the underlying diagnosis been made 20 years earlier?

A MOTHER'S PAIN: THE SON WHO STAYED TOO LONG

JAMES W. MOLD
University of Oklahoma Health Sciences Center

Mrs. C, a 69-year-old white, married female, was a somewhat sporadic user of medical services despite chronic, moderately severe, hypertension. Her first visits to me 2 years earlier were precipitated by medication side effects related to treatment of high blood pressure by another physician, and resulted in my referring her to a nearby medical center for confirmation and treatment of hyperparathyroidism. She had surgery to remove a parathyroid adenoma, and a nephrology consult to regulate her antihypertensive medications. She then returned promptly to my care.

She was seen two to three times over the next year, but then did not return for follow-up for 1 year. At the time of that visit, she had a blood pressure of 160/116 sitting and 154/110 standing, despite taking ESIMIL (guanethidine, 10 mg, and hydrochlorothiazide, 25 mg), 2 tablets per day. Her only complaints were of occasional headaches and dizziness, which she related to sinus problems and a recent upper respiratory infection. She had also gained 7 pounds since her previous visit 1 year earlier. She said that an abnormal blood pressure check at a local health fair precipitated the visit. Her medication was changed to guanethidine, 30 mg per day, and hydrochlorothiazide, 50 mg per day, and she was given instructions on a 1000-calorie, low-sodium diet. She made an appointment to return 3 weeks later to check her blood pressure and weight.

At her return visit, Mrs. C told me that, contrary to what she had told me on the previous visit, she had been chronically tired and intermittently depressed for some time (at least 6 months). She also complained of getting weak with almost any significant activity. These symptoms had worsened since I had increased her medicines. In addition, she said that she had been bothered for some time by bilateral shoulder and neck discomfort aggravated by stress, but relieved by getting out in the sun or using a heating pad. When I asked her to elaborate on the stress aspect of those symptoms, and after some specific questioning about her family situation, she told me that her youngest son (28) was single and still living at home, and that he and her husband enjoyed working on cars in their yard in their spare time. As a result, the yard was full of old cars and the house was always a mess with dirty clothes, grease marks, and so on, despite her best efforts to keep it clean. She felt that her son was too old to still be living at home and that he had been overly protected, since he was much younger than her other children. She had discussed the situation with her husband to some extent but had not convinced him that things needed to change. She felt uncomfortable discussing the situation with her friends, and, although she had tried talking to her minister, she felt that he was too young to really understand. She also expressed concerns about her husband's health since he smoked heavily, had peptic ulcer disease, and hadn't seen a physician for a long time.

She had lost ½ pound since the prior visit, and her blood pressure was now in the normal range. Lab work was ordered, and I suggested that she ask her husband and son to come in with her for an information gathering/sharing session. She expressed doubts that they would come, but was very willing to ask them and seemed to feel much better at the end of our visit.

Ten days later, she returned with her husband (but not her son). To my pleasant surprise, her shoulder and neck discomfort had completely resolved, and she was feeling a little better generally, despite no change in her medication. Her blood pressure had remained in the normal range (checked at home), and she had lost another ½ pound. Her husband seemed genuinely concerned about her. I anticipated that he might be feeling somewhat villainized, so I tried to ally myself with both of them equally, and made a special attempt to avoid making him feel like an outsider in the discussion. He quickly agreed that the major problem in their family was trying to get their son to leave home, and he expressed a real interest in pursuing that. He acknowledged that he and his son had become quite close, to the partial exclusion of his wife, but he acknowledged that the family would be better off if the son was given a nudge in the direction of being more independent. Mrs. C was allowed to express her concerns about her husband's health, and he acknowledged those concerns but no special arrangements were made for him to seek medical care for himself at this point. Mrs. C cried some during the encounter and spoke mostly to me, while Mr. C addressed most of his comments to Mrs. C. By the end of the visit, both of them seemed somewhat relieved and, at least verbally, committed to working toward positive change in the family. I was very comfortable throughout the discussion and felt that progress had been made.

I think that my willingness to ask about her family situation and to pursue those issues to the extent of having her husband come in had a very positive effect on Mrs. C's overall health and well-being. I hope I was able to make an impact on the larger family system and therefore benefited Mrs. C as well as her husband and her son.

EDITORS' COMMENTS

The patient experienced considerable relief prior to the family conference, probably because of two events: the discussion of the family stress that was exacerbating her symptoms, and her husband's show of commitment to her by his willingness to come to a family conference. Sometimes most of the work has been done before the family meeting. When he got the couple together, Dr. Mold skillfully engaged the husband in order not to "villainize" him. He encouraged them to discuss ways of changing their family so that their marital relationship could be primary and their son could leave home. And, he avoided the mistake of aligning with Mrs. C to get her husband to change his health habits; Mr. C had come to the conference to discuss his wife's health, not his own. Although no follow-up information is available, this intervention may have helped this family move into the empty-nest phase of the family life cycle without unnecessary casualties.

A HYPERACTIVE CHILD

E. LEONARD ROBERTS
Wake Forest University

Barney, a 10-year-old white male, was seen for the first time. His mother was in the room with him and offered the chief complaint about Barney, "He is hyperactive. He's so fidgety he just can't be still." This had been going on for about 6–8 months. There was no previous history of hyperactivity. Barney's mother stated that his schoolteachers were complaining because the quality of his schoolwork had dropped. She also said that they complained of his being "fidgety" at school, getting up and walking around, and not concentrating on his work. I asked how this affected the family. She described how it bothered her more than his father, but occasionally his father became very angry and yelled at Barney. She had been married to Barney's father for 11 years and had two older sons from a previous marriage. She requested medication and/or referral to a child psychiatrist for Barney. When I asked her to describe exactly what happened at home, Mrs. S described the following:

> Barney comes home from school about 3:30 or 4:00 P.M., and he either does his homework or plays. Then, about supper time, his father comes home

and the worst problems are usually at the supper table. Barney finds it hard to sit still. I usually tell him to be still at this point, and then his father yells at him to do as I have told him or leave the table. So he usually leaves the table and goes to his room. This cycle seems to repeat every evening around supper time.

When I asked Barney what happened, he said that he just did not feel like being still, and he particularly did not like his father yelling at him, so he left the table. He said that school just was boring, and he was tired of sitting and having to work.

I asked Mrs. S to leave the room so that I could examine Barney and continue to explore the story with him. He had no crying spells or sadness, although he expressed frustration at getting yelled at. He said that it seemed that his mother and father were either "yelling about me or at me" most of the time. Results of his physical examination, including a careful neurological exam, were all normal. I met with Mrs. S and Barney again and said that I needed more information and would like to meet with the family. Mother stated in a rather sarcastic tone, "Well, you'll never get his father to come. And I don't see the point of asking the other boys to come because they're just not involved." I asked permission to call Mr. S, and she had no objection.

I called Mr. S and attempted to arrange a family meeting. He was not interested in a family meeting, although he offered to come and see me himself. I met with Mr. S and his story was that Barney's mother had it all wrong. Barney was "not hyperactive"; he was "hypoactive." In fact, he was "lazy and disrespectful, especially to his mother." He said, "I can tell how much he doesn't like his mother just by his attitude." I recommended that Mr. and Mrs. S bring the whole family to see me. I offered the observation that these types of problems affect everyone in the family, and it might be best to see everyone and design a plan for dealing with the problems. Mr. S hesitated, then somewhat reluctantly agreed, but never arranged for this appointment. A follow-up telephone call to both Mr. and Mrs. S was unanswered. I did not press at this point, but hoped that I had left open the door for possible discussion.

In this case, the statements by both Mr. and Mrs. S suggested a tense conflict at home with ongoing tension between Mr. and Mrs. S. Barney seemed to be the common focus that precipitated expression of this tension. This case illustrates several common concepts in family systems medicine.

1. Conflict diversion: Barney's symptoms seemed worse in the presence of both mother and father. Mr. and Mrs. S seemed to "yell at" each other by "yelling at" him, enough to have made any 10-year-old fidgety. Thus, their conflict never reached a confrontation (or resolution) and was continued in their struggle over Barney's behavior.

2. Unresolved issues and conflicts: I could not prove, but only hypothesize at this point, that the issues of unresolved conflict between Mr. and Mrs. S were those of stepfamily or blended-family issues. Barney seemed incidental to the struggle. Certainly, the emotional valency and reactions of both Mr. and Mrs. S seemed much greater than his behavior warranted. In addition, the nonresolution of this problem by two people who were organized problem solvers in other aspects of their life suggested another more important agenda.

3. The identified patient: Barney was identified as the problem or patient in this family system. However, the whole story from each family member and from the exam in the office did not suggest hyperactivity. Barney's behavior seemed to be a response to the distress he experienced in the family system. It would have been easy to treat this behavioral response symptomatically, that is, the fidgety behavior; however, I suspect the treatment would bring only temporary relief at best.

I was concerned that I was unable to connect with this family and arrange a family meeting for whatever reason. I was afraid that they might find a physician who would be willing to put Barney on medication or in "therapy" and reinforce the idea that Barney was the main problem. I was also concerned that Barney would internalize most of this conflict as his fault; this may have already been occurring, as indicated by Barney's statement that his parents either "yell about him or at him" most of the time. Finally, I was concerned about our traditional lack of training for diagnosing and managing such problems.

This scenario presents a serious illness—a seriously dysfunctional, unhealthy interaction pattern in this family that may eventually emotionally cripple one or more of the family members. These unresolved issues can smolder and grow just like an emotional cancer, and then present as a more medically acceptable or "diagnosable" disease, for example, tension headaches, alcohol abuse, child or spouse abuse, depression (child or adult, or both), and so on. Yet, when I present this case, or others like it, to many of my colleagues, the responses typically are: (1) These are problems of living not disease. Don't get involved until medical illness occurs. (2) These are emotional problems. Refer to a psychiatrist.

Both of these alternatives I find lacking. The first strikes me as discounting the seriousness of the situation. The mother and son are here asking for help and my response is, "These are problems of living not medicine. Therefore, come back when things have worsened to the point of physical breakdown." This seems analogous to ignoring a fever until someone is toxic, or not suggesting that one quit smoking until a heart attack or lung cancer presents. In addition, even when medical illness occurs, the management is often directed to relieve the symptom (medication, advice to relax, diagnostic testing, etc.), rather than addressing underlying patterns that repeat and produce the symptoms.

The second response recognizes a problem but fails to recognize several practical difficulties with such referral. Psychiatric referral is not always practically available. It is unusually expensive if not prohibitive for some of the families who need it most, and most medical insurance severely restricts reimbursement for counseling. Many families will not go until some crisis precipitates a complete dysfunction. Some of my psychiatric colleagues see such cases as problems of living, not mental illness, and therefore not in their domain.

Ideally, my plan would have been to see this family for the expressed purpose of working to improve Barney's schoolwork and decrease the fidgety behavior at home. This would involve Mr. and Mrs. S working together toward a therapeutic goal. I suspect that this family at some point would require referral to or consultation with a family therapist or other counselor for dealing with other major issues. It has been 6 months since I've seen the family.

EDITORS' COMMENTS

Dr. Roberts did not collaborate with the parents in making a "patient" of Barney. Nor did he simply "punt" by telling the parents that their son was "normal." Rather, the physician attempted to intervene where the most progress might be made—at the family level. Although rebuffed by the family, he remained their family physician and could wait until a further crisis would bring the family back. Thus, the physician has provided skillful primary care family treatment, despite the family's reluctance to accept intervention. Unfortunately, if this family reenters the health care system through a professional who does not know how individuals' symptoms are connected with family systems, the family may get the wrong treatment. Dr. Roberts also describes poignantly the isolation that a family systems-oriented physician can experience in a health care system that orients to biological illness in individuals. The only antidote we know to such isolation is to surround oneself with family therapists and with like-minded health care colleagues.

A HOSPICE PATIENT AND HER FAMILY

ROGER P. BERMINGHAM
Family Physician Associates, Lamar, Colorado

I first met Mrs. S in February 1982. At that time her daughter, Mrs. L, who was a regular patient of mine, brought her in to see me at our office. Mrs. S had been discovered to have cancer of the colon a month previously and had undergone removal of a segment of her large intestine and colostomy placement by a physician in the central part of Colorado. Prior to that illness, she had owned a grocery store in a small town in central Colorado. She was a widow and was very independent. She struck me when I met her as being the epitome of the western frontier woman. She was gaunt, white-haired, very reserved in her manner, and a woman of few words: almost a female version of Gary Cooper. After her surgery, she seemed unable to care for herself, and with some reluctance had moved down to live near her daughter in Lamar. She was coming to see me now so that she could have a physician contact in the area. She had two other children, both boys. One lived in Oklahoma and the other in a town approximately 70 miles away. Because of this, I saw Mrs. S mostly in the company of her daughter. Mrs. L was married to a farmer in Lamar, and they had two children. One was a boy in high school, and the other was a grown daughter who was teaching school in Lamar. Mrs. S, her daughter and son-in-law, and her two grandchildren formed the nucleus of the family with which I had to deal as her disease progressed.

Mrs. S actually did quite well for some time. She went back to central Colorado 2 or 3 months after I first met her for a brief period to have her colostomy reversed, and for many months she seemed to get along quite well. She visited the office periodically for complaints related to coughs or colds or urinary tract infections, but it appeared initially that her cancer operation had been successful, and that her disease had been cured.

In the fall of 1983, Mrs. S began to experience increasing lower abdominal pain accompanied by bloating and a feeling of excess gas. She then began to notice that her bowel movements had decreased in diameter and she suffered from persistent nausea. It was about this time that she began to admit that this might be some recurrence, and said, "This is exactly like I felt when my colon cancer first started."

She underwent a barium enema, which surprisingly was normal, but an ultrasound of her upper abdomen showed rather enlarged gallstones and some abnormal shadows in her liver. After further noninvasive tests were negative, it was decided that she would undergo exploratory surgery, which did indeed show gallstones but unfortunately also showed three large metastatic lesions in the dome of her liver.

When I informed Mrs. S of her diagnosis after surgery, she accepted it stony-faced without any comments or questions at that point. Her daughter was also in the room and became quite tearful and concerned about her mother's care at that point. She pulled me out of the room, and out of the hearing of her mother asked if I thought her mother was going to last or if the cancer was going to kill her. Since her cancer was isolated to her liver, I explained to Mrs. L that there were techniques of chemotherapy that might help prolong Mrs. S's life and make her feel more comfortable, but that it was impossible to prognosticate until she decided whether she wanted to undergo further treatment. When I explained this to Mrs. S., she again accepted it with few words other than to say yes, she did want to undergo further therapy.

In view of this decision, Mrs. S was sent down to see a medical oncologist in Pueblo, Colorado. There she had a Hickman catheter placed and was begun on constant infusion of intravenous 5-fluorouracil.

It was at this point that Mrs. S began to get extremely tired, rundown, and depressed. She would come in the office to be seen, but in addition had to go weekly to a town 60 miles away to have her constant infusion replaced. March 13, 1984, she came in with these symptoms and when I discovered that she was anemic, she was admitted to the hospital. She was very upset about her constant infusion pump and asked if I thought it was necessary and if there was any way she could do without it. I informed her that there was no other treatment we could offer for her cancer, but she stated, "I really don't want to live like this." In the course of her hospitalization, it was discovered that despite her chemotherapy, her liver metastasis had increased in size. In accordance with the patient's wishes, I removed her Hickman catheter and stopped her chemotherapy.

At this point, Mrs. S began to wonder about her future. She knew she couldn't go home to live alone, and she was very adamant initially that she did not want to be "a burden to her daughter." She said, "Just put me anywhere, keep me in the hospital, or put me in the nursing home, I don't care where." She said this initially both to myself and her daughter.

About that time, we had started an outpatient hospice program in Lamar. This basically involved having terminally ill patients cared for by their family, with support from nursing personnel, social workers, the clergy, and their physician. I was the medical director of the hospice and was familiar with it, so I offered the service to Mrs. S and her daughter. Her daughter seemed interested in it but was very reluctant to have her mother "die at my home." Mrs. S was also very reluctant to consider this, but then a very interesting thing happened. She had to be kept in the hospital for a period of about a week to stabilize her anemia, and during that time she had two separate, rather loud, demented roommates. She was unable to get a private room at the nursing home because one was not available. She then began to seriously question whether she wanted to stay either in the hospital or a nursing home where she could not have her privacy. It was at this point in time that she agreed to try staying at her daughter's home to see how things went. Her daughter was very glad to do this and agreed to act as the primary provider for our hospice program.

It was at this point that the real "therapy" of Mrs. S and her family began. In looking back on it, it seems that the therapy was divided into several components: that of Mrs. S herself; joint therapy between Mrs. S and her daughter; and therapy of Mrs. S's daughter, in conjunction with her own nuclear family and children. These various therapies were conducted by me, one of the clergy in town, our hospice nurse, and a volunteer, and lasted for approximately 2 months, until Mrs. S's death.

Mrs. S was moved out to her son-in-law's ranch house outside of town. We got her a hospital bed, and put her in the guest room, which had close access to her daughter and son-in-law's bedroom. At first, I think Mrs. S had every intention of dying immediately and "getting things over with." I was very frustrated in my attempts to get Mrs. S to open up. I used the various open-ended questions suggested by Dr. Kübler-Ross, such as, "Is there anything you want to talk about? Is there anything you're worried about in the upcoming future? Do you have any thoughts that you want to discuss with me?" For the first month of her therapy, Mrs. S refused to discuss anything; she simply responded, "No." I left it at that point and spent most of my time dealing with the family subgroup consisting of Mrs. L and her family. They were very amenable to therapy, and we found ourselves doing family therapy as it applied to Mrs. S's effect on them. Mr. L was very supportive of his wife and seemed to be glad to have the opportunity to help his mother-in-law. The grandchildren however were very concerned about how things would effect their mother: Would her health be impaired? Would she develop back problems from lifting Mrs. S? Would she be able to handle her mother's rapidly progressing illness? They all had questions about what Mrs. S's prognosis was and how to deal with her. We spent several family sessions dealing with Mrs. L's emotions about her mother's impending death, and tried to train her in some of the Kübler-Ross techniques of talking with her mother. When it became apparent that Mrs. S was going to take some time to die, the whole issue of resentment and anger came up. Initially, Mrs. L denied this as did her daughter and son, but after a few sessions the following came out. Mrs. L had had to take care of Mrs. S's mother when she was ill. Mrs. S was too busy to help at that time, and the whole burden of care fell to Mrs. L. Mrs. L also resented the fact that her brothers were absent from the current situation. She said they were always looked on as "the fair-haired children," and Mrs. L felt that her mother had more affection for them. She viewed her agreement to take Mrs. S into her home as a way to prove that she was indeed a good daughter, but now that Mrs. S was taking so long to die it was bringing back old memories of how she had had to take care of her maternal grandmother, and the resentment that accompanied this. She was encouraged to express these feelings of resentment and was assured that they were very natural. Our hospice team, including myself, each shared experiences with Mrs. L and her family when we had felt resentment and/or anger toward patients who were ill. In addition, we set up a system whereby Mrs. L's daughter would come in and help more frequently, or our hospice volunteers would come in and help more frequently, particularly to spend the night, when Mrs. S tended to be the most demanding, needing help to go to the bathroom, asking for drinks of water, and requiring pain medications.

At this point, Mrs. S did need help in doing all these activities. She was having chronic abdominal pain, and eventually required morphine injections to be given at home. Frequently, these injections would "snow her" for several hours, and she would appear waxen and lifeless. On two of these occasions, it seemed as if she was likely to die soon, and we did a great deal of counseling with Mrs. L and her family about what to anticipate. It was about this time that two major breakthroughs occurred. First, Mrs. L accepted the fact that dying was a natural process, and she really wanted her mother to be able to die at home in the room she had now occupied for the better part of a month and a half. Her family was also very accepting of this. She was much less resentful now that she had been able to ventilate her feelings and had even accepted weekly relief visits from her sister-in-law, who came in from 70 miles away to visit Mrs. S.

In addition, Mrs. S began to talk about her upcoming death. It started in a rather interesting fashion when she pointed out to one of our volunteers that the picture hanging on the wall of her room was the Indian portrait "The End of the Trail." Mrs. S commented, "That's a rather appropriate picture for my room, isn't it?" This obviously was a key statement on her part and was used by the volunteer and later by me to get Mrs. S to talk more about her impending death. She said that at this point she was quite accepting of death although it still depressed her and she wished it could be otherwise.

She was encouraged to ventilate her feelings about this, which she did first only in the presence of the hospice team. The last week of her life, however, she was finally encouraged to talk with her daughter about her impending death, something she had refused to do previously. She and her daughter had three "good talks," one in the presence of the hospice volunteer, in which she expressed to her daughter her fear of dying, but also her thankfulness for being allowed to be near her daughter and grandchildren. Two days later, Mrs. S died in her sleep.

Mrs. L initially reacted very well, as we all had been anticipating Mrs. S's death. The hospice team came out to the house and was present when the mortuary service came to take Mrs. S's body away. It was at this point that Mrs. L realized the finality of Mrs. S's death. She was finally being taken from the room where she had spent the last 8 weeks under Mrs. L's care. We had several follow-up sessions with Mrs. L and her family, and they all appeared to be grieving normally. They were thankful that Mrs. S was finally out of her suffering, and that she had been allowed to die at home.

Mrs. S's case for me was very much a learning experience. I saw her change from a woman who did not want to talk at all about her impending death to someone who gradually began to share her feelings with her family and others. I saw Mrs. L change from someone who was very worried about having her mother die at home, and who had a lot of underlying resentment about her relationship with her mother to someone who was very accepting of having her mother die at her home. She was relieved at being able to talk with her mother about Mrs. S's upcoming death. I wish Mrs. L and Mrs. S had been able to talk about the problems associated with Mrs. L's caretaking of Mrs. S's mother, but neither of them seemed to be able to talk about this in the presence of the other. I personally am thankful for what both Mrs. L and Mrs. S taught me about the dying process.

EDITORS' COMMENTS

We find it hard to comment objectively after being emotionally moved by this case. In addition to the powerful drama of Mrs. S's final weeks with her family, we were struck by two issues. First is the importance of gentle perseverance when the patient's pace of accepting death is slower than the physician's. Dr. Bermingham did not conclude prematurely that Mrs. S was never going to talk about her dying process. He accepted her reluctance but kept on inviting her; meanwhile, he worked constructively with the rest of the family. The result was that when Mrs. S was ready, the family was ready too. The second issue is the role of the health care team. This kind of work is too much for any single professional, just as caring for a dying person is too much for any single family member. Dr. Bermingham engaged in mutually supportive relationships with members of the hospice team, and the patient and family were beneficiaries—as was Dr. Bermingham himself.

FATHER AND DAUGHTER ALCOHOLICS MOVE TOWARD RECOVERY

TERENCE McCORMALLY
KATHERINE COLE
Private practice, Wapello, Iowa

In our rural Iowa town, population 1,800, multigenerational families are the rule. Sometimes it's hard to tell who is the index case.

Susan R was a 32-year-old woman, divorced, with a 7-year-old daughter. She presented with a sore throat, but at the end of the interview she announced, "There's something else I need to talk to you about. I'm an alcoholic." She tearfully related that she had just had her first alcoholic blackout, and she had quit drinking. She was terrified that she would be unable to stay off alcohol. After an emotional half hour, she decided that she could handle things "on her own." She agreed to start seeing an alcoholism counselor, and to consider inpatient treatment if she couldn't stop drinking.

A month or two later, she called to ask if we would see her father, a 68-year-old man who had never been to the office before. "He's an alcoholic, too. He's so sick he can't get any booze by himself, but he badgers my mother so much that she buys and pours it for him. My brothers bring him drinks, too."

George P came into the office accompanied by his wife, Mary. His problem list was impressive. He had hypertension (blood pressure 220/120), chronic obstructive pulmonary disease, and cor pulmonale. His laboratory tests showed liver and renal dysfunction, as well as hyperglycemia, hypokalemia, and macrocytosis. Most impressive was his 4+ peripheral edema to mid-thigh, and bilateral severe stasis ulceration. He had been sitting in his chair all winter because he was too short of breath to lie down. On the right side, the ulcer was clean, but the left was definitely infected. He was unwilling to enter the hospital, despite my suggestion and his wife's pleadings. Outpatient therapy was started. During the next few weeks, some progress was made in controlling his blood pressure, heart failure, and the infection, but the edema and ulceration were resistant to our efforts. He continued to drink and did not elevate his legs. Mrs. P continued to complain about his lack of compliance, and his drinking.

While we were struggling with the parents, Mrs. R began drinking. After a brief binge, she appeared in the office, requesting inpatient treatment for alcoholism. She was hospitalized at our local residential treatment facility. She did extremely well in the program. After 3 weeks, she was ready to attempt high-quality sobriety, in place of the white-knuckle abstinence she had had before.

The program places an emphasis on family involvement, but Mrs. R's family did not participate much. Mrs. P had been down to one of the family group sessions. There, she was exposed to the illness concept of alcoholism, the role of the enabler, and the potential for improvement.

When Mrs. P presented at the office with fatigue, the interview quickly turned to the stress at home with her ill husband. We made multiple suggestions on how to improve things, but were continually met with rationalizations. "No, he wouldn't sleep in a hospital bed if we got one." "If I didn't give him the booze, someone else would." As a last resort, and expecting another negative reply, we offered the possibility of a family conference to confront Mr. P with his drinking and insist that he go into the hospital. To our surprise, Mrs. P immediately agreed. We arranged to meet at the office on Saturday morning.

When we walked into the exam room, the entire family—George, Mary, Susan, the five other siblings, and several in-laws—were present.

Mrs. P had marshaled the entire clan. Mr. P looked at me and grinned, "They've all ganged up on me." He immediately agreed to enter the hospital, as long as there was a television to watch the Cubs game that afternoon.

During his 5-day hospital stay, the edema melted away with simple elevation. His laboratory studies improved, and he felt better. At his discharge conference, also well-attended, there was general agreement that Mr. P would both keep his legs elevated and abstain from alcohol entirely.

We made three house calls in the next month for Unna boot changes. Mr. P improved remarkably and eventually was able to go outside for a walk for the first time in a year. His ulcers cleared entirely. His thinking became more clear and his personality became more pleasant. He and his wife expressed satisfaction with the improvement. Mrs. P said that she was never tempted to give Mr. P a drink, and Mr. P did not ask for one.

It was over 6 months from Mrs. R's first visit until Mr. P's hospitalization. Initially, we were quite discouraged and pessimistic about Mr. P's illness. We realized that our outpatient treatment was not optimal, but we didn't have the status to confront George. We remain curious as to whether a family conference immediately after the initial refusal to enter the hospital would have been effective.

We were impressed that the critical change in Mr. P's care came after his daughter was treated for alcoholism. This allowed the family to see that improvement was possible, and armed at least two members of the family with insight into how dysfunctional family relationships perpetuate alcoholism.

EDITORS' COMMENTS

Mrs. R was that rare patient who comes to the clinic saying, "I'm an alcoholic, help me." Her father was the more typical alcoholic patient, staying away from the health care system unless forced by physical symptoms. Drs. McCormally and Cole demonstrated flexibility with Mrs. R by going with outpatient alcoholism counseling initially and then moving to inpatient treatment when she relapsed. They demonstrated persistence in the face of pessimism about the father's health status and his unwillingness to get treatment for his advanced alcoholism. Even though they were getting nowhere with this man's wife in suggesting that she get her husband into the hospital, "as a last resort, and expecting another negative reply," they offered a family conference. In a stunning about-face, Mrs. P accepted the invitation, rallied the family, and the patient began his recovery. This family is not without serious risk of relapse, but the family physicians have demonstrated their ability to hang on with flexibility.

THE FAMILY SEIZURE

WILLIAM L. MILLER
University of Connecticut

On a cool October afternoon, 9-year-old Heather C appeared with her mother in my office, complaining of a cold. She indeed had a viral upper respiratory infection, and a treatment plan was rapidly negotiated. As we were preparing to leave the room, Heather pulled at her mother's coat sleeve, "Don't forget my tummyache, Mom!" Hesitantly, mother turned towards me and asked, "By the way, doctor, Heather has been having stomach pains two or three times a week for the past 4 months." It is unnerving how often the hidden reason for visiting the family physician exposes itself when you are running late, and the impatience level in the waiting room is beginning to echo in the hall. With this echo in my left ear and Heather's obvious plea for help in my right ear, I acknowledged their concern and recommended that they keep a diary of her pains for the next 2 weeks and schedule a 30-minute appointment at that time. Heather had already resumed her seat on the exam table, but with prodding from Mother, they agreed to my plan and reluctantly left the office.

Two nights later, at 11:00 p.m., Heather's mother called, sounding quite desperate. Heather's pain was getting worse, and tonight she had dry heaves. She was resting comfortably without fever now, but Mother was worried. We agreed to just observe the situation. I prescribed some antispasmodic medication and reminded her of my availability if further problems should arise. At this stage of the case, my working hypothesis, based on my previous exam and the nonverbal behavior noted, was that Heather was experiencing recurrent family pain in her abdomen. I felt she was protecting Mom, probably from Dad.

This hypothesis was rudely jolted, when over the next 10 days, I was called nearly every day by Heather's paternal grandmother with the latest news bulletins on Heather's pitiful condition, and what I wasn't doing about it. According to Grandma, Heather's mother could do nothing right; she didn't care for Heather, fed her improperly, ignored her, and never listened to mother-in-law's "good" advice. By now, my own stomach was getting upset; however, buried in Grandmother's musings, were some diagnostic pearls. Her observations on Heather's behavior were remarkably accurate, and she clearly described a postictal state following the episodes of abdominal pain. A call to Heather's teacher confirmed that Heather was also having "daydream periods" lasting 2 to 3 minutes in class. An electroencephalogram was ordered, proved positive, and a working diagnosis of complex partial seizures with visceral phenomena was made.

Finally, the 2 weeks passed, and Heather and her mother reappeared in my exam room. Also present, at my request, were the paternal grandparents. (My stomach, as well as Heather's, pleaded for resolution.) Father apparently was unable to come because of work conflicts. During the first 15 minutes, we discussed the seizure diagnosis and the antiepileptic drug that we were going to use. The grandparents would repeatedly interrupt, at which time Heather would immediately attract attention by opening a drawer or falling backward on the exam table. Mother was silent. Indeed, Heather was protecting her mother, not from Dad, but from in-laws. Intentionally, I sat Heather on Mom's lap and directed all further conversation to just Heather and her mother. The grandparents were asked to leave and given an appointment for the next day so that we could discuss their specific concerns separately.

Over the next few weeks, Heather's mother became more assertive at mothering, and Heather had no further seizures or abdominal pain. I saw the grandparents twice, and we were able to divert their energies away from Heather, back to themselves as a retired couple.

For the next year, Heather and I were pain-free. Then on a cold December morning, I received nearly simultaneous telephone calls from Heather's mother and Heather's teacher. Heather's school performance was deteriorating, and she was having "spells" in school and at home, characterized by headaches, staring, and "heart pain." They were worried that her seizures were recurring. We checked her antiepileptic drug levels and they were therapeutic. Not eager to repeat last year's abdominal distress, I convened Heather, Mom, and Dad at my office the next day. Father again claimed work conflict, but I persisted and he managed to find time for the visit. Heather sat between Mom and Dad and consistently intervened, with headache or "heart pain," whenever I challenged either parent about their husband–wife relationship. When I revealed this behavior, they both acknowledged marital troubles. Further negotiation resulted in referral to a family therapist, where, after 2 sessions, Heather exclaimed, "I feel pain—right here (pointing to her heart) . . . my heart . . . the place where love grows . . . is cracking."

Another year has passed. Parents and grandparents are communicating better. Heather and I are again pain-free. The family seizure is again at rest. Another cool October is passing into the cold of December. . . .

This case reminded me very poignantly of how the family physician quickly becomes a part of the family system. Heather was a very sensitive family lightening rod. When the family system experienced pain, Heather absorbed it. When Heather felt pain, I felt pain, and the source of her pain within the system usually was the source of my pain. Initially, Heather's pain reflected her mother's suffocation by the in-laws. When this pain was relieved and the system readjusted, Mother and Father were left with each other. No longer having the grandparents to divert attention from their faltering relationship, their direct conflict escalated, and Heather once again came to the rescue and absorbed this new pain. Only by joining the family process were we able to achieve very rewarding and satisfying results.

EDITORS' COMMENTS

The opening of this elegantly written case is vintage family practice: the "real" symptom appearing at the end of the office visit when there is no time to deal with it. What is unique and special here is how the physician used himself and his own emotions as a diagnostic sign of what was happening with the patient and family. Having experienced his own pain, Dr. Miller did not rush forward to quell his and the family's pain. Rather he proceeded systematically to work with the parts of the family system that would work with him, first the grandparents and mother, and then the mother and father. Nor did he try to handle this difficult case by himself; the referral to a family therapist allowed Dr. Miller to stay in a primary care role with the family. The therapist was important to help with both the doctor's pain and the family's pain, lest they all develop seizures.

THE SYMPTOMATIC AGED

ALEXANDER PREKER
St. Pancras Hospital, London, England

Mrs. D was a small, frail, 77-year-old widow. Her clothing scarcely concealed the sharp angulations of her near-protruding skeleton. She had maintained the same weight since 1975, when she dropped 15 pounds following the death of her husband. She experienced periodic incapacitating bouts of abdominal pain and dizziness. During these attacks, she became totally dependent, neglecting self-care and spending most of her time in bed.

Medically, she suffered from a number of illnesses, none of which were seriously threatening to her life, but all of which caused her symptomatic discomfort: Ménière's disease with dizziness, hearing loss, tinnitus, and slight nausea; spastic bowel syndrome with constipation and diarrhea, and bouts of diverticulitis associated with abdominal cramps; a hiatus hernia with gastroesophageal reflux, dyspepsia, and gas; early cataracts and macular degeneration with mild visual blurring, and loss of enjoyment in reading; and osteoarthritis in the knees and back with pain on walking or sitting for prolonged periods of time in one position. The polypharmacy instituted by her many independent specialists had been tapered and maintained at a bare minimum but was hard to control due to her refilling old prescriptions.

An examination of her mental status revealed a tense woman with an anguished, drawn expression on her face. Her hands were either continually writhing or closed in a tight fist. Although she would neglect self-care when ill, she otherwise dressed well and had a tidy personal appearance. Her mood was frequently depressed and anxious, and her speech was often pressured with racing of her thought process. She had a volatile affect with frequent tearful spells and had periods in which she was preoccupied by suicidal thoughts. These occurred most frequently when her somatic complaints were at their worst, but this had not been persistent. She had no other disorders in thought content, both hallucinations and delusions being absent. Her cognitive functions were excellent, with good orientation and no evidence of memory loss. Both judgment into her life circumstances, and insight into her illness were poor.

A functional review revealed an independent woman, her physical disabilities not preventing her from performing daily activities. When well, she was mobile, performing a full range of domestic duties such as housework, preparing meals, and shopping. She was able to maintain good personal care of both toilet and hygiene, being even on the meticulous side in these areas. Her social interaction was limited by lack of desire rather than inability to get out. Although her hearing and sight had deteriorated, she was able to communicate and interact with others without difficulty and could use the phone and write letters. She still managed her own financial affairs.

Despite her many apparent legitimate medical reasons for periodic somatic complaints, a peculiar pattern had emerged in the timing of her relapses, which most frequently expressed themselves as dizziness from her Ménière's disease and bowel discomfort from her spastic bowel syndrome: "My head is full. I don't know what to do. I don't think I will be able to manage. I think I'll have to stay in bed. No, I don't want to go to the hospital or into a home. No, I don't want help at home; I'll just have to manage on my own, but I don't know how I'll do it. It hurts all over. I cannot eat. When will it all end. There is no one who really cares. Oh, it hurts all over. I just can't stand it any longer." Full medical consideration had always been given at the time of any physical exacerbation. Psychiatric consideration was always adamantly refused by the patient, who "resents the image of psychiatrists" and denied any psychological causes for her somatic complaints. She claimed that drugs with any degree of psychotrophic effect worsened the dizziness of her Ménière's disease, leading to poor compliance.

Socially, Mrs. D lived by herself in a subsidized apartment complex for the aged; her living quarters were clean, though somewhat sterile, consisting of a bedroom, a bathroom, a living room with an attached kitchenette, and a balcony facing the parking lot of an aquatic center. Despite the ample free space and pleasant green environment, she preferred to remain in the confines of her dwelling, waiting for phone calls from her family. In an attempt to stay close to the phone she spent most of her day pacing back and forth between the living room and the bedroom, or sitting watching TV wearing her dressing gown.

Mrs. D had four children, three sons and one daughter. Two of her sons lived in the same community as she, while the other two children lived elsewhere. William, her second-youngest son, had two children (8 and 15), and one stepchild (14) from his wife Joan's previous marriage. Mrs. D claimed to be close to all of her children, but had more contact with William, who was going through a marital conflict with his wife. When William lost his job, Joan decided to go back to work. He in turn, stayed at home and looked after the children while she was at work. They both resented this role change; William felt that it had emasculated him, and Joan felt that she was neglecting her family by not being at home during the daytime. She saw her husband as being "pathetic" in his "helpless state." This, in the past, led her to press for separation and divorce, which William desperately refused to accept. Her own ambivalence prevented her from carrying through on her plans, but she was successful in periodically ousting her husband, who on these occasions would take refuge with his mother. She, in turn, would receive her son with mixed relief at a break from being alone but despair over his domestic difficulties.

One such episode occurred when William received an eviction notification from his wife's attorney. This was followed by Mrs. D experiencing a severe bout of abdominal pain and dizziness that led the whole family to rally around her when she claimed that she was dying. Joan dropped her divorce charges for the moment, and Mrs. D became less symptomatic. This pattern continued to repeat itself, being worse before Christmas and other holidays when family activities might not include Mrs. D. Her complaints were always somatic, with a persistent denial of psychological causes of her distress.

An initial interview was carried out in Mrs. D's home. Present at the time of the interview were Mrs. D, her two sons who lived locally and their wives, a community health nurse, a social worker, and a volunteer worker, all part of the local community health services team. I performed the dual function of physician and therapist. Together we formed a therapeutic quadrangle. New generational boundaries were established between the younger couple and Mrs. D. (Minuchin & Fishman, 1981). This was achieved by encouraging the different members to become less enmeshed in inappropriate aspects of each others lives, and actually establishing a physical barrier by encouraging Mrs. D's son not to use his mother's apartment as a retreat from his own marital problems. This physical boundary reduced the destructive contact between Mrs. D and her son, thereby improving the quality of the time that they spent together.

The feuding couple were successfully engaged in couple counseling to work on their marital discord. The full family was encouraged to relate in a more direct and positive way with Mrs. D, thereby reducing her sense of isolation.

To prevent overloading the family with instrumental tasks such as housekeeping and nursing duties, the social service network was engaged. These services were primed to be readily available to step up their involvement for short periods of time in the event of sporadic worsening of Mrs. D's condition. Involving the community and social services in conjunction with family therapy has been found to be particularly important when treating problems of chronic disability, compliance, and major lifestyle realignments (Doherty & Baird, 1983). As Mrs. D became less desperately demanding on the family, her sons and their wives started seeing her more frequently, thereby further decreasing her sense of isolation. At the same time, William was receiving enough support through his counseling that he also became less demanding on his mother during his visits.

The counseling received by William and Joan led them to try a period of physical separation following an episode of domestic violence in which Joan assaulted William with a knife. This initially caused an exacerbation in Mrs. D's somatic complaints, but these quickly subsided when the tension in the family diminished following the separation. Only when the separation period was coming to an end did Mrs. D once again relapse into a crisis of dizziness and abdominal spasm. These again subsided when the couple decided to move back together.

Symptomatic behavior, long recognized in children as having significance beyond the identified patient (Haley, 1976; Madanes, 1982) should be equally well recognized in the elderly. But due to the smokescreen created by concomitant biological and social changes accompanying senescence, it is frequently missed as a sign of underlying dysfunction in interpersonal relationships. Using a family-oriented clinical approach, families have been engaged in the diagnostic and therapeutic process when the symptomatology displayed by the elderly is suspected of being caused by underlying family dysfunction. The results have indicated that symptomatic behavior reflecting underlying family dysfunction may have three underlying modes of expression in the elderly (Preker, 1984): social symptomatology (abandonment, victimization, and scapegoating), emotional symptomatology (self-destructive behavior, autonomy crisis, and psychiatric illnesses), and physical symptomatology (malnutrition, obesity, excessive or lack of exercise, abnormal toilet habits, accidents, and sudden deterioration in general physical health). Symptomatology not related to underlying disorders cleared when family dysfunctions were eliminated. It is therefore felt that the symptomatic aged present an extremely important indicator of underlying family dysfunction requiring treatment through a family-oriented therapeutic environment.

A frequent oversight by mental health workers dealing with the aged is not appreciating the very important impact that slow erosion of physical health (disease, debility, and impending death) may have on the emotional well-being of the elderly (Seelbach, 1978). Environmental and social manipulation will not alter the course of an illness, although they may make the illness more bearable for both the aged and the family. A similar frequent oversight of physicians is to not recognize symptomatic behavior that is an expression of dysfunction in the interpersonal and social circumstances of the family (Minuchin, Rosman, & Baker, 1978). In treating the aged, these oversights may go hand-in-hand, since physical problems may set off a chain reaction of difficulties in interpersonal relationships, while dysfunctional interpersonal relationships may inversely aggravate physical problems by not allowing proper nurture, motivation, and calls for outside help.

This was a difficult case with clear evidence of how family stress may cause symptoms in the symptomatic aged. The therapeutic quadrangle consisted of the patient, the family, the physician/therapist, and the social services network, all indispensable when dealing with such multiproblematic situations. Mrs. D will no doubt continue to have relapses in her condition, for which a purely physical approach will be ineffective. Conversely, ignoring her physical complaints could be dangerous. Her illness has become a family illness, which must continue to be treated as a whole.

EDITORS' COMMENTS

This case and the author's discussion show a sophisticated team approach to the "symptomatic aged." The multiple somatic complaints of the primary patient gave the physician access to the larger family unit. Through home health and community services, family and couple therapy, and an intervention to clarify generational boundaries, Dr. Preker led a concerted effort to ease the primary patient's discomfort. Throughout this process, he offered repeated physical and functional assessment and treatment for specific medical disorders.

The "therapeutic quadrangle" was created during a home visit. The idea of using the home visit to initiate a team approach has much merit for family physicians. Once established, this team was coordinated by the family physician, who served in both medical and family therapy roles. This complex therapeutic and administrative role is beyond the skill of most family physicians working alone. However, a physician and a therapist could accomplish the same task through close collaboration.

A WOMAN PREPARES TO DIE

RUTH POWELL
W. WAYNE WESTON
University of Western Ontario

Mrs. Z was an elderly woman who came under our care while visiting London with her daughter and her daughter's family. She was seen at the Family Medical Center with abdominal pain and admitted to the hospital for surgical assessment. Several years previously, she had had a mastectomy for breast cancer, and had recently been started on chemotherapy for lung metastases. Metastatic spread to the liver was found to be the cause of her abdominal pain. She and her family were each informed of the diagnosis separately, and all knew that she would probably not live long.

We treated Mrs. Z with analgesics and antiemetics. After about 2 weeks, we were surprised to find that she was requiring less analgesia and was regaining her appetite. We were optimistic about discharge from the hospital so that she might have some pain-free time at home with her family.

As her pain settled down, we began to talk of other things with Mrs. Z on our hospital rounds. She knew that she had little time to live. She told us of her husband's death from cancer 2 years earlier. The pain of this loss had been heightened for her by his inability to talk with her about his cancer and impending death. She seemed to be struggling with wanting to avoid replicating this situation with her family now that she was dying. One morning, she told us that she had not been able to sleep the night before, not because of pain, but because of all the things going through her mind. At first we thought that she was confused, as she seemed to be mixing up past and present. On closer listening, we realized that her mind was clear, but she had much to think about before she died. She spoke of her relatives in Winnipeg, and wanting to get back to Winnipeg. She realized she could not go to her own home, but wanted to be transferred to the hospital there. She was worried about the cost to her daughter of transporting her body should she die in London. Her estate would cover the costs eventually, but how would her daughter manage in the meantime? She had not been able to talk to her family about these worries.

During Mrs. Z's hospitalization, we talked with various family members. While having her warts treated, her granddaughter expressed feelings of guilt for asking Mrs. Z for money just before she became ill. She expressed anger at the nurses for insisting that her grandmother try to eat when she felt ill. She was quite aware that Mrs. Z was dying, but was very upset when one day Mrs. Z told the family she was going to die on the following Tuesday. The granddaughter felt that this was an indication that Mrs. Z was becoming confused, losing her mind.

We received several phone calls from Mrs. Z's son-in-law, who expressed his distress through demands to know exactly how Mrs. Z's illness would progress, what was causing her nausea, why she was confused, and so on. When Mrs. Z mentioned going back to Winnipeg, he thought this obviously crazy idea was a sign that she was losing her mind.

Although all knew that she was dying, neither Mrs. Z nor her family members were able to acknowledge it openly to one another, thus allowing preparation for her death. As it seemed that Mrs. Z and her family had things they needed to say to each other, we suggested a family conference in Mrs. Z's hospital room. All agreed to this.

When we and the family arrived at the hospital the next morning, Mrs. Z at first seemed to be avoiding the conference with an urgent request to use the washroom, where she stayed for a long time. Meanwhile, we talked with her sister, daughter, and son-in-law. There were a lot of words about why it was impossible for Mrs. Z to go back to Winnipeg, and how they could not possibly look after her at home if she were discharged from the hospital.

Finally, Mrs. Z returned to the room. At first, the conversation remained superficial. We helped the family ask her why she wanted to go back to Winnipeg. At first, she offered the excuse that she did not want to rely on her daughter for money for shampoo and kleenex. The family was bewildered—why worry about such minor things? At that point, Mrs. Z became nauseated and began retching, which diverted things for a few moments. Then, Dr. B redirected the conversation and asked again what her worries were. She replied that she was "worried about money for . . . " and then halted. Dr. B asked, "Are you worried about funeral expenses?" This opened up communication. She was able to tell her family of her worries about the expense of transporting her body home. This worry was allayed by her daughter, who assured her that all the arrangements had been made. She was somewhat relieved, but still seemed to have other things on her mind. When asked what her other concerns were, she revealed that she had never told her 90-year-old mother that she had cancer. She had wanted to tell her when it was first diagnosed, but had been dissuaded by her sisters, who felt that the news would be too much for their elderly mother to handle. She felt that she had betrayed her mother by not telling her. Mrs. Z's daughter then told her mother that when the mother was told that Mrs. Z was in the hospital, she had said, "Doris has cancer, doesn't she?" This was a great relief for Mrs. Z. They went on to talk about helping Mrs. Z write letters or make phone calls to other family members and friends to whom she wanted to say good-bye. We left them making these arrangements. Shortly thereafter, Mrs. Z began to deteriorate rapidly, and she died several days later, having taken care of her final "housekeeping."

We first met Mrs. Z when her care was transferred to our team from the surgical team that had assessed her abdominal pain on admission to the hospital. While on rounds, our tendency at first was to ask Mrs. Z about her pain and nausea, and busy ourselves with managing these. Apart from the fact that we had just met Mrs. Z we think this shows our own difficulty in looking at death, and the tendency common among doctors to avoid doing so by keeping busy with medical details. When we finally started listening, we learned from Mrs. Z that, although control of symptoms is important, dying people have other important issues to deal with. While we were considering the relative merits of parenteral versus oral morphine, she was reflecting on her life and trying to prepare for her death from a hospital bed where her physical weakness, intravenous lines and catheter, and well-meaning health care workers prevented her from carrying out her unfinished business. At the same time, her and her family's difficulty in talking about the taboo subject of death, and their wishes to protect each other, kept them from communicating important things to each other. This "conspiracy of silence" is common, leading to isolation of the dying patient at a time when closeness with family and friends is most important.

As emotionally uninvolved outsiders, we were able to hear Mrs. Z's cues to our team about some of the issues she was struggling with, and her need to talk openly with her family. From this the role of family doctor as mediator or facilitator between patient and family members followed naturally. The case of Mrs. Z and her family demonstrates the usefulness of convening family members together and allowing them to talk about the issues they have to deal with in preparing for their loved-one's death in an environment made safe by a doctor's presence.

Kübler-Ross talks about patients who have accepted death and are ready to die but are prevented from doing so by unfinished business, usually with family members. Mrs. Z had let us know that she was ready to die early in her hospitalization. Once her unfinished business had been taken care of, she was able to die.

EDITORS' COMMENTS

This case and the authors' comments reinforce the value of convening the family at the time of one member's serious illness. How easy it was for everyone to underestimate the importance of the dying patient's possibly irrational statements. With the physician there for support, the patient's deepest concerns were explained to the supportive family. On a busy day, it would have been easy to skip the family conference because of the bathroom delay or the vomiting. With significant effort, however, Drs. Powell and Weston orchestrated a discussion that completed the patient's life tasks. Was that just as important as chemotherapy at an earlier stage in her illness? If this process is of such value, then why is it unusual for physicians to create time and a setting for it to happen? We hope this case example encourages us all to move past the usual limits of medical care, and to assist patients and families with intimate communications at times of serious illness and death. Everyone benefits from such efforts.

DEATH BRINGS A "CUTOFF" DAUGHTER BACK

RUSSELL J. SAWA
University of Calgary

Mr. S, a 78-year-old gentleman, had an acute myocardial infarction after being told that his wife would die from her liver cancer. Her illness had been sudden, and she died shortly thereafter while Mr. S was still in the coronary care unit. He then became depressed about his wife's death.

I did not know Mr. S or his family, but he became my patient after his infarction. I was visiting him in his hospital room after he had been discharged from the post-cardiac care unit. He was doing well. Several of his middle-aged children were present, including his only daughter, Irene. She seemed quite upset and angry about something, but we weren't in a setting where she was willing to talk. I asked her to drop in and see me if she would like.

Irene made a half hour appointment that week. During the visit, she opened up quickly, as if she had been waiting for an opportunity to talk to someone. During the discussion, she disclosed how she had felt cut off from her mother, and she felt cut off from her father and her brothers, as well. "You know, I have five brothers, and I feel that they are all on one side, and I am on the other. I have always felt that way, since I was small. I have never felt that they cared for me at all." Irene told me that she had tried to cut herself off from her family. "They all just make me so thunderin' mad that I just don't want to be anywhere near them!" She said as far as her relationship with her mother was concerned, "She didn't die just this week. She died 3 years ago. She turned on me and I still don't understand why. I have always gone over backwards to do everything possible I could for her. It just seems to me the more I did, the more I got kicked for it, you know?" Irene felt that she could never do anything right for either parent. She talked about times when she had been misunderstood and hurt as a child, and how she had been afraid of her father since she was a little girl. She described how she had made attempts to open up communication with her father, but she always felt rebuffed. She admitted that her feelings about her family were a present strain, even though she tried to ignore them. Her parents had interfered in her home life, causing stress for her husband and children. This was why she had tried to disassociate herself from her family.

Irene found the session quite helpful in releasing feelings and getting a clearer idea of what was upsetting her. She said that she would like to be able to sort things out with her father before he died.

After Mr. S was discharged, he was seen frequently because of his frail health. His problems included heart failure and moderately severe diabetes mellitus. He continued to be depressed, so time was set aside to talk about his feelings and his family.

During the session, Mr. S disclosed that his mother died of cancer when he was a child. His stepmother was cruel to him and kicked him out of the house when he was 14. He acknowledged that he was not close to his daughter and was upset about his daughter's poor relationship with his deceased wife and his sons. He agreed that he would like to make peace with his daughter and among his children, but he wasn't ready to sit down with his children and work things out. They weren't either.

Over the course of a year, Mr. S's relationship with his daughter improved. He refused to come in for family counseling, despite the fact that he was becoming preoccupied with family quarrels.

Mr. S's health began to deteriorate. At this time, Mr. S and his children and some in-laws agreed to a family session in order to discuss their father's illness. During the session, the family was able to talk about past hurts and Irene's isolation. They also discussed getting their father into a nursing home.

After this session, Mr. S's health improved somewhat, and he moved in with Irene and her family! One month later, he died peacefully in her home.

After his death, Irene came in to talk. She said that in the final months, her father had come to terms with his life and with his relationship with his stepmother. Irene had gained much insight into her father's attitudes and behavior through discussing his past life. She was able to forgive him when she found out what hardships and hurts he had endured.

Irene had come to peace with her father and her siblings. The family auctioned off their parents' belongings, and Irene experienced a new closeness with them during this time.

During the various encounters with family members, I urged them to forgive one another. They all recognized that the hurts they were harboring were affecting themselves and their own families. Their spouses encouraged forgiveness of past family hurts, as they and their children were feeling the impact of the negative feelings.

The family as a group never really sat down for family counseling. Yet, through a series of encounters with various individuals, as well as one family session focusing on their father's illness, many family members were able to make peace with each other.

I learned through this encounter that I can work with families during time of illness to facilitate healing and connectedness. I learned that I need not necessarily sit down and do family therapy per se to be effective. I also learned that I can work with families during the final stages of the parents' life and promote health in the new family units, and that when people are ready to change, a tremendous amount can happen without much work on my part.

EDITORS' COMMENTS

This is a story of a family healing itself at the eleventh hour, and of a physician's patience, compassion, and persistence that allowed this healing to occur. Families must be ready at their own time to break through old hurts. If Dr. Sawa had given up after failing to engage the family, he would not have done the necessary individual counseling. Nor would he have tried one more time to gather the family. The final outcome may help this family for several generations. And, as so often happens in family-centered medical care, the family's breakthrough led to the physician's breakthrough in learning how to help families with wounds that last a lifetime.

A FAMILY WITH CHRONIC CRISIS

BARRY L. R. GILBERT
University of Toronto

The J family had been patients in the practice for 15 years when I took over their care in 1980. Fifty-three-year-old Mr. J was a ticket collector in the subway and his 49-year-old wife worked as a clerk at city hall. They has 2 children: a daughter, 16-year-old Cathy, who lived at home, and a son, Ray, in his 20s, who had left home many years before. Their medical history, from the charts, was unremarkable except that Mr. J had had an uncomplicated myocardial infarction in 1976, from which he apparently had made a complete recovery.

In my first 2 years as their family physician, I saw only Mrs. J when she came in for her annual checkup. Then, in the fall of 1982, she came to see me with a 4-week history of sleep disturbance, fatigue, and a feeling of being "slowed down." Things were good at work and at home, except that Cathy had been seriously injured in a car accident in October, sustaining multiple fractures and a head injury. Though Cathy was going to live, she would have a long road to recovery. I gave Mrs. J some imipramine, which seemed to help, though 10 weeks later she insisted on stopping them since she felt so well.

My next contact with the family was in March 1983 when Mr. J came to see me for the first time. He was having episodes of chest pain and was tired most of the time. I diagnosed angina, and over the next few weeks tried to stabilize him on nitrates and beta-blockers. He responded poorly, so I referred him to a cardiologist for an angiography, which revealed two bypassable lesions. We elected to treat him surgically and scheduled the operation for July 1983. I explained all of this both to Mr. and Mrs. J, and they seemed to accept it fairly well.

Then, several weeks before the surgery, Mrs. J came to see me alone. The symptoms she had in the fall had returned with a vengeance. Before I could respond to this, she went on to say that she was terrified of losing her husband; that she felt completely alone and always had; and that her mother had been cruel and critical of her. Despite this, she and her husband had cared for her mother until her death. The family continued to live in her mother's house. I felt quite overwhelmed by all this. She refused my suggestion of a joint meeting with her and Mr. J, saying she couldn't burden him with this. I assured her that I would be available during this period of crisis. She again requested imipramine, which I again prescribed.

Mr. J's surgery went without a hitch, and he started cardiac rehabilitation in September. Over the next 4 weeks, both Mr. and Mrs. J came to see me separately several times complaining about the other. Mrs. J said that her husband had undergone a personality change and was always angry and critical; he complained that she was lazy, putting on weight, and trying to irritate him. I insisted on meeting with them together, whereupon Mr. J went on a half hour tirade criticizing his wife. We had several other sessions like this in which I unsuccessfully tried to get them to talk to, rather than at, each other. In the fifth session, I finally managed to break this pattern briefly by suggesting that Mr. J stop complaining about his wife's inadequacies and take a look at his own. For some reason he heard this and stopped. He became teary and started talking about his first heart attack and how they had taken away his license to drive buses as a result. For him, it had been like losing his manhood. Mrs. J began to cry when she heard this. Although they never showed this level of feeling in any later sessions, by Christmas both were saying that things were much better.

We stopped the sessions, though I was skeptical about how good things were with Mr. and Mrs. J. My fears were confirmed by Cathy, whom I had been seeing since August for management of her complex rehabilitation. She reported continued fighting between her parents and even some physical abuse of her mother. Both parents have minimized this, saying they are much happier, and all three have refused further family meetings for the present.

What I gained from all of this is a sense of what to expect next. Discussing this case with a family therapist clarified my feelings that both parents have low self-esteem that at best helps them protect and support each other, and at worst allows him to blame and abuse her. My effectiveness in this kind of system has been and will be limited to support each time they enter a new turning point in their life cycle. Issues currently on the horizon include: Mr. J's probable retirement, any illnesses, and Cathy's issue about leaving home (she may need some help with separation).

EDITORS' COMMENTS

Sometimes family physicians tangle with entrenched family problems that will respond only partially to primary care intervention. Dr. Gilbert was patient and persistent in trying to help this couple deal with painful personal and marital issues. They were able to use the counseling sessions to temporarily restabilize their relationship at perhaps a happier state. Significantly, the physician also got help from a family therapist, who helped him to understand why the couple did not respond to straightforward primary care counseling. Without this kind of consultation, some physicians get burned by a couple such as this and are reluctant to get involved with family problems again. Our only suggestion would have been that Dr. Gilbert involve a family therapist earlier in the counseling, either for consultation or referral. When the family physician is feeling "quite overwhelmed by all this," as Dr. Gilbert so refreshingly admits, it's time to call for help.

A BOY WITH RECURRING ABDOMINAL PAIN

GODFREY D. RIPLEY
Texas Tech University Health Science Center

Dave was a white, 9-year-old, only child, living with his father and mother in an upper-middle-class suburban home. I had been seeing him perhaps once or twice a year for school or camp physicals, or for minor upper-respiratory infections. He was brought in one day by his mother with the complaint that Dave has "tummy pains."

Dave, a bright, warm and open boy, told me that he often felt pains in his tummy. He was not sure how long ago they started, but perhaps over the past few months. At first, they were not too bad, and he just carried them about with him without telling anyone. Then, gradually, they became worse and made him feel real bad, and he told his mother. In response to my further questions, Dave gave me a more comprehensive review of his symptoms, with occasional and appropriate additions and qualifications from his mother.

The pains were felt in and around the umbilicus, and were cramping in nature, making him want to double up. Once they started, they progressively built up becoming stronger and stronger over about a half hour. The pains did not radiate any place else, but did make him feel sick to his stomach. Although he did not throw up, he usually passed plenty of gas up through his mouth, which seemed to help him. His mother's hand on his abdomen also helped to ease the pain, and it would tend to gradually disappear after perhaps another half hour. There were no bowel or urinary symptoms, and no abdominal discomfort between the episodes of pain. On a scale of 1-to-10, with 10 being the most severe pain Dave had ever experienced, the pains usually built up to a 9 or 10 before they cleared. His appetite was not affected, and his general health was excellent. His activities were not restricted except that when he had the pain he, "could not move." The pains occurred more commonly in the evenings or during the night, occasionally preventing him from getting to sleep and sometimes even waking him from deep sleep. They occurred perhaps once a week, but not on regular days.

His medical review of systems was completely negative, and his past medical history was essentially normal including complete immunization. Dave's family history was also essentially negative; both parents were well with no significant medical conditions, his grandparents were alive and well, apart from both grandfathers having moderate hypertension, and his maternal grandmother being somewhat overweight and having mild diabetes controlled by diet and tablets. Dave had spent all of his life in this city just a few hours drive from the city where both sets of grandparents and various uncles, aunts, and cousins lived. He attended the local public school, was in the upper third of the class, and told me that he enjoyed both the work and play at school. He had some good friends with whom he enjoyed "passing the time of day," and denied that there was anyone or anything that could be upsetting him.

I had seen Dave's parents in the past with the same frequency, that is, no more than once or twice a year for checkups or minor complaints. From the medical point of view, they were an excellent family; caring for themselves in an appropriate fashion, no tobacco, moderate alcohol—usually wine with an evening meal—reasonable physical activity, and good family time together. They always buckled up when they drove, and kept no firearms in the house. Dave's father was a highly regarded engineer with a petroleum exploration company; his particular expertise was troubleshooting machinery that failed. Dave's mother was a homemaker, and she stated that this, together with some occasional daytime volunteer activities, satisfied her. The family income was fully adequate for them to live a comfortable lifestyle. I have more than a passing acquaintance with them socially.

I asked Dave's mother to leave the room. While I examined Dave, I asked him if he would care to tell me anything else "about things." No, he said, there really was nothing on his mind. No one was bugging him, school was fine, and his parents were okay. His last episode of pain had been the previous night, and right then he felt fine. His physical examination was entirely normal.

With his mother back again, I told them my findings and my assessment. I could not give them a "proven" diagnosis right then. However, it was my opinion that the episodes of recurrent abdominal pain could represent some stress in Dave's life. The pain, for sure, was real pain, and was the result of the intestinal muscles knotting up, rather like colic, in response to emotional pressure. There were other possible explanations, such as a low-grade infection, and I wanted to have some tests performed on his urine and blood, but these were much less likely. I felt that Dave was showing a fairly classical presentation of stress-related, recurring abdominal pain, and I asked them to return to see me 3 days later when I would be able to let them know the results of the tests. Then, perhaps, they would be able to think of some possible cause for Dave's distress. In the meantime, I prescribed no treatment, and suggested that they might call me if he had another attack of pain. Both seemed to accept my comments well, although both repeated that they had no idea what could be giving Dave a problem.

The following day, I had the lab results. His urine was clear and free of any abnormalities, and his blood count and differential were also within normal limits. That night at 11:30 p.m., I had a phone call from Dave's father, who sounded as though he was attempting to control his anger. His son had developed another attack of pain about a half hour earlier, and it had rapidly built up to be the worst ever. Dave was doubled up in agony and crying, and would I please see him right away. This, I felt, was a clear indication for a house call. I already had the lab tests, and unless there was a new indication for an x-ray or some additional laboratory work, a clinical examination as soon as possible was clearly indicated.

An obviously hostile father in his pajamas opened the door and led me to the beautifully furnished living room where Dave lay curled up on his side on the sofa crying quietly, with his mother, in her gown, sitting by his side with a most disturbed look on her face and her hand on Dave's abdomen. Through his sobs, Dave told me that the pain had started in its usual way while he was trying to get to sleep, and that it had built up stronger and stronger until it had become the worst pain he had ever had. It was centered right at his navel, was crampy, and did not radiate. He felt a little sick to his stomach, was passing a little gas without much relief, and had no other symptoms. He had eaten his regular meal that evening, and please, could I do something to take the pain away. He groaned loudly as he turned onto his back to allow me to examine his abdomen, at first keeping his abdominal muscles as tight as a drum. As I talked with him about this and that with my hand gently on his abdomen, he slowly calmed down, allowing my hand to press deeply without any signs of discomfort on his face. Once again, Dave's physical exam was negative.

Dave's mother had been sitting on a recliner to the side of the sofa while his father had been standing over me. I sensed a great deal of urgency and some pretty strong feelings radiating from him. Dave was now sitting up, and I asked his father to sit by his side so that we could all discuss the situation—Dave's pain, my opinion, and the remedy.

We relaxed a little, now that the crisis had, for the present at least, settled, and I noticed two travel bags standing by the door. "Are you going somewhere?", I asked Dave's father. "I am due to fly out at 5:30 in the morning to one of our rigs in the Persian Gulf. I was called this afternoon." The intangible contacts between the three of them vibrated in the presence of the physician. Anger, frustration, resentment, fear—the sideways glances from one to the other. The diagnosis became clear, and the four of us were able to have a most rewarding assessment and intervention session seated in their comfortable living room at midnight.

Dave's father was always on call to his company. He was their most skilled and most successful "malfunction fixer," and when the word came in that a problem had arisen in one of their Saudi fields, on a rig in the North Sea off Norway, in the bush of Nigeria, or in eastern Indonesia, he was the preferred engineer. His passport was filled with valid visas for virtually every oil-producing country in the world; his company's doctor kept him up-to-date with his travel shots and antimalarials, and he was always ready to go, virtually at a moment's notice. Sure, he missed his wife and Dave, but he really enjoyed his work. The challenge was exciting, and the reward most satisfying. He traveled first class, was treated in royal fashion, and always brought back some terrific gifts for the two at home. Yes, his wife respected him enormously and certainly enjoyed sharing the rewards of his labor. However, she could not deny that she felt some resentment when he flew off to such romantic places, sometimes for weeks on end, and sometimes, just as he returned, he would leave again, leaving her to deal with the home front alone.

Dave shared his mother's feelings, adding that he was always worried that there might be a plane crash, or that his father might be taken hostage like the people that he often saw on TV.

Now that they knew what to look for, the family was able to identify Dave's attacks of pain as often coming on at the beginning of one of his father's trips. Dave felt scared, and it was not surprising that his "stomach knotted up."

The diagnosis was accepted by all, and the suggested treatment immediately instituted. Each of the family members openly shared with the others his or her feelings. It was okay to express some fear, some joy, some resentment, and much love. Dave's abdominal pains occasionally returned, but they were never severe. Over the coming 6 months or so, the attacks became less frequent, and then there were no more. This family had experienced the reality of family systems theory.

EDITORS' COMMENTS

After a thorough office evaluation, Dr. Ripley was convinced that the young patient's symptoms were stress-related. The initial effort to identify the precipitating stress was unsuccessful. The physician waited patiently for the right time (11:30 p.m.) and the right place (the patient's living room) for a more productive interview. In that setting, the correct diagnosis and treatment suddenly became obvious to everyone. It may seem that an unusual effort was needed to resolve this medical and family issue. However, the family-centered approach in the context of sound medical care was productive only when the environmental setting for the interaction was the family's home. Perhaps we should consider this option of the home visit more often. We wonder what would have happened if the final scene had occurred in the emergency room.

LIFE AFTER DEATH

WILLIAM L. MILLER
University of Connecticut

Outside, the maple leaves were just starting to hint at changing color; the vibrant smells of summer were fading. Inside my office, I was being introduced to Hal H, a 52-year-old man, who, despite his emaciated hunched form, managed a smile and had a twinkle in his eye. "I'm here because I need a family doc to help me live before I die" were his first words to me. Before I could recover and respond, he continued, "Cancer is going to kill me by the day after Christmas, and I want you to keep me feeling as if I have something to live for." I sheepishly commented that the sparkle in his eye suggested he already felt and knew why he was alive. He paused, coughed, struggled for a deep breath, gazed directly into my eyes and said, "That's true for me, but not for my family." We spent the next few minutes reviewing his medical history, and drawing a family genogram (Figure 1). I recommended some nutritional adjustments, prescribed some medication for his cough and oral moniliasis, and established a return appointment for his family.

Five years after divorcing his first wife of 23 years, Hal H married Susan, a 30-year-old divorced woman with two children. This marriage caused immediate strain in Hal's close relationship with his 25-year-old daughter, Ellen, who, only 6 months before, had had a 2-year engagement broken by her fiancé. This strain was temporarily shelved

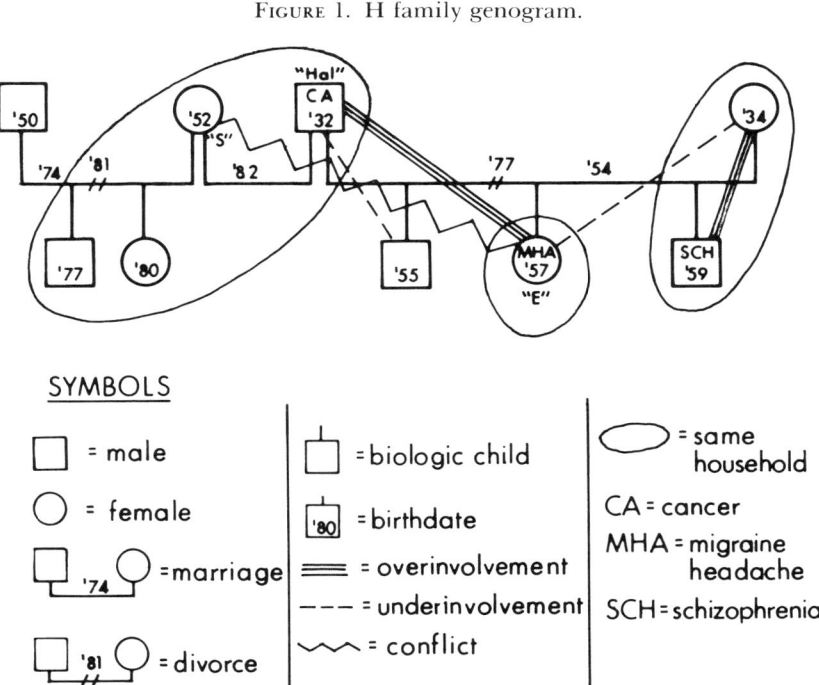

FIGURE 1. H family genogram.

when, 2 months after the marriage, Hal was given the diagnosis of renal cell carcinoma with diffuse pulmonary metastases. Over the next 2 years, Hal underwent chemotherapy, radiation therapy, and, finally, experimental interferon treatments at Sloan-Kettering, which he completed 2 months prior to appearing in my office.

Ellen, a respiratory therapist who had lived with her mother and schizophrenic younger brother, changed jobs and moved 100 miles to be near her father when it became evident his cancer was terminal. Living alone and with no new friends, Ellen spent nearly all her free time at her father's home. Superficially, Hal's new, young wife, Susan, tolerated Ellen's presence, but the old interpersonal strains were being intolerably stretched. Susan felt her position as wife was rapidly being eroded by Ellen's "inside knowledge" of the medical system upon which Susan's husband was dependent, by an undercurrent of sexual jealousy, and by a distinct lack of privacy. Meanwhile, since Ellen's departure from her home of origin, her younger brother was having increasing difficulty with his schizophrenia. Ellen, herself, was suffering from severe migraine headaches, which were becoming resistant to both prophylactic and abortive medical management. Hal H was indeed correct. He was coping well with his cancer, but the family pain was becoming overwhelming.

During the 45-minute family meeting, with Hal, Susan, and Ellen present, two groups of issues were defined. The first set dealt with problems that existed while Hal remained alive; the other set dealt with problems that might arise after Hal's death. The two principal predeath issues concerned the conflict between Susan and Ellen, and the deteriorating mental health of Ellen's younger brother. Postdeath, the concerns focused on the isolated vulnerability of Ellen, the restructuring of Susan's family as a single-parent family, and continued management of Ellen's younger brother's schizophrenia.

Using the genogram as a guide, the family, with only minimal assistance from me, devised its own strategy for managing the above issues. Ellen suggested that she visit her father only at designated times agreeable to Susan, and stay for only 2 hours. In return, she asked that Susan make it possible for Ellen and her father to be alone at those times, if they so desired. Both of these ideas were successfully implemented with a significant reduction in the conflict between Ellen and Susan, and a simultaneous lessening of Ellen's overinvolvement with Hal.

At Hal's recommendation, Ellen also spent more time with her older brother, made regular telephone calls to her mother, and became more involved with the other respiratory therapists at work. These changes improved Ellen's relationship with her mother and mobilized a support system to help Ellen after Hal's death. Hal also arranged and promoted Susan's contact with former friends, agreed to involve the local hospice in his home care, and rewrote his insurance policies to improve Susan's support after his death.

Ellen and her mother decided to renew contact with the younger brother's psychiatrist, who, after two outpatient sessions, recommended a brief return to the state mental hospital. The family agreed, the younger brother consented, and he was admitted without further problems.

Thanksgiving found Hal with a brighter sparkle in his eye and an envigorated wit that repeatedly transformed tragedy into comedy. He still coughed, he could barely walk, his breathing was more labored, but he and his family felt specially blessed as they shared the dinner turkey together.

Two weeks later, Hal's condition seriously deteriorated. He could no longer swallow, and was admitted to the hospital with moderate dehydration. Within 24 hours after admission, he suffered a pulmonary embolism and soon developed a complicating pneumonia. We all had previously agreed not to use CPR or mechanical ventilatory support, and this request was followed. Two weeks before Christmas, with Susan and Ellen at his bedside, Hal died peacefully in his sleep.

Outside, the trees are now bare and the air is cold, but the smells are crisp and the sun's reflection is especially radiant. Inside my office, there is a quiet warmth. It is Christmas and Hal gave his family and his physician a very special gift. I received a lesson in healing; Hal's family received hope and their life after death.

Whenever I have worked with a family in my practice, my satisfaction quotient has risen. Usually, in the beginning, the plot thickens and the problems multiply. But, in the end, the resolutions feel more definitive and the sense of healing more complete. I am needed less, and I like that. This case followed the pattern but was uniquely satisfying because so much was accomplished with such little effort on my part. Hal made the diagnosis, convened the family, outlined the treatment plan, and then achieved treatment compliance. I was listener, occasional moderator, and always a learner. Hal reaffirmed that death and sickness are not enemies to be feared and battled alone; they are the storm's eye through which we and our families can see more clearly how to nourish life and become better healers.

EDITORS' COMMENTS

The beauty of the writing matches the beauty of the family drama enacted in this case. Dr. Miller plays down his role in this family's healing, and indeed, the family did most of the work. But Dr. Miller was able to understand that they desperately needed to talk as a family about living, dying, and relating. He skillfully used the genogram process to allow the family to decide how to reorganize themselves to face life after death. He blamed no one and understood each member's needs, thereby giving them permission to do likewise. Significantly, he also was happy to step back and not be responsible for how they carried out their family decisions. It takes considerable skill to do as little as Dr. Miller did with this family.

AND BABY MAKES THREE

THOMAS GILBERT
Brown University

Twenty-four-year-old KM first presented to the Family Care Center (FCC) at 20 weeks in her first pregnancy. She was single but living in a stable relationship with 28-year-old SE. The pregnancy progressed normally, and the couple attended childbirth preparation classes provided at the FCC. In addition to the pregnancy, the maternal problem list included chronic petit mal epilepsy controlled with medication. KM went into labor at term and, after secondary arrest of dilatation failed to respond to usual management, underwent primary cesarean section for cephalopelvic disproportion. I first became involved in the family's care at the onset of labor.

SE's response to his partner's labor problems was to physically threaten the nurses and physicians attending her. Frequent, direct reassurance allowed him to turn his attention to supporting KM. Threatening behavior continued postpartum, whenever SE perceived that KM or M, his daughter, were not receiving the care he felt they deserved.

Better history data, obtained postpartum, revealed that the couple were living in a single-room apartment and sharing bathroom and kitchen facilities with three other families. They had no baby food, supplies, or clothing, and no money or food for themselves. SE had worked in the past, but was presently unemployed; KM had never worked. While they were aware of their needs, they had no idea of where to turn for help in meeting them.

SE had a tested IQ of 69. He had been frequently depressed after the death of his grandmother when he was 12 and had attempted suicide twice. He had been physically abused by his father as a child; his brother and physically handicapped mother had been abused concurrently. The family was now scattered, and SE had only occasional contact with any of his relatives. KM had an IQ of 88. She had been sexually abused by an uncle both as a young child and as a teenager. Her father had left, but the rest of her family was still together and allowed her little autonomy. KM's family history included epilepsy and intermittent paranoia (her mother), autism (her brother, 18-years-old), and drug abuse (her sisters, 20 and 22-years-old). The family's genogram is shown in Figure 1.

A number of hospital personnel, including nurses and family medicine residents, were concerned that SE and KM would be unable to care for M at home. They feared that SE's threatening behavior would be directed at the child in times of stress. The possibility of immediate foster placement was raised by several. My colleagues and I felt, however, that such a judgment was not justified, and we resolved to provide the maximum possible support in the hope that the family could survive.

Emergency requests to the welfare department, the Women, Infants, and Children (WIC) program, the Salvation Army, and the local community action program yielded formula, baby furniture, clothing and supplies, food, and financial support. The FCC social worker, a worker from a local family service agency, and a visiting nurse agreed to provide daily home visits at least for the first 2 weeks. The local

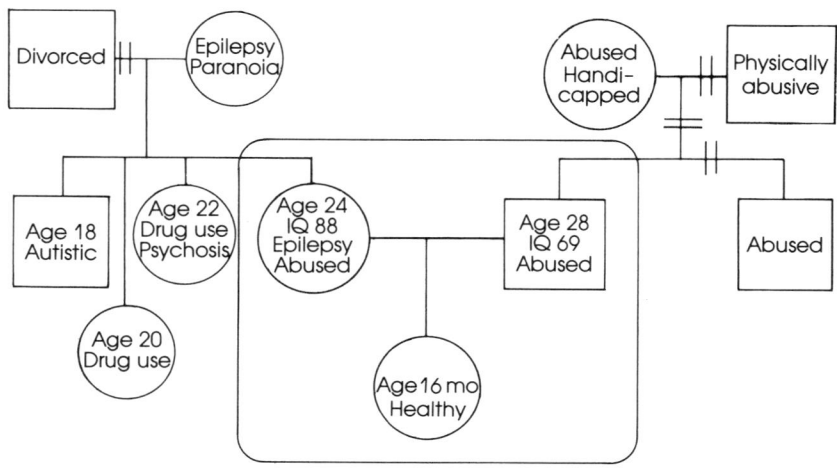

FIGURE 1. Genogram of the E family.

child protective agency was notified of the family and of our efforts on their behalf.

SE and KM needed concrete advice about all aspects of child care. We provided frequently updated feeding instructions, for example, adjusting formula amounts for M's growth. We found we needed to offer menus and cooking instructions for the food we provided, because even such common dishes as macaroni and cheese were beyond the couple's experience. Shopping and money management were other areas in which we needed to provide concrete help. Some needs exceeded all agencies' abilities to help; we provided small amounts of emergency food, cash, and transportation in times of crisis.

Early on, we identified the need to coordinate the efforts of the many agencies caring for the family's needs. An interagency meeting was held in the first month. Agency representatives were able to identify adequate housing and continuing instruction in parenting and child care as the most pressing needs. Supporting SE and KM in their growth as a couple, and helping them learn such basic living skills as shopping and money management were also listed as important priorities. Most representatives had experienced SE's threatening behavior and agreed with us that it vanished with reassurance and support.

The group agreed that the FCC would be the coordinating agency. Each representative took on responsibilities appropriate to his or her agency. A striking aspect of this and subsequent meetings was that few agencies could view the family as their primary focus. The Division of Retardation, for example, could not provide any help for the identified problems because it only served individuals, and the problems were all family problems.

Over the next several months, as basic needs were met, and as housing and financial problems gradually came under a degree of control, a new focus of our work with the family emerged. SE and KM got married. Visits were dominated by discussions of the demands placed on them by K's family. K's mother often asked that they come to live with her for a time to "protect" her. It became clear that S and K were being asked to protect her from her delusions, not from any real threat. K's addicted sister lived with the couple for a time immediately before she (the sister) gave birth to a premature infant, who died soon after. S's father returned for a visit as well. Our efforts were directed to helping S and K develop an identity as a family separate from their families of origin. Concrete advice was necessary in this area, as in others, and we made a special attempt to coordinate our efforts to provide appropriate specific suggestions. The conflict between original family and new family became too much for K, and she and S separated for a brief period. She returned to her mother while S managed alone with their child. K was able to resolve her conflict in favor of her husband and daughter, however, and the talk of difficulties with K's family faded as S and K were reconciled.

Currently, the family is living in a nicely kept apartment in a poorer urban neighborhood. S goes to work daily in a training program from which he hopes to be placed in a real job. According to his supervisors, he needs to work on his dependability. His threatening behavior remains a problem for him in unfamiliar or anxiety-provoking situations but has never been directed at M, to whom he is devoted, and has not been part of his contacts with any of us for over a year. K remains at home, but gradually is becoming more able to venture out on her own. M has grown and developed normally. She has been brought in for each of her well child visits on time and is entirely up-to-date in her immunizations. Both our social worker and the family service social worker who have been working with the family from the beginning have recently moved on to new jobs. The physician and nurse practitioner are now the only care providers who have remained involved with the family since M's birth (20 months). The couple are happy with the progress they have made. Each reported great pride in returning to a recent school reunion and showing off spouse and child. They are now seeking counseling help to deal with their more difficult problems of past abuse and poor self-image.

EDITORS' COMMENTS

Commitment to the family when most professionals would have withdrawn support; extra effort when some would have done less; and leadership provided by the family medicine team—these issues are beautifully exemplified in this case. Anything less may have been futile, although the resources for this energetic treatment are not universally available outside of university teaching centers. The family might have succumbed to overwhelming forces had the assistance been less aggressive. We have intensive care for newborn children and seriously ill individuals of any age. Why not for families? Our belief is that the benefits to individuals, families, and society would be at least as great as for medical intensive care.

A HUSBAND WITH DEMENTIA, A WIFE WITH TERMINAL CANCER, AND A CARETAKING SISTER

JOSÉ FRIEYRO
Unidad de Medicina de Familia, Madrid, Spain

Mr. F, a 78-year-old man, and his 71-year-old wife came to our family and community medicine program in September 1982.

A few years after their marriage, Mr. F had developed presenile dementia, which brought him to full physical and mental incapacity.

Mrs. F became his personal nurse, with the responsibility of keeping him clean, nourished, and comfortable, day after day. In this task, she was helped by her sister, Miss A, who offered her support in such a difficult situation.

The couple had no children.

After an initial evaluation, the family was assigned to Dr. E, a third-year resident, and included in our home care program for the elderly, which offered periodic family home visits, as Mr. F was completely bedridden. At the same time, therapeutic measures for benign essential hypertension and osteoarthritis were recommended for Mrs. F after evaluation at the family practice center.

In November 1983, Mrs. F was seen at the emergency room for vaginal bleeding. A pelvic mass was found at physical examination. She was referred to the Department of Gynecology, where a diagnosis of endometrial leiomyosarcoma was established. Hysterectomy, followed by local radiotherapy, was performed.

In May 1984, she consulted for costal pain. Clinical and radiological studies showed multiple pulmonary and bone metastases.

Management of this new situation was discussed at one of the weekly group meetings in the department. In order to offer a holistic approach to the patient and the family, the following aspects of management were considered:

1. Providing chemotherapy if indicated.
2. Treating for pain.
3. Keeping the patient informed about her critical situation.
4. Mitigating the patient's and family's anxiety in the terminal days.
5. Arranging for care of the bedridden, demented husband after the patient's death.
6. Providing for technical and psychological support within the group to the resident and nurse directly involved in the management of the case.

Combination therapy with cytotoxic agents was ineffective and induced severe secondary manifestations; it was interrupted after two cycles of treatment.

Pharmacological control of pain was adequately obtained along the course of the disease; this proved to be substantially important in order to maintain a good relationship with the patient and her family.

The patient was informed about the nature of her disease. Diagnosis and prognosis were explained to her in some detail. Initially, she showed a characteristic denial reaction, which was followed progressively by a complete acceptance in the terminal days.

Having a thorough knowledge of her own situation helped the patient to establish a sort of contractual link with her sister so that care of her husband was assured after her death. The positive attitude of Miss A in accepting this responsibility was essential in contributing to the mitigation of Mrs. F's anxiety.

Management of this case was stressful for all members of the team, particularly the resident and nurse directly in charge of this family. Technical and psychological support were mutually offered among team members during periodic meetings for follow-up.

Mrs. F died on August 31, 1984. Since then, Miss A has taken care of Mr. F. She shows trust and gratitude and keeps contact with us on a regular basis.

In this case, a comprehensive approach to the management of the patient allowed us to also manage the family. It was evident that we could not deal with Mrs. F's physical problem without considering it in a family context.

At the initial evaluation, we recognized that the most important problem we had to face was Mrs. F's anxiety about who would take care of her husband in the future. She accepted her disease and collaborated with us when this responsibility was assumed by her sister. The positive attitude of a family member was essential and decisive in management of the problem.

This case was paradigmatic in showing us the importance of the family as a therapeutic tool to be used in treating health problems of any of its members. Miss A became a member of the team, and contributed in a substantial way to offer human and comprehensive care to her sister.

EDITORS' COMMENTS

It is rewarding to see Dr. Frieyro's case illustrating that family-centered care has practitioners beyond the North American continent. Wisdom, compassion, and attention to family and staff needs are displayed throughout the case, but especially in the initial care plan for the terminally ill patient: home visits; a home care program for the elderly; support for medical residents, nurses, and other staff as they cope with the dying patient; and specific attention to the patient's concern for her demented husband's care after her death.

The author's comments delineate the practical value of considering the family context in the management of Mrs. F's medical problems. We are grateful to Dr. Frieyro for this portrait of the Spanish medical system and are pleased that there is international support for the benefits of the family contextual approach to medical care.

A PATIENT WITH STOMACHACHE

W. WAYNE WESTON
University of Western Ontario

Hilda B was a 44-year-old woman who immigrated from Germany many years ago with her husband. Their two children attended college and lived away from home.

Hilda had had an irritable colon syndrome for many years, but generally had coped very well by watching her diet and using antispasmodic medication. She presented to the office one day with severe constant lower abdominal burning pain. She was exquisitely tender over her lower abdominal wall, but had no muscle guarding. A bimanual examination was normal, and her urine was clear. I was puzzled by this sudden exacerbation of her pain. She denied any changes in her life situation or stress. Thinking this could be related to her irritable colon, I increased her antispasmodic medication and reassured her.

Two weeks later she called imploring me to give her something to control the pain. She felt "out of control." I sent her some acetaminophen with codeine. One week later she appeared in the office with her husband. They were both desperate! The pain was getting worse, and was unremitting. Now, she also had severe pain in her right upper quadrant similar to what she had before a cholecystectomy 10 years earlier. At that time she had been in and out of the hospital numerous times for investigation of abdominal pain, and she ultimately had a normal gallbladder removed. Following that, she settled down for awhile, but the pain returned.

She and her husband were convinced that she had an organic problem, and wondered about having her admitted to the hospital. Again, there was little to find on physical examination. I probed deeper for sources of stress in her life, but she denied any problems. She seemed almost panicky that this pain was never going to let up. It was greatly interfering with her ability to do her jobs around the house, and work on a book she was writing. I reassured her that there was no evidence of any serious organic problem, arranged some investigations, and promised to stick with her until I had the problem sorted out.

She returned 3 days later and reported that the pain in her right upper quadrant had disappeared after her last visit. However, she continued to have the lower abdominal pain that she had presented with initially. I was puzzled, and wasn't sure which way to go next. While exploring the effects this pain was having on her functioning, she mentioned she had some trouble sleeping because of vivid dreams. At last, here was a clue! At first she was reluctant to discuss the dreams, but finally told me about a recurrent dream of five European cathedrals. She finds herself inside one of these, and it is dirty and full of soot from the burning candles. She struggles to find a way out and finds herself in one of the other churches. It seems that she can never escape from them. She then told me that the first 5 years of her life were spent mainly in bomb shelters during World War II. She was raised very strictly as a Roman Catholic, and her mother was extremely rigid. The nuns at school were not much better. Eventually, she rejected the church altogether but continued to feel some guilt and confusion about this. A few years ago, her mother had come from Europe to live with Hilda and her family. After 2 years of fighting with her mother, Hilda finally had sent her back to Europe to live in a nursing home. Hilda felt very guilty about this, but could think of no other solution. Ever since then, Hilda had phoned her mother every week, although most of what she heard from her mother was complaints. I suggested to Hilda that she had "a belly full of her mother." She readily agreed and asked if I thought that her abdominal pain was related to her inner conflict. I suggested it might well explain this chronic pain better than any other theory and asked her to think about this and return to see me in 1 week.

On her next visit, she was dramatically improved. Although she still had some pain each day, she had pain-free periods from 4 to 6 hours on many days and, in fact, had been able to write a 40-page chapter for her book. She told me about her mother. Hilda was an only child, and she had always felt that her mother wanted Hilda to be more like herself. In so many ways, Hilda chose to be different, and she felt her mother's disapproval. She crossed the Atlantic to try to escape this oppressive criticism. Hilda dreaded the day when she was well enough to go back to Germany to visit her. "As long as I am sick I have an excuse not to go." As Hilda put more and more of the pieces of the puzzle together, she realized that the recent flare-up of pain coincided with Christmas. It was 2 years ago, just after Christmas, that she put her mother on the plane and sent her back home.

Control was an important issue for Hilda. Although she had rejected her parents' religion, she adopted their rigid style, which became a major defense mechanism for her. When the pain became worse and she was threatened with loss of control over it, she panicked. The doctor provided temporary external control for her, which allowed her to mobilize her defenses again and regain control for herself.

She was initially very reluctant to consider possible psychological causes for her distress. Whenever physicians had suggested this in the past, she interpreted this to mean that it was all in her head, and that nothing could be done. I explained that if stress was the cause, then we would have something to work on. She casually mentioned dreams that were keeping her awake, but she was very reluctant to discuss them. It was only after repeated questioning that she finally gave in and talked about the dreams. She expressed surprise that I would be interested in that aspect of her life. Then, her internal conflict poured out. She told me later that she had been angry with me for suggesting that the pain could have a psychological explanation, but she stuck with me because she felt I believed she truly had terrible pain. Referring a patient in this situation to a specialist is fraught with peril. Referral to a psychiatrist would be experienced as rejection; referral to a surgeon or internist would lead to a series of tests, and perhaps hospitalization, and even needless surgery, as had happened to Hilda before. Patients with problems like this are usually best helped by a physician who can look at body and mind together, within the broader context of the patient's life history and family circumstances.

Hilda came to see me alone, except for one visit when her husband accompanied her (a clear message to me to take this problem very seriously). But in another sense, Hilda never came alone—she was always accompanied by the family within her. Her abdominal pain was rich in meaning; it represented the unbearable pain in her relationship with her mother; it was punishment for not fulfilling her mother's expectations, and for finally rejecting her mother by shipping her back home; it gave Hilda a legitimate excuse for not visiting her mother; it was a way to defuse her anger at her mother—she truly had a "belly full" of her mother. While it can be invaluable for the family doctor to see the patient within the whole family, it is much commoner for him or her to see the family within the individual patient. This "family" is always present if we will look for it. Sometimes it is like a Chinese puzzle. Hilda first presented me with her pain and asked me to take it away. Then she shared with me an image of her experience of "family"—being trapped inside a European cathedral full of soot. Finally, she gave me her confession—she had not been a proper daughter to her mother, who was rigid and rejecting.

Laing (1969) challenges us to understand the family in the patient this way:

> The family as a system is internalized. . . . The family may be imagined as a web, a flower, a tomb, a prison, a castle. . . . The "family" set of relations may be mapped onto one's body, feelings, thoughts, imaginations, dreams, perceptions; it may become scenarios enveloping one's actions, and it may be mapped onto any aspect of the cosmos. (pp. 4, 6, 18)

EDITORS' COMMENTS

The "family within the patient" is a powerful theme amply discussed by Dr. Weston in the author's comments. We choose to comment on a less obvious but important issue in this case—courage. The physician had the courage to stay with the uncomfortable patient without a clear-cut diagnosis until the interactive process led to a more well-defined pattern. Dr. Weston could have used a number of common, medically acceptable techniques to extricate himself from significant involvement with this uncomfortable patient whose diagnosis was not clear: repeated referral to the surgeon, in spite of the failure of this in the past; referral to a psychiatrist, which might have suggested to the patient that she was crazy and undesirable; another major technological investigation in spite of the fact that the physician felt strongly that only a modest biomedical investigation was appropriate; or, in spite of the patient's clear discomfort, giving her patronizing reassurance that "nothing serious is wrong," without further planned follow-up or support. Instead, Dr. Weston declared that he would do a responsible reevaluation, and "stick with her until I had the problem sorted out."

Risk-taking can become contagious. Even though she may have been losing control of her pain, Hilda had the courage to share very personal data and uncomfortable feelings with her physician in order to help him understand her complaints more fully. With mutual respect and trust as a bond, these two came to a useful interpretation of her abdominal symptoms as related to unique family conflicts that had never been resolved. This time the problem was understood well enough to approach it directly—accepting painful feelings no longer equated with anyone being a "bad" person. Courageously opening the door to the patient's family context led to a concrete identification of the underlying discomfort with interpersonal relationships that had been intertwined with physical pain. Less effort by the patient or the physician might have failed to open these heavy doors.

LOWER ABDOMINAL PAIN IN AN ADOLESCENT

MARK MENGEL
University of Washington

I met Sally T, a 12-year-old girl, on a Saturday night in the emergency room of a small rural hospital. She had been there for 2 hours already and had been evaluated by the 4th-year surgical resident on duty. He signed the patient out to me saying that she had lower abdominal pain, fever, and leukocytosis. He also mentioned that he didn't think it was appendicitis, but didn't know what was going on, and asked me if I would take a look at her since I was a family practitioner. The chart revealed that she had had abdominal pain for 3 days, a fever to 101.3°F, and a white blood cell count of 18.2, 80% polymorphonuclear leukocytes.

As I entered the room, Sally's father leaped out of his chair and challenged me in an angry tone of voice, "Who are you?" I realized that he hadn't been told that a new doctor was taking over his daughter's care, so I answered politely that I would be seeing Sally since the other doctor was going off duty. He then went on to complain that they had been in the emergency room for 2 hours and that nothing had been done. He stated that he just wanted the best for his daughter. I apologized for the time delay and explained that I would do everything possible to help Sally. He sat down with a "hrumph."

Sally was lying on the table, looking up at the ceiling. She had not responded to my discussion with her father in any way, even by looking at us while we were talking. I went over to her, introduced myself, and sought permission to ask some questions. She answered, "Okay" in a weak, fearful voice. During my introduction, the father did not look at his daughter or respond to our conversation, but remained quietly in the corner.

Family systems theory teaches that you can learn much about a patient's symptom simply by looking at his or her relationship to other family members. In my first 2 minutes with this family subsystem, I noted that the father seemed rather distant from his daughter (disengaged), with interactions between them being nonexistent. The father had expressed concern over the daughter's health to me, but had shown no concern or support directly to his daughter. I speculated that his anger and concern were motivated by his own feelings (perhaps guilt that at some point in her illness he had not done the best for her) rather than out of a true sympathy for his daughter's plight. I went on to speculate from his disengaged stance with his daughter that perhaps he was disengaged from his whole family as well. I wondered, too, if this disengagement could have prevented him from correcting a family problem that might have contributed to his daughter's illness. Was that why he seemed so guilty to me? And then there was the matter of Sally's fear.

Most adolescents are shy when meeting a new doctor, but most do not exude fear. Since there was nothing in my behavior to cause fear, was there something that she was trying to hide from me that would make her father angry?

I sought to confirm some of my tenative hypotheses by taking a history. Briefly, Sally had had constant bilateral lower abdominal pain for 3 days. The pain was not associated with any other gastrointestinal or genitourinary symptoms. She had not had any previous episodes of this kind of pain, no previous abdominal surgeries, and had not taken any medicines to ease her pain. She had begun menstruating a few months before, but was not now.

During this history, her father remained unresponsive unless asked a direct question. When I asked why it took so long for him to bring Sally in to be checked, he replied that his wife usually handled such things. "Why did you bring her in now?" "Because my wife told me to. I didn't think there was anything wrong with her." "Why didn't your wife come in with her?" "Because she is watching a baseball game that my son is playing in." "Don't you go to baseball games with your son?" "Every now and then."

A clearer picture of a disengaged father was emerging. Also, as Sally's fear eased only slightly with my questioning, I decided to dig deeper to see if indeed there was a family secret that would explain Sally's fear, and perhaps the reason for her illness.

The results of my digging bore some fruit. Both parents were in their mid-40s. Fourteen years previously, they had lost all four of their biological children in a house fire. After the fire, they tried to reconstruct their family through adoption, because the wife could not conceive after the fire. The reconstructed family consisted of an 18-year-old boy, adopted at age 6, who had just been inducted into the army a week ago; a 15-year-old boy, and a 9-year-old girl, in addition to Sally. All but the 18-year-old had been adopted shortly after birth. None of the children were biologically related. Sally felt closest to her mother, farthest from her father, and disliked her 18-year-old brother most because he treated her "bad." Both parents were active and well respected in the community, and all the children did average to above-average work in school.

I was quite shocked to hear about the loss of the first four children and wondered if that was the family secret everyone was hiding. Yet, the story was told in such a straightforward, sad way by the father, without prodding from me, that I felt it was not. No doubt such a trauma had had a significant impact on this man and might even explain some of his current disengagement, but without the mother present I could not confirm this hypothesis. However, the comment about the 18-year-old brother by Sally was interesting to me. Did his leaving have something to do with the family secret?

At this point, I did an abdominal exam and confirmed that Sally had significant lower abdominal pain in both lower quadrants, with mild rebound tenderness. Running the differential diagnosis through in my mind, I began to focus on a condition that, had it occurred in an older woman, would have been an easier diagnosis to make. Perhaps, that was the family secret?

I then explained to both Sally and her father that I would have to perform a pelvic exam. I explained in some detail to Sally what that would entail, I asked her father to leave the room, and went to get a nurse. Upon my return, Salled seemed even more fearful. At that point, I decided to ask some more questions. After introducing the topic by saying that it was quite personal and that she didn't have to talk if she didn't want to, I asked, "Do you understand what sexual intercourse is?" "Yes," came the reply. "Have you had sexual intercourse recently?" "Yes," came the tearful reply. "Was it forced upon you?" Another tearful yes. "By who?" "My brother," she said. "The one who just left for the army?" "Yes," she said.

The family secret was out. I gave both myself and the patient a chance to compose ourselves. The pelvic exam, although painful for the patient, went well and confirmed the diagnosis of pelvic inflammatory disease (PID), secondary to incest.

I went out and talked with the father about my diagnosis. He confirmed the daughter's story, saying that it had happened before, but that he thought it had stopped when he severely punished the boy. I referred the case to their personal physician, recommending that Sally be admitted to the hospital and placed on intravenous antibiotics. Sally recovered quickly except for mild dysmenorrhea during her next three menstrual cycles.

The father called his son's first sergeant and told him that the boy had a social disease. The first sergeant understood and said he would take care of it. The son reportedly was cultured positive for gonococcus (GC) and treated. Sally's GC culture was also positive.

Despite numerous attempts by their personal physician, the father has consistently refused any form of family therapy, saying that he can handle the problem on his own and that the son is no longer welcome in his house.

This case confirmed for me the value of viewing the patient in the context of her family. The value in this case was the aid that information gave me in making a diagnosis. My interpretation of the family dynamics, as the interview progressed, led me to consider the unspeakable and to make an accurate diagnosis. Specifically, the father's disengagement and Sally's fear caused me to search further in the family history for an answer to those two visible dynamics. That search revealed the story of the terrible tragedy of the four children's death by fire, and the efforts of the parents to deal with it by reconstituting the family (four for four). That story added to my "gut feeling" that the eldest boy's recent departure had something to do with the family secret that I suspected existed and would shed light on Sally's illness. Some would probably argue that I could have dispensed with these observations, as the pelvic exam would have led me to the same diagnosis. In fact it might have, as the history, physical exam, and laboratory data were classic for the diagnosis of PID. However, the issue of incest could have been easily missed if the family dynamics hadn't piqued my interest. In fact, I would argue that if Sally had presented with anything less than classic findings, the outcome would have been vastly different, as it was the visible pattern of interaction between father and daughter that eventually led me to the complete diagnosis.

EDITORS' COMMENTS

We have little to add to this elegant case. Dr. Mengel was able to gather data simultaneously on the biomedical and family systems aspects of the patient's presentation to the emergency room. He had the wisdom to pursue the family data until a hypothesis occurred to him, and the courage to ask directly about this frightening hypothesis. The result was a biopsychosocial diagnosis rather than a narrowly biomedical one. The family secret is now exposed, but all that the family's physician can do now is continue to invite the family to deal with the aftermath of the revelation.

FAMILY DYSFUNCTION AND PEPTIC ULCER DISEASE

STEPHEN J. SPANN
University of Oklahoma Health Sciences Center

RR, an 18-year-old white male, came to see me for the first time because of severe epigastric abdominal pain and nausea. He had previously been evaluated by another physician for similar symptoms. An upper gastrointestinal radiographic contrast study had shown duodenal ulcer disease, and he had been appropriately treated with cimetidine and antacids. Now, several weeks after completing his course of therapy, he was having recurrence of symptoms. He denied symptoms of intestinal blood loss. He did not smoke or drink coffee. Despite the fact that he appeared quite anxious, he denied any sources of anxiety in his life. He lived at home with his parents and a younger sibling, and worked in a grocery store as a stocker. He could not identify any major stressors at home or work. He had a steady girlfriend, and things in that relationship seemed stable. On exam, he was noted to be rather anxious, and difficult to engage in conversation. He was tender in his epigastrium and had no evidence of intestinal blood loss. I told him that I was available at any time to talk about any problems that he might have, and started him back on cimetidine and antacids for a diagnosis of peptic ulcer disease.

Two weeks later, before his scheduled follow-up visit, the patient presented late one evening to the emergency room with severe nausea and vomiting, and inability to keep down any oral intake. He had been taking his medications as prescribed. On exam he was found to be mildly dehydrated and still very tender in the epigastrium. He still appeared very anxious, but denied any anxiety-provoking factors in his life. His parents were both with him, and they too denied knowledge of any problems at home or at work. The patient was admitted to the hospital with the diagnosis of gastric outlet obstruction secondary to peptic ulcer disease. He improved after 2 days' treatment with nasogastric suction and intravenous fluids and cimetidine. During this short hospitalization, he admitted to feeling anxious and had insight that he somatized his anxiety to his gut. He was unable, however, to discuss the source of his anxiety. Following improvement, he was discharged home on cimetidine, antacids, and a short-term course of diazepam in hopes of decreasing some of the physiologic manifestations of his anxiety.

A few days after his discharge, WR, the patient's mother, came to the office to see me for the first time. Her chief complaint was fatigue. She admitted to insomnia, increased appetite, and a loss of interest in life in general. When asked about her libido, she admitted that her marriage had been on the rocks for years, that her husband was having an affair with another woman, and that the only reason that she remained married and lived in the same house with him was for financial support. Past history and review of systems were otherwise negative. On physical examination, she was found to be mildly obese, and she appeared depressed. Her general examination was unremarkable except for the abdomen, where she was found to have a large ecchymosis in the right upper quadrant. When asked if this might be the result of physical abuse from her husband, she replied that she had been bruised when wrestling with RR. When I asked her if she had been fighting with him, she replied that they got along well and were very close, and that the wrestling was their way of expressing affection for each other. My assessment was that the patient's fatigue was secondary to depression, probably situational in nature, related to chronic marital discord and unhappiness. The patient accepted this diagnosis, but when asked to return to her husband to discuss the possibilities of marriage counseling, replied that the marriage was dead and could not be saved.

The pieces of a puzzle were beginning to fall into place. Here was a middle-aged woman with a severely dysfunctional marriage, who admitted to wrestling affectionately with her 18-year-old son. I began to wonder whether RR's anxiety could be related to this; perhaps he interpreted his mother's behavior as incestuous advances and was being literally frightened sick. The thought of confronting him with this possibility made me feel anxious, but I knew that I must explore this with him.

Less than 2 weeks after his discharge from his previous hospitalization, RR had to be readmitted for symptoms and signs of gastric outlet obstruction. After he had stabilized with nasogastric suction and intravenous fluids and cimetidine, I decided to test my hypothesis.

"I saw your mother in the office the other day," I said.

"Yes, she told me about it," replied RR.

"It sounds like she and your dad don't get along too well," I said.

"No, they have been fighting for years," he responded.

"It sounds like she's a lonely lady."

"I guess so." RR admitted.

"You know R," I said, "sometimes when parents aren't getting a lot of love from their mates, they may seek affection from their children. Your mom was telling me the other day that you and she wrestle playfully sometimes."

"Yeah, sometimes," he said.

"I'll bet getting that close to your mom could cause some scary feelings, like sexual feelings."

"You'd better believe it can!" he exclaimed. He then went on to relate that he was afraid that his mother wanted him to be her lover and that it did, indeed, worry him sick.

I felt exhilarated that my hunch had proven correct, yet apprehensive about confronting his mother and father with these facts. I reassured the patient that anxiety was a normal reaction to the situation, and asked him if he thought that he could confront his mother with the fact that her affection made him anxious. He agreed to tell her, with my help.

The next day, I met with RR and his mother. With my support and direction, the patient was able to tell his mother that he perceived her affectionate behavior as incestuous advances, and that it worried him sick. I pointed out to her that we really needed to make some effort to work on her relationship with her husband; she was, again, pessimistic. Both mother and son agreed to a joint meeting with the patient's father. It was obvious from the outset of that meeting that mother and father had nothing but contempt for each other. Rather than bring up the real issue of incestuous feelings, I framed the problem in terms of R's need for independence and emancipation from his parents. Mother and Dad agreed to this, but steadily refused marital counseling for themselves.

R was discharged from the hospital the next day and moved out of his parents' home to his own apartment. Over the next 3 years that I followed the family, his ulcer disease was controlled with maintenance single-dose daily cimetidine therapy. He never had to be readmitted to the hospital for this problem. His mother continued to refuse marital counseling or to leave her current marital situation. She continued to manifest symptoms of chronic depression and was seen frequently with varying somatic complaints.

This case history illustrates the utility of caring for the entire family. Even when we strongly suspect that a patient's somatic illness may relate to family stress, it may be difficult to elicit corroborating information from the patient. The patient may be able to admit this information over time, or we may be able to elicit it in a family conference. Sometimes, however, it can only be obtained in the course of taking care of another family member who is being affected by the family problem. In this case, I suspected the possibility of family stress as a contributing factor to the patient's recalcitrant peptic ulcer disease from the beginning. Despite careful probing for corroborating information, I was only able to solve the puzzle after I saw the patient's mother and linked her problem with his. Other family member's health problems often provide valuable clues to the solution of a patient's medical problem. Caring for the entire family increases the physician's chances of discovering those clues.

Even when one solves the diagnostic puzzle, one is not always able to intervene to the benefit of every symptomatic family member. In this case, identification of the problem and institution of a fairly simple intervention resulted in symptomatic improvement in the teenager. His mother, however, was unable to work on the more chronic, and difficult, marital problems; consequently, she did not benefit from the identification of the problem and remained chronically symptomatic.

EDITORS' COMMENTS

It is difficult to imagine many situations scarier for the clinician than this one. The family secret concerned a budding incestuous relationship between mother and son, along with a marriage held together by contempt and dependency. A less courageous physician might be forgiven for treating this case biomedically, and leaving the frightening family material alone. A key to Dr. Spann's success here was his ability to bring up the incest issue with both the boy and his mother in a nonjudgmental manner. He was able to be nonjudgmental in part because he understood how these things can happen in a family where the parents do not give much love to each other. Although "pathological," the problem was also human and worthy of respectful handling. In the full family meeting, it was wise to frame the issue as one of autonomy for the boy, since Dr. Spann had no contract with the parents to open up painful marital and family issues. This primary care family counseling succeeded in reducing the casualties in this family by one third.

ENURESIS: A DOG IS A BOY'S BEST FRIEND

THOMAS J. GRAU
Family Practice Residency, Sioux Falls, South Dakota

Tommy was a 6-year-old white male who was referred to me for primary care family counseling. Four months before I first saw Tommy, he was playing with friends and hiding in a cardboard box in an alley when a car hit the box. He sustained a fracture of the right lower leg. Emotionally, the accident was a very traumatic experience for him because he was trapped in the box for some time. Other than the fracture, however, there were no other significant physical injuries. He was hospitalized for an appropriate amount of time and discharged.

Tommy had frequent nightmares about the accident, which were still occurring when I saw him. The most difficult problem for the family was that about 1 month after the accident, Tommy began having daytime enuresis, three to four times a day. Tommy's mom indicated that he was not aware that he was wetting his pants, but had no difficulty initiating urination when he felt the urge. The family reported no nocturnal enuresis, even during the nightmares.

I would like to thank Michael Bloom, PhD, for his assistance in treating this family.

Prior to his visit to me, Tommy had a complete urologic workup, the results of which were normal. He also had a complete neurologic workup, in part because Tommy's teacher had reported that he was day dreaming and seemed unable to concentrate. Initially, it appeared there might be neurologic abnormalities, so referral was made for a second opinion. That physician, however, felt the questionable findings were within normal limits. He also felt that Tommy's problem was probably functional and referred Tommy to me for counseling.

The initial interview was with Tommy and his parents. In addition to the above history, the parents reported that Tommy was still having nightmares, although they seemed to be lessening in frequency. The enuresis was still the major problem, and the parents stated that they had tried a variety of things to remedy this situation. These included restricting fluids, reprimanding him, putting him on a schedule of going to the bathroom, and frequently reminding him to do so. They had given up on everything, but still frequently reminded him to go to the bathroom.

The parents also reported that Tommy's behavior had showed a marked change. Primarily, he was very demanding. When asked what they were doing about this, the mother reported that, since the accident, she felt very bad about all that he had been through and found it difficult to discipline him.

After a detailed discussion of the problems, I came to the following conclusions: (1) The nightmares were probably related to the traumatic stress of the accident and, as would be expected, were becoming less frequent. (2) Tommy had received a lot of attention in various ways following the accident, and, now that he was home from the hospital and life was returning to normal, the added attention was no longer present. I felt new symptoms were an unconscious effort to perpetuate the attention.

I then made the following recommendations. I suggested that rather than receiving a great deal of attention for wet pants, Tommy should receive very little attention, and actually get special rewards for dry days. Specifically, I set it up so that rather than telling Tommy to go to the bathroom frequently, they would not tell him at all. If he wet, he was told one time to change his pants. If that did not occur, he was not allowed to sit down anywhere in the house except his bedroom. The parents were not to fight with him over changing his pants. I recommended the same for the teachers at school. If he made it a full day without wetting his pants, the parents were to do something special with him at the end of the day I suggested that, if he was able to be dry for 3 consecutive days, they make arrangements for him to stay at his friend's house (during the interview, Tommy had expressed a desire to visit a friend's house, but hadn't been able to for fear of wetting his pants).

As for disciplining Tommy, I recommended that the parents treat him as they had done previously. There was no need to be lenient because of what he had been through. In fact, if he acted badly, they should put him in his room alone as a way of denying him attention. The mother was relieved to receive the okay to discipline her son and was willing to do so.

I informed the parents that, initially, we expected things to get worse as Tommy would likely try harder for attention. If they could be firm in their plans, however, I anticipated he would do well. (The family had functioned well in all respects prior to the accident and did not have the characteristics associated with psychosomatic families. Therefore, we were optimistic about his recovery.)

A telephone call 1 week later indicated that things were much better. The ultimate therapy was revealed at their next meeting, approximately 3 weeks after the first visit.

At that time, Tommy and his parents reported things to be going very well, and he had no further enuresis and fewer nightmares. Both Tommy and his parents were extremely pleased at this success (and I was, too), but I was surprised at the speed with which things got better. I was then told how this happened.

After our first meeting, Tommy's father bought a puppy. One of their first goals with the puppy was to housebreak him. The dad said, "This is my dog and you can play with him, but only when you have dry pants. I would also like you to help me housebreak him, but in order to do so, you will have to set an example." He implied that there was no way Tommy could housebreak the dog if he himself was not trained. According to the parents, the problems resolved practically overnight and their lives returned to normal.

When therapy goes poorly, it is usually easy to formulate an explanation, perhaps many explanations. When therapy goes well, however, an explanation is often more difficult. Here are my thoughts on this case.

Following the accident, the parents were told (by physicians) how to take care of their son. They followed the advice closely. As the physical injuries healed, the other problems developed. The parents again followed doctors' suggested treatments, but the problems persisted. What I did in my counseling was to transfer the primary responsibility for the care of the child back to the parents. Once in the responsible position, they created their own ways to help their son. The parents were the best therapists in this setting and we liked their idea. I jokingly asked if I could use their plan should a similar situation present to me in the future.

EDITORS' COMMENTS

The author has already commented well on this charming case. We focus our discussion on the context of this primary care family counseling. Tommy was referred to a family physician/family therapist team by the physician(s) who did the urologic and neurologic workups. In our fantasies, we imagine this situation being repeated routinely in medicine: Family physicians, often in teams with other health professionals trained to work with families, would be used as consultants to other physicians for cases that cannot be adequately handled through a biomedical approach alone. Indeed, this casebook contains the work of many pioneers in this new referral area. The present dominance of the biomedical model will not be changed without leadership from within medicine, and the primary care disciplines of family practice and pediatrics probably are the best hope for leading this change toward a biopsychosocial model. In Dr. Grau's case, the "referral treatment" was brief, primary care family counseling that returned control back to the family. Dr. Grau probably could have done this counseling alone, but Dr. Bloom's presence added assurance that together they could cope with complications that might occur in the primary care approach.

FUNCTIONAL SYMPTOMS IN RESPONSE TO STRESS

ANTHONY ROSTAIN
University of Pennsylvania

I first met the T family in the emergency room one afternoon when Kerri was 20 months old. She was suffering a prolonged bout of acute otitis media and pharyngitis, which had not resolved after several courses of antibiotics. Mr. T seemed very anxious about his daughter's illness. He had been to see a physician in the neighborhood, had followed the prescribed treatments carefully, and was particularly worried that despite everything, his daughter remained irritable, refused to eat, and slept more than usual.

After carefully examining Kerri and finding nothing remarkable in the way of physical findings, I pursued more information about the family situation. I learned that Kerri's mother had just given birth to a son, Joey, and that the baby had recently come home from the hospital. After hearing a little bit more about the "new" baby, I gently suggested to Mr. T that much of his daughter's behavior seemed to be a reaction to Joey's arrival. I said that I understood how difficult it must be to have both a new baby and a sick toddler at home, and I reassured him that his daughter was not seriously ill, that she would be fine in a matter of days, and that he could expect several weeks of "immature behavior" before she would adjust to Joey's presence. Visibly relieved, Mr. T thanked me and took my name and phone number. I encouraged him to call me if any other problems developed.

The next day Mr. T and Kerri returned to the emergency room and asked to see me. Kerri had developed a rash and was still irritable, and her father was even more worried than before that something terrible was happening. Her physical exam remained essentially unchanged except for a maculopapular rash on most of her body, which appeared to be a viral exanthem. I patiently explained my diagnosis to Mr. T and again reassured him that his daughter was going to improve in a matter of days. As an added measure of support, I invited Mr. T to bring Kerri and Joey in for well child exams. I had the feeling that he liked me and that he was looking for a pediatrician for his kids. My hunch was confirmed at the follow-up visit 2 weeks later.

Both Mr. and Mrs. T were present for the visit. Mr. T was tall, thin, blond-haired and blue-eyed with a toothy smile and a hearty laugh. He held Joey comfortably on his lap and obviously enjoyed contact with the baby. Mrs. T was short and slightly rotund, with an attractive face, large blue eyes, and a somewhat tired expression. She held Kerri in her arms, and she cried and fussed during the entire visit. Mr. and Mrs. T were friendly, talkative, and responsive to my queries about the family and the children.

I learned that they lived in a small row house, which they rented in a working-class neighborhood several miles from the hospital. Both of them had been born and raised in this neighborhood, and Mrs. T's mother and siblings lived nearby. Mr. T's parents had died when he was a child, so he was raised by his aunt and uncle and various older sisters.

Mr. T was presently unemployed, having worked for several years as an inventory control manager at a warehouse. Although he was having a hard time finding a job, he seemed optimistic that sooner or later he would meet with success. Mrs. T described herself as a housewife, and although she planned to go back to work at some point in the future, for now she was happy to stay at home and raise the kids. Mr. and Mrs. T felt their relationship was basically good. They agreed about most things and generally were able to settle their differences. Affectionate and communicative with each other during the visit, there was a playful and teasing quality to their interaction. I asked them to discuss any concerns they had about the kids.

Mr. and Mrs. T were worried most about Kerri's behavior. Since her brother's arrival from the hospital, she had become a whiny, irritable child prone to temper tantrums and crying fits. For example, the previous evening Kerri became extremely upset when Mrs. T put Joey to sleep in what had formerly been her crib. Although they explained to her that she was now a big girl and could sleep in a bed instead of a crib, Mr. and Mrs. T were simply unable to comfort their daughter. They were confused and anxious about how to handle her tantrums, which were growing more frequent and more intense with each passing day. Furthermore, whereas Mrs. T tried to ignore these outbursts, her mother believed Kerri should be disciplined for her negative behavior and was openly critical of her daughter's more lenient approach. As was fairly typical of his style, Mr. T had not yet taken any sides in this dispute.

After listening to their concerns, I asked each parent what they believed was going on, and what they thought they should do about it. Mrs. T explained that Kerri was probably very jealous of the baby, and that she needed time to get used to him. She also felt her mother was being intrusive and unhelpful, but she wasn't sure just how to stand up to her.

Mr. T wasn't sure how to deal with Kerri, although he sensed that they needed to be firm with her and not give in to her tantrums. He agreed with his wife that they could take care of Kerri's behavior themselves, and that she needed to tell her mother in a nice way not to interfere. I suggested that the two of them work out a plan whereby Kerri could have time alone with her mother. This meant that Mr. T would have to take care of Joey by himself from time to time.

Both of them looked at each other and laughed. Mrs. T remarked that she had wanted her husband to learn to feed and change the baby but that he had been resistant. I replied that in order to help Kerri, Mr. T was going to have to learn a few new routines. In this day and age it was appropriate for men to take more of a role in caring for their babies. I also explained that this would be the only way to get Mrs. T's mother to stop interfering with her daughter's parenting. If she saw how helpful Mr. T was being, she might be less prone to try to help her daughter out. Mr. T laughed good-naturedly and agreed to give it a try. I turned to Mrs. T, complimented her on her choice of husbands, and proceeded with the physical exams of the children.

During the remainder of the visit, I took several opportunities to comment upon what wonderful parents Mr. and Mrs. T were. I expressed my belief that they knew the right way to raise their children, that they didn't need experts to tell them what to do, and that as long as they could communicate with each other and work together, the kids would thrive. Predictably, Kerri's adjustment reaction proved to be short-lived.

As I followed the T family over time, I always made a point of focusing part of each visit on parenting issues. For the first 2 years, Mr. T accompanied his wife to every appointment, in spite of the fact that he had found a job as a carpet installer. They seemed to enjoy coming to the office and sharing their joys and their concerns about the children. I looked forward to these visits as well.

Things continued uneventfully for the T family until 2½ years later. At a routine well child visit, I learned that Kerri, who had recently started nursery school, was developing recurrent abdominal pain. It was classic in its presentation. Without any apparent reason, she would suddenly start to complain that her tummy ached. Located diffusely in the periumbilical region, the pain was not associated with recent meals, nor with vomiting, diarrhea, or other gastrointestinal symptoms. It usually responded promptly to rest and aspirin. At home, Kerri's belly pain would occur at times of stress, for example whenever her father would get angry at her or her brother for misbehaving. In school, at various times of the day, Kerri would suddenly start to cry and complain that her tummy hurt. Mrs. T would be called to come and fetch her daughter; upon returning home, the pain would subside.

Kerri's physical exam was completely benign. Her urinalysis and stool heme test were unremarkable, and a urine culture proved to be negative. When I asked her what she thought was going on, Mrs. T replied, "It could be her nerves," although she didn't understand what in particular was making her so upset. Kerri enjoyed school and was well liked by her teachers and her peers.

I asked Mrs. T if anything had upset *her* recently. She grew quiet for a moment and replied that her mother had passed away 2 months previously. Growing visibly sad in the office, she confessed to not having fully resolved her feelings of grief. Her husband had been somewhat supportive, but with his busy work schedule there hadn't been enough time to talk together.

After listening for a while, I suggested to Mrs. T that Kerri's pain might indeed be a reaction to seeing her mother sad and depressed. I told her to keep a record of the episodes and to keep her daughter in school despite the complaints of pain. I also strongly urged Mrs. T to spend some time talking to her husband, and I recommended that the two of them come in alone to discuss Kerri's problem in more detail. We made an appointment for the following week.

The T family arrived on time for our session. I began by explaining to them that I thought Kerri was basically a healthy little girl, and that there was nothing medically wrong with her. I was concerned that she was having stomachaches as a a reaction to the stress she was experiencing both at home and in school, and I made it clear to them that the purpose of this meeting was to see if they could figure out exactly what might be bothering their daughter.

Mrs. T began by stating that Kerri was nervous all the time, was easily upset, and was extremely sensitive to criticism. She expressed frustration at the fact that whenever she would try to discipline her daughter, Kerri would cry and go running to her father. She also admitted to having felt quite sad after her mother died, and to having kept much of her feelings to herself, for fear of upsetting the kids. She also complained that her husband was working too hard and that he wasn't helping her enough around the house or with the children. Apparently he was laying carpets 11 to 12 hours a day, 6 days a week, leaving for work before the kids awakened, and arriving home after dinner, shortly before their bedtime.

I asked Mr. T what he thought about the situation. He readily admitted to feeling guilty for working so much and for not being around more. He defended his actions by stating that he wanted his wife to be able to stay home with the kids, and that in order to bring home enough money, it was necessary to work overtime. He also claimed that Mrs. T was too harsh with Kerri, and that she picked on her for "little things" that really weren't very important. He thought it was his wife's constant nagging that was making Kerri upset most of the time.

After listening to their discussion, I suggested that there seemed to be several issues over which they were disagreeing, and that they needed to start talking through these one by one in order to arrive at some resolution of their conflicts. I agreed with both of them that Kerri was a sensitive child, then added that her recurrent bellyaches were probably a reaction to their discord, which was all the more reason for them to start working out their disagreements. I instructed them to pick one topic and to discuss it right there and then in my office. They chose to focus on Mr. T's job.

After reviewing the pros and cons of the situation, Mrs. T started to challenge her husband's reasoning about overtime. Although the family could use the money, it seemed to her most important to have him at home more in order to take care of the children and help her out with the chores. Mr. T finally admitted that although it would be better to do so, he was afraid of telling his boss that he was unwilling to work all the hours that were being asked of him because it might put his job at risk.

At this point, I suggested that if Mr. T didn't find a way to reduce the number of hours he was working, Kerri's problem could get worse, and Joey might also start to show symptoms related to stress. Mr. T asked me what he could do to convince his boss that it was important for his family's sake that he not work so much. I offered to write a letter on Kerri's behalf explaining that her medical condition necessitated that Mr. T be home *at least* 2 hours each evening. Furthermore, should this fail to convince him, I was prepared to talk with his employer directly in order to dramatize the urgency of the situation. I quickly added that I believed Mr. T would be able to make the case for less overtime without my help, but that it was there if he needed it.

Mr. T was extremely appreciative of my offer and stated emphatically that he would find a way to cut back his hours at work. Mrs. T looked visibly relieved to hear her husband's words, and the two smiled at each other for the first time during the session. Noticing this, I commented that I believed the two of them would be able to resolve their other areas of disagreement once this basic obstacle had been overcome. As far as Kerri's belly pains were concerned, I suggested that the parents continue to treat these as they had been doing in the past. The most helpful changes for Kerri would be for her to see her father around the house more, her mother less overwhelmed and upset, and her parents interacting in positive ways. I cautioned them to work together on issues of discipline, and to stop their daughter from playing one against the other. I was confident that they could do this providing Mr. T was home enough to be involved with raising his kids. I repeated several times that both his wife and his children needed him now, and that things would improve for the entire family if he was more available to them. Mr. T nodded in silence as he looked tenderly at his wife.

I concluded the session by asking Mr. T to give me a call in 2 weeks to let me know how things were going. I was willing to meet with them again to continue discussing some of the parenting issues they were raising, but I was fairly certain that it wouldn't be necessary provided they continued working out their differences on a consistent basis. I asked them to schedule an appointment for both kids in 1 month's time so I could follow up on Kerri's progress. At the 1-month follow-up visit, Kerri was having no further episodes of abdominal pain, Mr. T was spending more time at home, and both parents were pleased with the new situation.

This case highlights the importance of getting to know the family's issues and context in order to effectively handle functional problems. Kerri became the symptomatic child in a family undergoing predictable but stressful life changes. The pressures of earning a living had forced Mr. T to give up spending time with his wife and children at precisely the point when they needed him to be around. By getting the parents to set their priorities and settle their differences, I helped eliminate the underlying causes of Kerri's symptoms. A firm but supportive stance toward each parent provided a basis for promoting positive changes.

EDITORS' COMMENTS

The T family represents a basically healthy family undergoing stress stemming from developmental transitions. The family's stress presented classically in the illness of a child around whom parental fear and conflict centered. Dr. Rostain demonstrates here several important charactertistics of primary care family counseling: first, the advantage of continuity with a family, since successful physician–family collaboration during one stressful episode paves the way for similar collaboration the next time; second, the value of early intervention, since by the time this family saw a therapist the couple might have been ready to divorce, or the older child completely unmanageable; third, the optimism with which the physician can approach a family undergoing painful but predictable life-cycle stress. The details of primary care counseling interventions naturally must be adapted to the physician's style. Dr. Rostain was more directive about the father's work situation and more willing to intervene with the employer than we might have been. But especially in the context of a long-term relationship with a family, a variety of physician styles can be helpful.

A GIRL WITH UNCONTROLLED DIABETES

DANIEL P. RAINS
Private practice, New Castle, Indiana

Ms. C, a 13-year-old girl, was brought to my office by her mother after she complained of vaginal and perineal irritation. I had not seen this young woman previously, but was acquainted with a half sister who had come to the emergency room with a pyelonephritis, got well, and subsequently became pregnant but did not come to me for care. Ms. C's history revealed that she was a juvenile diabetic on insulin. She denied previous problems of this sort, had some knowledge about yeast infections, and denied any sexual activity. Examination included findings of Tanner Stage II sexual development, and rather severe vulva irritation with nonspecific findings on potassium hydroxide and saline preparations. A random blood sugar was taken and was over 300.

After Ms. C dressed and the lab reports returned, I spent some time talking with her further about her diabetes control, and outlining a plan of management for her perineal and vulvar irritation. She understood quite well what type of diet she needed to be on and when she should take her insulin, but was not complying with either diet or insulin therapy. The mother had gone to do some shopping, and when she returned to pick up her daughter, I visited with her very briefly and told her that I wanted her and Ms. C and all of the family members who were available to come in for a visit the next week.

I cannot explain exactly what messages were given to me by this young woman. It was clear to me that she didn't need to be told how to manage her diabetes; she was just unable to manage it in her current life situation. Therefore, I decided not to concentrate on diabetes management at all until I understood further her and her family's environment. As we will see, this hunch was an accurate one, and, to this day I believe that I avoided falling into that trap, that is, hospitalization, regulating insulin, and so on, without fully assessing the environment.

For the family session, a younger sibling, and two older half siblings accompanied Ms. C and her mother. Missing were the oldest daughter, who was married and not living in the area, and Mrs. C's three ex-husbands. All five of the young women were neatly dressed, and seemed bright, alert, interested, and happy to be there. The mother appeared somewhat nervous but quickly relaxed and warmed to the discussion. I had, with the permission of Ms. C and her mother, asked that our family therapist sit in on the discussion (with the full expectation that she might indeed prove to be the more important member of the health care team). The father of the older three daughters was not in the picture at all. The father of the younger two daughters was in the area and was helping with their finances and other needs but was not in attendance. The third ex-husband had been divorced recently. When we asked the mother the circumstances of the divorce, after a brief period of silence, she struggled for words and, beginning to cry, calmly told us that she had discovered that he had been sleeping in turn with each of the older daughters. Not only had she divorced him but he had been turned over for prosecution. As this was discussed, the older daughters rather bravely held their chins up but cried softly, and Ms. C relaxed. The youngest sister, who was about 7 or 8 years old, from time to time tried to ease the tension by making some jokes or acting out a little, but was taking all this in and obviously knew this family secret. Neither of the older three sisters involved in the incest had received counseling, but the two present expressed a desire to do so.

The family came back for several more sessions, and at the third session we followed up with Ms. C's complaints of vaginal irritation and also diabetes control. The vaginal irritation had cleared and she was managing her diabetes much more actively and appropriately, with occasional lapses one would expect of an adolescent wanting fast foods and pizza like her peers.

I learned several things from this situation. It no longer surprises me to uncover such secrets in a family. This was one of the first times I ever followed a hunch like this instead of being overwhelmed by the medical side of a situation and getting bogged down in what would have no doubt been a frustrating and inadequate attempt to control

Ms. C's diabetes. It seems quite likely that as her secondary sex characteristics developed, she was coping with the expectation that she would be next in the family to fill the role of the daughter active in the incest. This role was confused by the prosecution of her stepfather, the move away from him, the presence of her natural father, her older sister's pregnancy, and so on. The vulvar irritation pointed in its own way to the source of the problem, and the diabetes turned out to be a good barometer of the stress level of the whole family. It could have been a smokescreen instead.

EDITORS' COMMENTS

A desire to understand the context of the adolescent's medical complaint led Dr. Rains to assemble the available family. A clinical hunch moved him to collaborate with a family therapist before there was definite evidence of a serious family problem. When the terrible family secret was exposed, no one was overcome. Contextual medicine and a collaborative approach protected this family physician from the pain of being overwhelmed by discovering an explosive diagnosis—incest—and helped him avoid the frustration of addressing a medical problem without a hope of patient compliance.

Dr. Rains has evidently learned to trust his instincts. When he felt that treating the patient required a larger circle, he convened the family and the therapist before vigorously pursuing the medical treatment. By doing this, he established a setting in which a potent issue could be discovered with minimal damage to himself, the patient, and the other family members. In a parallel manner, a skilled surgeon would demand that the proper surgical instruments and support staff be present for a complex surgical case. As family physicians pursue family and other social contexts, we must learn to set up the "operating room" to support us in case complications arise from the interview.

Many times the issue for discussion is less potent than incest. In those cases, the physician may not want a therapist in the room but may call one for consultation or referral. Sometimes, a different community resource is needed eventually, but not urgently. In that instance, the family physician may call familiar resources for assistance after the family interview. However, such an option is realistic only if the needed resource is relatively familiar to the primary physician before the need arises.

Familiarity with the "tools" of family-centered care is critical to satisfying outcomes. Most family physicians currently do not have a family therapist available to join them in an office interview. However, every family physician can become familiar with local family therapy, mental health, and other community resources in order to be most efficient and effective in their utilization. In doing so, the family physician will become proficient in practicing family-centered primary care.

A FAMILY WITH RECENT LOSS

ALVAH R. CASS
University of Oklahoma Health Sciences Center

Mrs. B was a 46-year-old woman who presented in the clinic complaining of numbness in the fourth and fifth digits of her left hand. Her history was negative except for the fact that each morning while driving to work she would rest her elbow on the armrest of the car. Her physical exam was consistent with an ulnar neuritis secondary to compression trauma. I explained my findings and reassured her that she would likely experience a full recovery if she avoided repeated or continuous pressure to her elbow. She seemed satisfied, but as she was leaving she asked, "Doctor, do you think this could be caused by my nerves?"

I responded, "Why do you ask?"

She answered by saying, "Six weeks ago my husband died suddenly and unexpectedly of a heart attack at home. Since then my daughter, Becky, and I have been fighting constantly." Breaking into tears, she continued, "I'm afraid I am losing her, too, losing her love and her respect. I just can't take this anymore! Do you think she needs to see a child psychiatrist?"

I explained to her that her daughter was feeling the same type of loss and grief over the death that she was experiencing, but that children sometimes express this in terms of anger more than sadness. I suggested that before she involved a psychiatrist, I could meet with her and Becky, and we could discuss what this experience of an unexpected loss had been like for both of them. Mrs. B thought this would be very helpful, and a family conference was arranged for the following week.

Mrs. B, her 10-year-old daughter Becky, a 4th-year medical student, and I were present at the first meeting. I opened the family conference by asking Mrs. B and then Becky what their understanding was of why we were meeting. They agreed it was to talk about why they were arguing so much. Throughout the discussion, Mrs. B and Becky had a difficult time talking without arguing. An interaction pattern emerged in which Mrs. B would make a statement, Becky would disagree and correct her mother, and Mrs. B would respond by modifying, justifying, or rationalizing her initial statement. Becky was frequently disrespectful of her mother and would behave similarly when I would try to engage her in conversation. In the midst of one of these interactions—an argument about whether Mrs. B had the right to go out as an adult and leave Becky with a sitter, something she never did while her husband was alive—Mrs. B, in a frustrated voice said, "Sometimes I don't know who the mother is in this relationship, Becky or me!" I agreed in a sort of joking manner that they acted much more like rival sisters than like mother and child. The conference ended with instructions from me for Mrs. B not to engage Becky in arguments, and with Mrs. B and Becky negotiating a time when Mrs. B would go out one evening and leave Becky with her older married sister. In retrospect, this was a tactical error on my part because it empowered Becky with control over her mother's behavior. They agreed to return in 2 weeks.

At the second meeting, I invited Dr. Doherty, a family therapist, to observe me and to participate in the family conference. The conference was opened by asking how the last 2 weeks had gone. Mrs. B responded quickly and said her evening out was a disaster, Becky was becoming more rebellious, and had embarrassed her several times in public. Becky pouted and refused to engage in conversation except to correct her mother and degrade her. Midway through the conference, I was engulfed in a struggle to engage Becky, and after repeated failures, I turned to Dr. Doherty and said, "I'm lost. I don't know what to do."

He quickly aligned with the mother, and clearly defined her role and responsibilities of being in charge as the parent. He pointed out that Becky could choose not to talk, but her participation was welcome if she would speak with respect. He also instructed that no one should respond to her if she shouted or was disrespectful. He went on to label Becky's behavior as fear of losing control, and not rebellion. This produced outbursts from Becky, and the issue of losing control became more evident. The session ended with an agreement that Mrs. B would set and enforce one simple rule for Becky, continue to resist engaging in arguments with Becky, and decide on the circumstances under which she would go out as an independent adult. We agreed to meet in 2 weeks.

The third meeting did not occur until approximately 3 weeks later. Mrs. B, Becky, Dr. Doherty, and I were present at this meeting. Mrs. B had followed through with her assignments and was proud of taking a more parental role. She appeared confident that she could be an effective parent. Becky had responded, and was acting more like a 10-year-old child. During the interview, she was polite, respectful, and said that she was happier with the relationship she now had with her mother. Mrs. B was starting to go out with her friends, Becky was making new friends her age at school, and had joined the New Kids In School Club. The interview ended with supportive statements regarding the progress they had made in such a short time. We also indicated they could return for further counseling if they felt it was necessary, and that I would continue in my role as their family doctor.

I have had limited follow-up with Mrs. B through telephone conversations. Mrs. B accepted a new job and enjoys it very much. Becky is doing well in school. Mrs. B's job allows her more time with her daughter, and more time for herself. She has met some new friends, goes out regularly, and enjoys this new degree of freedom. Mrs. B feels that their relationship is very stable now and that she is being an effective parent.

The first lesson I learned from this case was that without meeting as a family I could have easily labeled the problem as a grief reaction, and not recognized the struggle for control. In retrospect, Becky had always enjoyed a significant amount of control in this family, and with the death of her father, she took on more of his role and behavioral characteristics. Having them together allowed me to experience their interaction patterns, and understand each of their roles in maintaining this system. It also helped me avoid thinking of Becky as a spoiled child who was rebelling against her mother's authority. The family conference allowed me to recognize these issues, and, with the help of Dr. Doherty, deal with them more effectively.

The second lesson learned from this case was a greater appreciation of the role of a family physician in dealing with this type of problem. Bringing a family together demonstrates the doctor's willingness to work with them and limits the fragmentation of medical care. Even if the case is ultimately beyond the skills of a family doctor, as was the case here, I believe the ease of recommending a referral, and the likelihood of success is greatly enhanced.

EDITORS' COMMENTS

Dr. Cass has already commented nicely on the primary care aspects of this case. Although this family needed a brief intervention from a family therapist to help them get unstuck, the bulk of the case was assessed and handled at the primary care level by a family physician who met with the family and looked beyond conventional ways of interpreting the mother's stress and her daughter's anger.

A WOMAN WITH FIBROMYOSITIS

ALVAH R. CASS
University of Oklahoma Health Sciences Center

Mrs. M was a 40-year-old black woman who first came to my office in November 1984. Her chief complaint concerned a painful lump on the back of her neck. She went on to state that for the last 7 years she had had diffuse muscle aches and pains, and a few associated joint pains. The pain began in 1976, and gradually and progressively increased until she had to quit her job as a filing clerk in October 1983.

Since 1981, she had also had insomnia, which was characterized by trouble falling asleep as well as frequent awakenings throughout the night. In the morning, she felt tired and unrested. In the past 2 years, she was also bothered by generalized stiffness, particularly of her hands and neck. The stiffness was worse in the morning and after prolonged periods of rest. It would improve with motion but would never completely clear. Her symptoms gradually progressed to the extent that, at her initial visit, she was unable to perform simple, routine housework.

She denied any redness or significant swelling in her joints. In addition, she denied anorexia, constipation, diarrhea, heat or cold intolerance, or suicidal thoughts.

Mrs. M's past medical history included a peptic ulcer diagnosed in 1960, and a series of surgical procedures including an appendectomy, a hemorrhoidectomy, an ectopic pregnancy, and a hysterectomy.

Mrs. M was married in 1974 and divorced in 1976. She had had three children. Her 22-year-old son, Tony, is married and has three children. Her 16-year-old daughter, Sherry, is severely mentally retarded, apparently from asphyxia at birth, and lives with Mrs. M. In 1971, Mrs. M had an infant die at 12 hours of age after a premature birth. Her father died in 1944 of unknown causes, and her mother died in 1973 of a stroke. Her oldest sister died in 1979 of alcoholic cirrhosis.

Physical exam revealed a 40-year-old black woman who was moderately obese and had a depressed affect. The remainder of her exam was unremarkable except the musculoskeletal exam, which revealed a limited range of motion of the neck and a large lipoma over the nape of the neck. Trigger points were identified over the spinous processes of the lower cervical spine, trapezius muscle, and lower lumbar spine. Additional points were found including medial epicondyles of the elbows, popliteal space, and tenderness along the fascia lata. The neurological exam was normal, including muscle strength.

At the time, my assessment was that Mrs. M was suffering from fibromyositis, a chronic condition characterized by generalized stiffness, muscle pain and tenderness, insomnia, and tender trigger points. It is frequently worsened by psychosocial stresses and is often associated with symptoms of depression.

I explained my impressions to Mrs. M, and she was relieved that I didn't think that she was making up her symptoms, as other physicians had implied. I recommended that she should start on amitriptyline and explained that this might help with the sleep disorder and ease some of her pain.

She returned in 2 weeks for a follow-up visit, and she was moderately improved. She went on to say that her friends and family were avoiding her because they thought she was faking her illness. We discussed this at some length, and I suggested that it would help to understand her illness better if I could meet with her and her family, and that it might be helpful for her to have me explain her illness to them. She felt this would be a good idea, and I asked whom she would like to invite. She quickly listed several people including family, friends, and a social worker. I also suggested she continue on the amitriptyline, and she agreed.

In January 1985, Mrs. M, her daughter, and her son came in for the family conference. I invited Dr. Doherty, a family therapist, to join us. During the conference, I explained the nature of Mrs. M's illness and discussed the long-term outlook of her condition. Her son took a very active role in the discussions and demonstrated sincere interest in his mother's health. We discovered, and pointed out, that her son was a very helpful person who frequently overcommits himself to help others, including people at work, in the neighborhood, and at home. He admitted he was near "burnout" at times, and we focused much of the conversation on him. At this point, Mrs. M, who was always in a dependent and demanding role with her son, offered to help him by coming to his house or watching his children. We also discovered some of Mrs. M's fears regarding her daughter and how a full-time job would prevent her from caring for her daughter in the manner she wanted.

Tony said it was easier to be around his mother since she was feeling better, and he wanted to help her and his sister. The family meeting ended with Mrs. M feeling understood, her son with fewer demands on him, and both with a better understanding of fibromyositis.

I continued to see Mrs. M every 2 months for follow-up visits. She did well and her symptoms were adequately controlled. She continued to take amitriptyline, which helped with the sleep disorder and some of the pain. Additional pain control was afforded by exercise, massage, moist heat, and nonsteroidal antiinflammatory agents. Mrs. M was able to take care of routine household chores, care for her daughter, and care for herself. She frequently found innovative ways to get tasks accomplished and demonstrated a degree of pride in her accomplishments. The relationship with her son was less strained. She asked less of him, and he was more willing to help with chores that were too difficult for Mrs. M to do. She wanted to eventually return to work and be more self-sufficient, but was afraid that her daughter would not get the care and supervision she needed.

Working with this case demonstrated the benefits of convening a family conference to discuss a complex and/or chronic medical illness. I gained a better understanding of the ramifications of this illness on the other people involved, including the effects on relationships, in and out of the family, and what concerns and fears are involved in caring for a severely retarded teenage girl. Mrs. M's illness allowed her to be totally dedicated to caring for her daughter and reduced the fear of having her taken away or having something happen to her while Mrs. M was away. This, however, was not without a price. Mrs. M had lost a lot of self-esteem; she had compromised other relationships and had endured a lot of pain and suffering. By convening the family, and establishing a patient–doctor relationship of mutual respect, I was able to negotiate a therapeutic plan with the patient, which led to some improvement and lessening of the negative effects of her illness.

It also would have been easy to view her son as noncaring, but the family meeting demonstrated just the opposite. The conference also helped Mrs. M feel understood and provided the context in which she and her son could talk about and better understand each others' feelings.

EDITORS' COMMENTS

The family conference was called to get the physician, the patient, and the family on the same track about Mrs. M's condition. This basic goal was accomplished. The unexpected payoff came from the openness of Tony and his mother in discussing their relationship. By spending time talking with Tony about significant stresses in his own life, Dr. Cass and Dr. Doherty facilitated a more balanced mother–son relationship in which each could help the other. Allying with Mrs. M by trying to get Tony to help her more would probably have increased Tony's defensiveness and sense of burden. Optimal treatment of this patient and family required a level four understanding of family systems. A brief family intervention such as this should not be expected to produce massive change in long-standing illness patterns, or in long-standing family interaction patterns. In this case, Mrs. M's attachment to her retarded daughter was not addressed. However, Mrs. M and her son were able to shift their interaction pattern in a subtle but significant way. As a result, Mrs. M took more responsibility for herself and was able to better handle her illness.

LEVEL FIVE CASES

FAMILY THERAPY

KNOWLEDGE BASE

Family systems and patterns whereby dysfunctional families interact with professionals and other health care systems.

PERSONAL DEVELOPMENT

Ability to handle intense emotions in families and self and to maintain neutrality in the face of strong pressure from family members or other professionals.

SKILLS

The following is not an exhaustive list of family therapy skills but rather a list of several key skills that distinguish level five involvement from primary care involvement with families.

1. Interviewing families or family members who are quite difficult to engage.
2. Efficiently generating and testing hypotheses about the family's difficulties and interaction patterns.
3. Escalating conflict in the family in order to break a family impasse.
4. Temporarily siding with one family member against another.
5. Constructively dealing with a family's strong resistance to change.
6. Negotiating collaborative relationships with other professionals and other systems who are working with the family, even when these groups are at odds with one another.

FAMILY INTERVENTION IN FAILURE TO THRIVE

KAREN WEIHS
Brown University

This case involves a child with the diagnosis of failure to thrive who was managed by a 2nd-year family medicine resident. As the faculty supervisor for this resident, I addressed multiple levels of the system surrounding the problem, including the patient's immediate family, the extended family, the hospital team, the family care center team, and the community agencies. By using the forces at each level to create a clearer structure for the child's life, the problem of failure to thrive was resolved. The family also moved to a new evolutionary stage in which all of the members made better use of their resources.

Michael T was 4 months old when he was admitted to the pediatric floor with the problem of low weight gain. It was his third admission in 2 months. His primary care physician had done a thorough evaluation during the previous admissions for diseases such as hypothyroidism and malabsorption. As the attending physician on the family practice service, I was new to the case. The child had gained weight quite well (10% increases) during the previous hospitalizations. In the home environment, however, his weight remained the same. At the time of this admission, he weighed 9 pounds; low normal weight for his age is 14.5 pounds. I suspected failure to thrive, a syndrome that includes stunted growth, caused by deprivation of physical touching and personal attention.

During the first day of rounds in the hospital, I met Michael's mother, Mickey T. She was a 21-year-old mother of three who had never been married. She was involved with Ed R, the father of all three children, but he did not live with her. She said this was because she would not receive her welfare payments if he moved in. Mickey and Ed were planning to marry after he got a job and could earn enough money to support them. Mickey was a slightly overweight, poorly groomed individual who gave long tangential answers to all of my questions. She had worked part-time as a waitress between the birth of her first and second children. She lived with her children in a third-floor apartment of a building two blocks from her parents' house. I constructed the beginning of a family genogram during this interview (see Figure 1).

The hospital social worker and the resident both said that they felt hopeless about Michael and his mother. I realized that I was beginning to feel the same way and became angry at this young mother who was not, in my opinion, taking proper care of her child. My knowledge of systems broke through these hopeless feelings just enough to make me consider that something might be done if I knew more about the family. If I could understand *how* the baby was being deprived, then I could work with the family to give him more of what he needed.

I invited both of Michael's parents to talk with me and the resident the next day. They came for the interview and a picture of the problem emerged from a careful behavioral interview.

Michael's 4-year-old brother, Roger, was considered "uncontrollable" by his parents. His incessant explorations had involved such incidents as painting the front door red with paint left under the porch steps by the landlord, throwing plants out of the windows, and tearing most of the wallpaper from the walls of his bedroom. He was said to "behave" when his father was present, but both father and mother agreed that he required constant attention when only his mother was present. Mickey said that this sometimes got to be too much for her, and she would have to ignore him to keep her sanity. Michael's 18-month-old sister, Tina, was said to be a good baby.

In this chaotic household, Michael was described as having a quiet temperament, which was a relief to his mother. She could put him in a baby swing in front of the television and he would sit quietly between feedings, every 4 to 6 hours. He was sometimes taken out of the swing, but often fed by either his mother or his brother while sitting in the swing.

I thought this lack of physical contact and attention were the essence of Michael's problem and arranged an intervention with Mickey and Ed after explaining my understanding of the problem. My formulation of the problem was that the brother, Roger, had overwhelmed the mother's ability to care for her children, and that she,

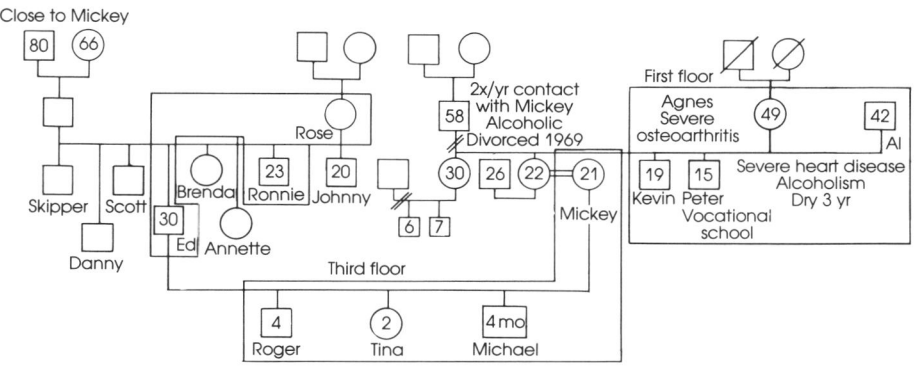

FIGURE 1. Family genogram.

therefore, had no time or interest left for Michael. The first task was to incorporate the parents' concept that Michael was sickly into a broader description of the entire family. They were aware of feeling generally overwhelmed, but had not connected these feelings to Michael's problem gaining weight. When I reframed it for them, they agreed to work with me and the resident to change things at home.

Secondly, the parents needed to arrive at a way to address Roger's behavior, and they agreed to begin using a behavioral reinforcement plan of rewards. They also agreed to go to a parenting class at the local YMCA. The family practice social worker, the resident, and the welfare social worker were all involved with the plan and began to work with Mickey during the hospitalization. Mickey and Ed agreed to come in weekly to see me and the resident for monitoring of the situation.

After 2 weeks in the hospital, Michael gained 4 pounds, but his parents had made no progress in taking control of his home environment. He was, therefore, sent to foster care under the auspices of the Department of Children and Their Families. This upset both parents very much. Mickey and Ed were told to solve the problem and create a home environment in which Michael could thrive. They clearly had no experience in managing an orderly home, but they were motivated to work with us to have Michael back at home with them.

The resident and I worked together managing the family over the next year. Our efforts were supported by the court, which required successful completion of parenting classes, as well as our approval before Michael returned home. We saw the parents weekly at first, then every other week for 30 to 60 minutes each session. Our goals were: (1) to improve the couple's problem-solving and management skills in order to allow them to have time for themselves as well as for their children; and (2) to reinforce the need for priorities and clear boundaries within their household. We used their motivation to be good parents, and we reinforced their strengths as individuals and as a couple to maintain momentum in the therapy. The experience of success and forward movement was new and exciting for them and improved the sense of hopefulness for us and the family.

Ed got a job at $5.70 an hour and worked from 8:00 a.m. to 4:30 p.m. After work, he spent time with Mickey and the kids from 5:00 p.m. to 10:00 p.m. Roger began preschool in the mornings, and Mickey accompanied him as a teacher's assistant. Mickey's mother took care of Tina during this time, and through this involvement, Mickey was able to change her relationship with her mother from one of rebellion to adult-to-adult cooperation. Mickey received good modeling for child-rearing and management techniques at the preschool and was encouraged by the teachers to study for her graduate equivalency diploma. She started a study program and received her certificate 3 months later.

Michael returned home after 7 months. He had reached the 60th percentile of weight for his age. We continued to see the couple one or two times a month, and made some home visits, which revealed a sparsely furnished, third-floor walkup with teenage neighbors dropping in frequently. These friends were appropriate to Mickey's stage of development, and she obtained needed peer approval from them. She had moved into the same building where her parents rented the first-floor apartment and was receiving some help in caring for Tina from them.

Although we realized that Mickey needed these outside supports, we were concerned that she might not continue to spend enough time with her children. During our home visits, we noticed that Ed was more in charge of child discipline and home care than Mickey was. Our ongoing goal was to work with Mickey to mesh her own developmental needs with the care of her children.

This case illustrates the effectiveness of structural interventions at the community level in conjunction with family interventions. It was only when we placed the child in foster care that we were able to activate the parents to do what was needed to change the home environment. Placement was a difficult step and was viewed by some of the hospital staff as a punitive action. However, it proved to be successful because we had formed bonds of support with the parents before legal action was taken, and we made a commitment to work with them to attain their goals. It was only by seeing the larger picture and having clear, long-term goals that *we* were able to feel comfortable making the recommendation for placement. We gained invaluable assistance from preschool teachers, parenting class teachers, and social workers from the Department of Child Welfare and the courts. We used the physician role as leader and coordinator of services to create forward movement in a previously uncoordinated family system in order to bring about the changes that ended the problem of failure to thrive.

EDITORS' COMMENTS

Sometimes a systematic approach to a difficult problem yields an unusually successful outcome. This case makes that point and demonstrates the impact of a primary care physician trained to work therapeutically with other physicians, allied health personnel, nonmedical community resources, and families. A key decision was to offer temporary foster care to this struggling family, even though it was initially opposed by other hospital staff. Dr. Weihs was convinced that removing the child from the parents temporarily was not a punitive act. To persist in that belief in the face of criticism was an act of courage and demonstrates the value of advanced training in family therapy and general systems theory. That the family accepted this without overt hostility suggests the high degree of trust and respect they had for the physician. The economic impact on the community of this successfully managed case is enormous. A healthy child is living with a functionally healthy family. Not all cases that are expertly managed will have such excellent outcomes. However, it is helpful to know that sometimes there are successes.

A PATIENT WITH ALOPECIA AREATA

MARK MENGEL
University of Washington

Mrs. H was an attractive, well-dressed, 28-year-old white female who came to my office complaining of hair loss. She had received the diagnosis of alopecia areata 8 months previously. Her disease initially had responded well to subcutaneous injections of dilute triamcinolone acetonide, but now was back. As her previous physician had left, I was to take over her care.

On physical exam, three bald spots were present. I injected those areas without difficulty, and asked if there was anything else I could do for her. She said, "Yes, could you give me another prescription for Furinol. I'm having pretty bad headaches and that's the only thing that works."

Review of the chart and questioning of the patient confirmed the diagnosis of tension headaches. Further questions directed at possible stressors in the patient's life yielded little. "Everything is going well," she exclaimed, "if only I could get my hair to grow back." "How is your marriage?" I asked. "Fine," she replied. I stated my reluctance to continue Furinol, but negotiated with Mrs. H that she could receive it once more, before trying other nondrug therapies. She agreed and left to make a follow-up appointment.

Six weeks later, Mrs. H returned with six bald spots. She was a bit more uneasy at this visit, but still would not give a straightforward answer to my questions. I injected the areas again, and asked her to return in 6 weeks. I felt very uneasy myself after the visit. Specifically, I felt that something was going on that knowledge of which would help me treat the patient, but I did not know what the something was.

I reviewed Mrs. H's family system in my mind. She had remarried 3 years ago to a black air force sergeant. She described their relationship as a good one, although she wished that he was home more often. She had two children from a previous marriage, who were now 8 and 5 years old. Both were doing well, including the 8 year old, who had epilepsy that was well controlled on Dilantin. Her previous husband was also in the air force in another state. She left him because he "didn't treat her well" and "was seeing other women." After an initial stormy period, their relationship had improved, with both keeping in loose touch with each other.

Mrs. H did not keep her next 6-week follow-up appointment, but returned 2 months later, distraught. She claimed that her husband had been drinking heavily and was "seeing another woman." She was also afraid that he would abuse her. She described him as a distant man who had difficulty in expressing his emotions. Needless to say, her alopecia areata had not improved. I asked Mrs. H to invite her husband to her next follow-up appointment, which I scheduled in 1 week.

One week later, Mr. and Mrs. H came to see me. The session began in a stormy manner, with Mrs. H leveling her accusations at Mr. H. He admitted to drinking "more than he should," but denied seeing other women. Mr. H also readily admitted to not being able to express his feelings freely, saying that his family of origin was a military family that did not allow such expressions. He mentioned that he had gone to a military high school. He then went on to defend himself by saying that Mrs. H wanted "too much" in their marriage, and that he felt pressed to supply more than he could.

A clearer impression of Mrs. H emerged during this session as well. Her family of origin consisted of an abusive, alcoholic father who had not only physically abused her mother, but Mrs. H as well. She had left home after high school because she "wanted out," and moved to Alaska where she met her first husband, who, as it turned out, also drank heavily and was abusive. I was impressed with this repeating pattern in Mrs. H's life, and referred the couple to a marital counselor who could devote more time to the case.

The marital counselor worked with the couple to set goals for their relationship and attempted to improve the pattern of communication between the couple. Therapy was interrupted once when Mrs. H's father died. This had a profound effect on Mrs. H, causing a very severe grief reaction. However, 1 month after attending the funeral, she appeared better and was able to continue therapy. After 6 months of therapy, Mrs. H's alopecia had resolved, her husband drank less, and she felt better about their marriage. She and her husband decided to terminate therapy at that point as "they didn't need it any more."

I still did not feel that lasting changes had been made in the relationship between Mr. and Mrs. H, yet I felt that I could do no more given the fact that neither partner wanted to continue therapy. As if to prove my point, Mrs. H had two more mild flare-ups of her alopecia areata during the next 6 months, though they rapidly improved with short courses of systemic Prednisone. During both flare-ups, she denied further family problems. Interestingly enough, the last flare-up began 1 month before I was scheduled to leave the clinic and necessitated some short-term termination work. That went well, and I learned that Mrs. H's alopecia rapidly cleared after I left.

Fortunately, further follow-up is available on this case. From her new physician, I learned that Mrs. H did well over the next year without any recurrence in her alopecia. However, 1 year after I left and 2 years after her last family crisis, Mrs. H presented to her latest physician stating that her husband had started drinking again, and "had pushed and shoved her." This time she stated that she was separating from him. Her physician referred her to a psychiatrist, whom she is seeing in group therapy "in order to understand why she is attempting reconciliation when he treats her so poorly." Interestingly enough, 1 month after she presented to her physician in a crisis state, her alopecia recurred, necessitating further steroid therapy. A few weeks after beginning group therapy with the psychiatrist, she said that she was thinking about getting back together again with her husband.

This case illustrates many interesting points. First, I was too easily taken in by the patient's statement that no significant family stress existed, and did not pursue a possible family problem until a crisis occurred. Second, there seemed to be a direct link between the patient's symptoms of alopecia and family stress. When relations between the patient and her husband worsened, the patient's alopecia brought her in to see the doctor, acting almost as a cry for help. When relations improved, either spontaneously or through therapy, the alopecia improved. Alopecia is thought to be caused by autoantibodies directed against the hair follicle. Therefore, it is possible that there is an immune mechanism through which family stress acts to exacerbate this patient's underlying condition. Third, there seemed to be a distinct pattern to the patient's relationships to men. She seemed to become involved with men who drank and eventually abused her physically (i.e., her father, her first husband, and her second husband). When such intergenerational patterns are in evidence, many family therapists have begun therapy by first dealing with the patient's family-of-origin issues. Once these recurring problems are faced and dealt with, the more immediate problems can be handled. Such an approach, had it been used, might have been successful in this case.

EDITORS' COMMENTS

Two issues strike our attention in Dr. Mengel's case. First, there are limits to what may be accomplished no matter what the approach to the patient. The physician in this case recognized that stressful family factors were related to the presenting complaint. Eventually, he met with the patient and her husband to clarify the issue. The couple was moved to the care of a therapist. In many cases, that is all that can be asked of the health care delivery system. The process was appropriate. There are never any guarantees about outcome.

The second point is less straightforward. The destructive impact of alcoholism is rarely modified for long when therapists, physicians, family, or friends advise the patient "cut down on your drinking." It is our conviction that once alcoholism or other substance abuse or dependency is discovered, specific attention to that problem takes precedence over other therapeutic issues. To struggle with other issues while the chemical problem remains unaddressed is to set the stage for frustration and failure. This is particularly painful for families who already feel hopeless after many years (or several generations) of failure to cope successfully with these disorders. Family- or individually-oriented therapy can be coordinated with a team of community resources designed to deal with substance abuse and dependency (A.A., Alanon, Alateen, community chemical dependency treatment centers, and drug and alcohol education centers). We strongly urge therapists and physicians to deal directly with alcoholism and all other substance-abuse problems. A more detailed discussion of this issue is available elsewhere (Baird, 1985; Doherty & Baird, 1983).

Postscript: Just before the book went to press, Dr. Mengel reported to us that although initial group therapy failed, later the patient was referred to another group therapy program that identified the alcoholism problem as a priority and moved the husband into a chemical dependency treatment program. At last report, both husband and wife were doing well.

VENTRICULAR TACHYCARDIA AND FAMILY EXPLOSIONS

JANET CHRISTIE-SEELY
Ottawa University

I first heard about the M family from a resident who was exasperated with them, as were most of the ward staff. She had tried to get the family of six together in the hospital, since Mrs. M was frequently on the ward, usually with congestive heart failure. The cardiologists were rather puzzled by her frequent admissions, since between admissions her heart function was reasonably good, with a systolic ejection fraction of 80%. The family medicine resident wanted to discuss this with the family, but on one occasion when they were all present one of the daughters stormed out before anything could be discussed. Newly arrived and labeled as the family expert, I have been getting the families with the most difficult problems as referrals.

The family genogram is shown in Figure 1. All four adult children were in frequent contact with the parents; two now lived at home. Throughout the first session, "Mom is dying" was repeated frequently. This is quite a contrast to my usual experience—families dealing with cancer—where death is a taboo subject, and the difficulty of working with these families is to get them to talk about death. In the M family, it was difficult to stop the topic. There was considerable confusion about the cardiac history, but she had been resuscitated at least once.

It took three sessions before there was sufficient trust in the process for all six members to be present. The reason they came was "to help Dad cope with Mom's dying." The most resistant was Ann, who had a history of manic-depressive illness: "We all have therapists, why can't we just talk about it with them?"

The protectiveness in this family was discussed, and was to me one prime reason for concern, particularly when I observed constant

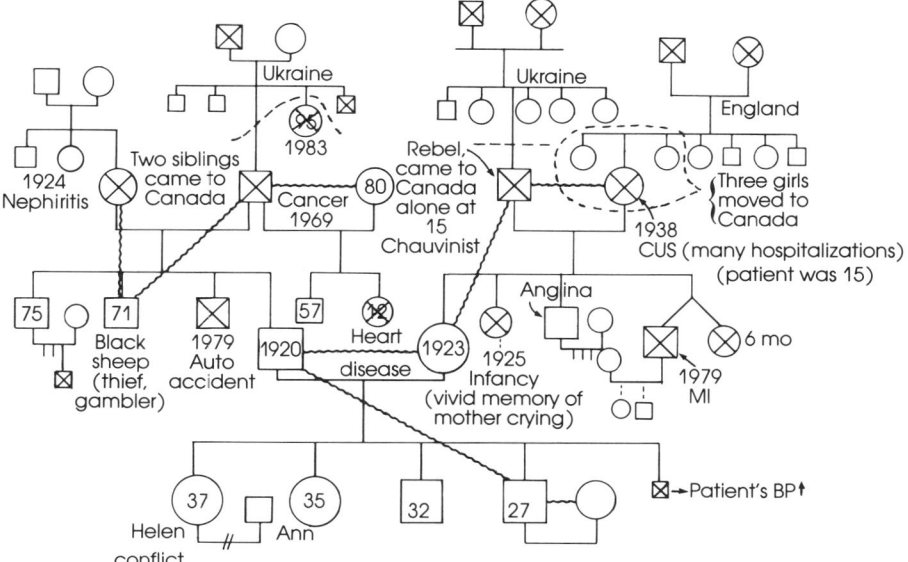

FIGURE 1. M family genogram.

monitoring of Mrs. M and statements like, "Don't get upset, Mom," whenever there was a mild increase in family tension. This protectiveness was labeled as one extreme in the family roller coaster. In fact, pussyfooting around any dangerous issue increased the tension level. At the other extreme were the violent explosions of anger that several members were prone to, particularly Ann. It appeared that both parents were reared to never express anger. Mr. M exploded periodically; he once threw a lawn mower across the basement. Helen was very afraid of angry men and felt that women were not allowed to get angry. Both of her grandfathers were authoritarian and highly controlling. Mrs. M was clearly very angry at her father, and was transferring a great deal of this anger indirectly to her husband, partly, I felt, through her illness and hospital admissions, which made him extremely anxious. He took time off work because of her symptoms, and as a result was having problems at work. He had even been threatened with early retirement.

The day of the second session, Ann moved home. Two days later, her mother was in the hospital again, following an argument that involved Ann. This time it was ventricular tachycardia that prompted the admission, and the family was very confused as to whether she had been unconscious on arrival in the hospital. She had apparently kept her eyes closed, her head lolling to one side, but had been conscious all the time. Several of the family members thought she had been resuscitated again.

During the next session early in the new year, when all members were present, there was a violent outburst by Jim. I had relayed what I learned from the cardiologist—that Mrs. M's cardiac function was quite good between admissions, and that she had a reasonable prognosis provided she did not have another heart attack or a fatal arrhythmia. This provoked a sudden, angry outburst at the medical professionals, who had never taken the time to sit down and explain to the family what had been happening since Jim was 3 years old. His anger could be heard down the hall by the secretaries, who were afraid that I would send the offending patient out of the room and that they would have to deal with him! He swore vociferously, then dropped his voice briefly to say, "Not you personally, I mean," and again raised his voice and expressed the family's frustration and fury at the years of ambiguity and stress from their mother's illness. He described having to sneak up the backstairs of the hospital when his mother was in for "what seemed like a year" when he was 11 years old: "Don't tell me she's not been seriously ill. I *know* she's dying."

When Jim had ventilated all this long-standing anger, I commented that coping with uncertainty and with a mother constantly in and out of the hospital must be an extraordinary chronic stress and one that they may have dealt with by premature burial. I also commented that anger at the illness must be enormous, but that the medical profession was a more satisfying target, even though (or perhaps because) it had saved their mother's life at least once.

I suggested that the illness was producing stress, and that this stress might, in turn, be producing more illness. I was aware of the fine tightrope I was walking by clarifying to the family that their response to the illness might well be aggravating it and triggering hospitalization. I didn't want them to be so scared of their emotions that they would increase the already excessive protectiveness, nor did I want repeats of outbursts such as Jim's in either the office or at home. The family agreed to the contract of trying to reduce the roller coaster extremes of this family, and to learn to "act as barometers" by monitoring each others' reactivity at a higher level than the current protectiveness, but effectively enough to prevent explosions. I commented on my own tension level after Jim's explosion, and inquired how everyone else's blood pressure was faring. They all recognized that the anger, rather than being dissipated by this expression of it, tended to be perpetuated, and certainly would increase Mrs. M's catecholamine level. Again, I felt that my role was to give the family my perception of the facts, without producing a situation in which guilt would be enormous if she did in fact die during one of her admissions. I told them of a study indicating that family crises can precipitate congestive heart failure, and added that adrenaline could trigger ventricular tachycardia.

In an individual session with Mr. M, I discussed his response to his wife's symptoms, and this proved illuminating. The minute Mrs. M showed any minimal sign of being off-color or symptomatic, Mr. M would stay home from work, or, if he went to work, he would phone her frequently to check on how she was. The only times that Mrs. M had been admitted to the hospital were after her husband had been home from work for 2 or 3 days because he was worried about her. It became clear that the couple was caught in a vicious cycle of mutually raised catecholamines that continued until congestive heart failure or ventricular tachycardia prompted the admission. Mr. M, a highly intelligent man, understood this explanation fully, and agreed to change his behavior. Since it was not necessary for her safety that someone be at home, because neighbors were readily available to take her to hospital if needed, we agreed that he should ignore her symptoms if they presented and go to work as usual. He agreed not to telephone more often than his once-daily routine. Mr. M also said that he was tired of the "doom and gloom" and the constant discussion of his wife's dying, and that he was going to take one day at a time. He felt that he had accepted the possibility of her dying, but that he would cherish her while she was still here. He was using a meditation method to deal with his anxiety, and in general struck me as coping very well.

It was difficult with this family, where an adversarial stance was frequent between family members, for me to walk the tightrope of neutrality, but I perceived that neutrality as essential to my being able to work with them. In particular, I saw being able to empathize with Ann, who generated incredible anger in all who came in contact with her, as crucial. She was essentially a very likeable, but very defensive and volatile, aggressive young woman. I began to see her behavior as the family's "solution" to her mother's decision, made early on in life, in face of a very angry controlling father, for "peace at any cost."

One difficulty with this family was their constant intellectualizing, an important part of their defense system and coping. I asked them to do a family sculpting exercise, in which family members depict their family nonverbally, in order to cut through the talk and look at the role of illness. When I first suggested this, Ann immediately declined saying there was no way she was going to let out any of her emotions or feelings about the family; she thought this would be very destructive. She then added casually that she was simply waiting for her mother's death so that she could commit suicide, and that the family knew this. To this bombshell, the family showed no response. Mine was dramatic internally, and I made a quick decision. I'm not sure if what I did next was going along *with* the family system, just trying to reduce my own anxiety, or a sensible strategy. I said that she overestimated her own power, perhaps as a response to her feeling of helplessness. Thinking about it afterward, I wondered if I should have suggested that this was her effort at keeping her mother alive (which it probably was), but I knew that she would discount that by stating that she wanted her mother to hurry up and die. I didn't want to risk that degree of negativity in the session. I then casually proceeded to ask the others how they felt about sculptures. The group agreed to do it, and surprisingly Ann agreed to take part, providing she didn't have to do a sculpture of her own.

I described sculptures as physical representations of the family emotions and relationships in space. Each member would produce his or her own sculpture, with a particular focus on how those images might be changed when Mrs. M was in the hospital. Mrs. M was elected by a daughter to do hers first. She placed her husband in a chair on one side of the room, with the four adult children facing him, and herself standing between, arms stretched out sideways, protecting him from an imaginary barrage from the children. She felt that he was very weak and vulnerable. (This position kept him from the dominating position her father had held, and kept her as the hub of the family.)

Her husband then chimed in that his picture was much more dull. He put himself and his wife in the middle of the room, back-to-back, with the four children in the four corners as "satellites." I asked what happened when she was in the hospital. He put her on the far side of the room in two chairs, and then she chimed in, "I am enthroned, and everyone is worshiping me." He put the rest of the family in the opposite corner of the room with himself close to them. John said, "Look at the payoff of her being in the hospital!" Helen added, "She really is getting a rest. And it looked like she needed one, given the position she was in when she was at home; now Daddy has the kids! It's better for both of them." Then Ann commented, "Helen and I have known for years that we both use illness as means of getting attention, and so does Mom." This had never been stated in the family, however, and it was interesting to hear Ann express it so easily about herself. Helen's sculpture placed the two parents in chairs leaning toward each other, her father's arm around her mother, with the daughters on one side and the sons on the other at some distance. Ann was holding her mother's hand, and Helen was touching Ann, "connected with a blood-to-blood connection," making the three women as the chief symptom bearers apparent. Ann and Mrs. M both used the threat of death to control other members as had Mrs. M's mother, who had also had cardiac disease, and had been in and out of the hospital as a means of dealing with her very autocratic and angry husband.

Subsequent sessions with the couple alone revealed another issue that was at the core of Mrs. M's low self-esteem and her hospital admissions. Mr. M had long complained that she was unresponsive sexually, but her father had impressed on her that responsive women were "sluts." I used Satir's "parts-party" technique to get at the issues of sexuality and self-esteem. (Each person picks six famous people who either impress or horrify them, and gives three adjectives for each; these then become the aspects of the person they either like or dislike in themselves.) Helping Mrs. M accept the "slut" part of herself, and get past her low self-esteem and anger at her husband over that issue (hospitalization helped avoid it) enabled her to stop wishing she was dead, just like her mother had before her.

Mrs. M's chronically sick mother had provided a role model of illness as a solution, and had generated its own anger at absent motherhood, a pattern that was being repeated. I find the illness history of a family and their experience with the medical profession an essential piece of family assessment that is often omitted. This may clarify sick-role models, repeated family patterns, illness and hospitalization as a way out of difficulty and as a way of gaining attention. The M family system reverberated around illness, and it seemed important first to get them to understand this, and second to give them some other alternative or to open up the system so that such a solution to the emotional tensions was not necessary. Helping Mr. M deal with his own mother's death, which he was reliving through his wife's illness, was another aspect of therapy that helped avoid history repeating itself—so far.

After five sessions, I accepted Ann's suggestion that I see Mr. and Mrs. M alone. I found it much easier to deal with the couple alone than with their volatile family. Mr. M, now close to retirement, seemed a very gentle man, incapable of throwing a lawn mower across the basement! I don't enjoy facing hostility, which was chronic in Ann and Jim. The couple boundary was clearly a problem, with two children in their 30s still at home (and linked to the problem of sexuality, as Mr. M slept downstairs in the living room in order to avoid stairs!) The meeting paid off in the surfacing of the sexual problem, and in the decision by the couple (not prompted by me) to have the children move out. Sessions were much more peaceful without the younger generation!

EDITORS' COMMENTS

As a well-trained family therapist and family physician, Dr. Christie-Seely comments beautifully on this case as she leads the reader through it. Working alone with such a difficult family is clearly beyond the skills of all but those few family physicians who receive postgraduate training in family therapy. More than most other cases in this book, this one demonstrates the intricate multigenerational processes involved in how families deal with serious illness. Dealing with this multigenerational family, as the author expresses at the end, was hard work, not recommended for the fainthearted. But the potential savings, both financially and humanly, far surpass the effort and courage that Dr. Christie-Seely demonstrated with this fascinating family. See also Christie-Seely (1984) for more case examples and conceptual development in family-centered medical care.

A SUICIDE GESTURE:
THE YOUNGEST CHILD BRINGS
HER FAMILY TO THE DOCTOR

GEORGIANNA S. HOFFMANN
PAUL S. WILLIAMSON
University of Iowa

Karen G, a 15-year-old high school sophomore, came to the office on Monday following a suicide attempt the preceding Saturday night. Dr. W examined Karen's wrists and found superficial wounds. When his attempts to explore the events leading up to Karen's action were unproductive, Dr. W suggested that he speak with her parents. She agreed, and said her father was in the waiting room.

When Dr. W called for Mr. G, whom he had never met, a muscular, middle-aged man in obvious pain responded. Mr. G's jaw was wired shut, and his left arm was in a cast. Karen had not mentioned her father's accident or injuries at all during her appointment with Dr. W!

Feeling that the entire family must be experiencing stress, Dr. W began a lengthy explanation of why the whole family ought to come in, thinking to himself that this burly guy wouldn't be interested in talking. To Dr. W's surprise, Mr. G and his daughter readily agreed to a return appointment for joint therapy with a family counselor.

Before the first interview, the Family Stress Clinic requested letters from the parents describing the family's problems. Mrs. G wrote describing five major stressors the family had experienced: (1) serious financial problems (in spite of hard work and ambition), (2) a seizure disorder in the eldest son, combined with (3) a life-cycle issue around his leaving home, (4) her husband's injury, resulting in fear of losing him, followed by (5) a role shift (his need for care, and her working to help with finances). She also had to write her husband's letter since his arm was immobilized. It was brief, but explicit about the choices he had made between business success and the family's need for his time and attention. Just as they were getting established financially, his accident occurred.

We requested that the whole family come for the initial session. They agreed, though Mrs. G was obviously reluctant to include the boys. When the family arrived to see Dr. W and Mrs. H, it turned out that the parents and Karen had come without the boys.

The story of this family's most recent (and overwhelming) crisis unfolded. They told us that Mr. G, a 47-year-old construction worker, had fallen from a second-floor scaffolding 6 months earlier. He had been hospitalized in orthopedics for 2 months, and had not been able to work for the past 4 months. Mrs. G, a registered nurse, was working the 3:00 p.m. to 11:00 p.m. shift on a medical ward, and wasn't home when the family was home as much as she would have liked. Because of conflicting schedules, she might not see the children for 3 days at a time. Karen was taking care of the house, doing the cooking, cleaning, and other chores.

Fighting between Karen and her brothers had escalated to the point where Karen was being bruised, physically and mentally. She was afraid of her brothers since they were older, bigger, and ganged up on her. The night of her suicide attempt, while her parents were away from home, Karen had become upset with her brothers for teasing and hitting her in the now-familiar pattern. Having thought of suicide before, and believing that her brothers would stop tormenting her if they thought she was crazy, she slashed at her wrists with a knife, and then went to the neighbor's, not telling anyone in her family what she had done. Late that night, when her parents returned, she told them what had happened. Mrs. G said that Karen, or perhaps all the children, needed help, so she called Dr. W's office for the initial appointment that eventually brought the family in for treatment.

Although Karen was the identified patient, it appeared to us that both parents were depressed, and that Mrs. G was the most demoralized family member present. She acknowledged that she "felt dead inside." There was virtually no eye contact between family members. They seemed isolated with little or no communication between them, something Karen said she especially missed. The parents had lost control of the children, who were now all adolescent and required different parenting skills. Mr. G's life-threatening accident frightened the family. Initially, the children had rallied around their mother and helped her cope. However, when Mr. G returned home for a long convalescence, he was unaccustomed to dependency and the family was not used to having him underfoot. The role reversal was hard on all of them. Mrs. G, who wanted to stop working, had to continue in order to help pay the bills. She loved her husband, but felt increasingly trapped.

On top of all this, the eldest son, who was closest to his mother and whose physical problems had worried the family a great deal, was trying to establish his independence. Both he and his family were threatened by yet another disruption in the family system. Since this family's primary mode of communication was action-oriented, this initial therapy session was the first time they had talked together and expressed the feelings that had been boiling beneath the surface.

We began treatment by putting the father in charge of bringing the boys for counseling, thus supporting Mr. G as head-of-household. He agreed that he could help arrange things with school and the coaches to get the boys in for the next session. His accident had demolished his sense of power, and he seemed to sit taller as he accepted his assignment. We encouraged Mrs. G to think of ways to take better care of herself and to ask for what she needed from her husband, her children, and her employer. We encouraged Karen to ask her parents for the protection she needed.

The second session opened with only Mr. and Mrs. G present. Neither Karen nor the boys appeared, though the parents fully expected them to be there. By phone, we found the 17 year old had "forgotten" he had a test, and the 19 year old, who was supposed to have brought Karen with him, had car problems. We continued the session with just the couple. Mrs. G's depression had begun to lift. She had started to improve her employment situation. They had talked with the youngest son about Karen's suicide gesture, opening up communication in the family.

A genogram revealed that both parents were the youngest children in their respective families, so they were both unaccustomed to taking a firm position of leadership. We supported the parents in their parental role, and gave options to help them get the boys to the therapy session either the next time or the time after that. We persisted with the assignment, expressing confidence in the parents' ability to gather the family together.

The parents elected to attend the third session by themselves. They told us that the boys had started helping with the cooking. Mrs. G said the food was "pretty weird," but they all ate it anyway. Mr. G had wine and hors d'oeuvres ready for his wife at midnight one night when Mrs. G came home from work, and she seemed pleased with the special attention. Mr. and Mrs. G were working to regain an intimate relationship in spite of the role changes. The whole family seemed to be getting closer together.

At the fourth session, the whole family finally came together. The session got off to a slow and difficult start, since the room was crowded and the seating arrangement chosen by family members interfered with eye contact. The two boys, strangers to the clinic, were boisterous and loud. They were clearly accomplices in causing trouble. We had a firsthand demonstration of the obstreperous behavior that Karen had experienced in dealing with her brothers.

The 17-year-old younger brother sat behind Mrs. H and mimicked her gestures. We suggested that he move his chair forward. After rejoining the family circle, he told his parents clearly and directly that he needed to be told how to behave. Mr. G let us know he had gotten the message. Karen's older brother also calmed down, and spoke about his plans to move out of the family home to begin junior college.

As the session continued, family members discussed Mr. G's accident, and the ways in which it had disrupted plans and patterns in the family. The following information emerged. Over the years, Mr. G was disturbed by the roughhousing of his two sons. To keep fights from escalating, he took the boys on himself, and, before his accident, he was able to settle them down. After his serious injury, the boys knew better than to continue this pattern. So they turned their aggressive impulses on Karen, who apparently did her share of teasing and provoking. Thus, the background behind the bruises and the tension that precipitated her suicidal gesture surfaced.

An indirect approach was necessary to keep the parents at the top of the hierarchy. Mrs. H told a story about a pair of male Siberian Huskies, littermates who habitually challenged each other. No matter how ferocious they appeared, neither ever injured the other, because they were equally matched in weight and strength. The dogs were trained, however, not to play with the family's female cat, a much smaller animal. And even though the cat could defend herself, two against one would be overwhelming odds. The whole family listened to this story with rapt attention and appeared to get its message. At the session's end, we expressed confidence in the parents' ability to work as a team to control and protect their children.

Although we met with this family only four times, in various configurations, the progress they made was remarkable. The daughter, who initially brought them to therapy, is doing well in school and is a star athlete. Her oldest brother successfully emancipated himself from the family. Her other brother is also doing well. Mrs. G is no longer depressed, even though she still works to help support the family, and Mr. G, though still disabled, is healing, and is able to function as head of the family. He plans to return to school to retrain for less dangerous work. The family's rapid response to brief treatment is an outstanding feature of this case—*G.S.H.*

This case illustrates how a previously functional family can be stressed by a medical trauma to the extent that each family member becomes dysfunctional. The youngest child in this family made a desperate and successful effort to obtain assistance for the family's problems. Brief but firm support of the parental hierarchy to restructure the family at a key point helped them get through a difficult time. Encouraging the parents to be in charge of their children, facilitating communication, supporting assertiveness in both Mrs. G and Karen, and redirecting the boys' aggressive behavior helped this family to return to effective functioning. This progress occurred in a shorter time than would have been possible with individual therapy for Karen. Indeed, it might never have occurred at all. This case illustrates how a family physician can team up with a family therapist to treat a family unit.—*P.S.W.*

EDITORS' COMMENTS

Here we see once more the value of the family physician and family therapist functioning on the same team. The presenting suicide gesture alone would tend to move the case into the level five therapy domain; only an unusually well-trained family physician would want to take on this case. In this instance, Dr. Williamson was able to make a preliminary assessment of the context of the girl's distress and move the family quickly into therapy with a trusted colleague, Mrs. Hoffmann. The family physician chose to continue with the family as a cotherapist, thereby adding power to the therapy team. In other similar cases, he might make the referral and provide supportive care from the background. Either way, teamwork is crucial to success: the family presented to the physician, not to the therapist, but the therapist's skills were clearly needed. For a physician who believes in treating problems such as this with a family systems approach, an in-house or at least readily available family therapist is an indispensable part of medical practice.

A BOY WITH ABDOMINAL PAIN

JERI HEPWORTH
University of Connecticut

John J, a 9-year-old boy, was referred to me by a pediatrician who believed that the boy's severe abdominal pains were related to problems in the family. The physician informed me of John's 2-year history of recurrent abdominal pain, associated with severe cramping and nausea, usually without vomiting or diarrhea. John usually complained of stomachaches 2 to 4 mornings each week. Sometimes he awoke crying from the pain, and at other times the pain came on more gradually, becoming severe enough later in the morning for him to go to the school nurse or to interrupt play activities at home. The pain did not seem to be related to eating or bowel habits. During painful episodes, John wanted nothing to eat or drink, and usually lay down, cried, and clutched his stomach. Severe pain usually ended after an hour or two, but John generally continued to feel some pain throughout most of the day.

John's mother telephoned and visited the doctor frequently regarding John's complaints. About 6 months prior to referral, John was hospitalized for evaluation and observation. During the 4-day hospitalization, John was evaluated by a pediatric gastroenterologist, and had a complete bowel workup, including nasogastric tube insertion to determine acid levels in the stomach. All tests were normal, with the exception of slightly higher than expected acid levels of the stomach. When John was discharged, his mother was told that there was no organic reason for the pain, and that the pain was probably due to some anxiety or stress that he was experiencing.

Mrs. J expressed her anger about these conclusions to the doctor, and complained that the health care system had not done enough to determine the true reason for John's pain. After further discussion, she confided that the boy's father had divorced her 3 years before, and had married another woman. She conceded that the situation might be making John nervous. Mrs. J agreed to talk to the boy's father and see if he might be able to help John feel more secure. The physician felt satisfied that he had helped uncover a stressful situation and also that Mrs. J's concern would enable her to help John. During the first 3 months following hospitalization, John reported fewer episodes of pain. However, after 3 months, Mrs. J began telephoning the physician more frequently, and complained that although she had spoken to John's father, the boy's episodes of pain were recurring more often. Mrs. J felt that either the father was not helping John, or that the abdominal pains were actually due to an undiagnosed physical condition. At this point, the physician decided that family therapy might be helpful, and discussed the option with the family and myself.

When Mrs. J called me for an appointment, she acknowledged her frustration with the medical system and her belief that family therapy probably would not help. She said, however, that she was so concerned about John that she was willing to try. I asked if all family members, including John's father, would be able to attend at least an initial family session. Mrs. J said that she and her 15-year-old daughter, Jane, would come, but that it would be very difficult for them if Mr. J was present because they both hated Mr. J and did not want to be in the same room with him. Mrs. J said that she would ask Mr. J to call me to discuss whether he would attend.

Mr. J phoned me and stated that he was very angry. He said that Mrs. J had told him that the doctors believed that John's stomach pains were his fault. Mr. J said that he was also very concerned about John, but that he felt certain that the pains were due to the stress that John experienced from his mother. Mr. J told me that John stayed with him and his new wife (Mrs. J_2) alternate weekends and for periods during the summer, and that John rarely complained of pains during those visits. I asked Mr. J to attend the sessions, and he said that he would as long as Mrs. J_2 could accompany him. I suggested options for meeting times and asked him to contact Mrs. J_1 and for one of them to call me. Mrs. J_1 telephoned me to arrange the appointment and to tell me again how difficult it would be to be in the same room with her ex-husband and his new wife.

At the first appointment, I met the J family in the office waiting room. Mrs. J_1 and her daughter Jane were sitting together. John had come with his mother and sister, but was sitting on the other side of the room, talking with his father and Mrs. J_2, whom he had not seen for a week and a half. I shook hands with all family members and escorted them to a large family meeting room.

Although there were many chairs in the meeting room, Mrs. J_1 and Jane sat close together on a two-person couch on one side of the room. Mr. J and Mrs. J_2 sat in chairs on the opposite side of the room, and John selected a chair on the third side of the room, midway between the two sets of people. I selected a chair opposite to John and commented on the striking positioning of people in this family situation. Mr. J said that that was the problem—Jane and her mother were completely against Mr. J and his new wife, and they made John feel that he was caught between two warring camps. Mrs. J_1 and Jane retorted that they had the primary responsibility for John, and that they were trying to care for him as best as they could without the support of his father. I asked John to describe what it felt like to be in the middle, and he described how he was caught between both families because he was the only one who lived in both homes. During the ensuing family discussion, all family members seemed to realize that John was in a very stressful position in the family. The seating arrangement and description of family life also allowed the family to realize and discuss the coparental position held by Jane.

Near the end of the session, I asked John and Jane to wait in the waiting room while I talked with the adults. At this time, I credited them for being willing to come together to see if they could help John, even though it seemed to be uncomfortable for all of them. The adults discussed how John seemed to be caught in their bitter war, and they agreed to meet with me for a few sessions to see if they could cooperate to keep him out of the middle. It was also decided to leave Jane out of those sessions to reaffirm that she was an older child in the family and not a parent.

The three adults attended three sessions, spaced over 5 weeks, and focused on ways in which Mr. J and Mrs. J_1 could communicate directly about their concerns without having the children (particularly John) be message bearers. At times, Mr. J and Mrs. J_1 were extremely hostile, and blamed one another. We discussed their respective anger, and acknowledged that the conflict and hostility in their relationship was likely to continue. However, since they were both parents of the same children, there would be times when they would have to consult one another and share information. At the third session, all three persons agreed that they were more comfortable with one another and that they had already begun to communicate more easily outside of the therapy sessions. They felt that it was time to include John and Jane in the sessions to demonstrate their new relationship.

At the following session, John looked far more relaxed. He and his mother reported that he was feeling much better and had experienced only occasional mild pains. However, Jane was very nervous and expressed annoyance about being excluded from the previous sessions. I encouraged her to express her angry feelings, and eventually she described how angry she was with her father for abandoning her but continuing his relationship with her brother. Mr. J described how he had tried to visit Jane, but had given up after feeling rejected. There was a tearful reunion between father and daughter, and plans were made for renewing visitation. Mrs. J_1 said she was very happy that Jane and Mr. J were going to see each other again. All family members agreed that there probably would be difficulties in maintaining these changes, but since they were now talking with one another, they wanted to see how they would do without further therapy. A follow-up session took place a month later with Mrs. J_1, Jane and John. The family reported that John's pains had almost completely stopped, and that both children were visiting with their father. Mrs. J_1 had not had much contact with Mr. J, but felt that if it were necessary, she would be able to discuss concerns with him. The family agreed to contact me if they had further problems, but there was no future contact.

I described in detail the way in which this family negotiated attendance at the initial family session because I think that their attendance was the primary reason that change occurred. Once the family members came together, the relationship patterns were evident to all of us. In this case, the content of the sessions was far less important than the message of those sessions—that all of the family members were able to put aside their differences and come together to help one of their members. It seems that the power of this message allowed John to give up his abdominal pains.

This case also illustrates problems that can occur when a physician does not consider all of the family members during diagnosis and treatment of a complex problem. The father's experience with John's pains was different from the mother's. The physician did not know that John's father thought the physician blamed him for John's pains. Thus, if the physician had tried to include the father in the treatment plan at that time, it is unlikely that the father would have been a willing or compliant participant. Perhaps if all family members had been included in early assessments, family stress might have been recognized earlier, and John's hospitalization might have been avoided.

EDITORS' COMMENTS

This is a family therapy case with important implications for primary care. As Dr. Hepworth observes, understanding of the context of John's abdominal pain might have led to earlier intervention and remission. Right from the beginning, the physicians could have benefited greatly from the father's information that John rarely complained of stomach pain when with his father and stepmother for weekends and summer periods. This crucial bit of data could have helped the physicians to diagnose more readily the family stress underlying the boy's pain. An expensive gastroenterology workup might have been avoided or at least postponed, and the probable cause of the discomfort might have been addressed before 2 years went by. The family still might have needed a skillful family therapist to help the parents take John out of their relationship conflict, but a primary care physician oriented to "context" could have proposed the most effective treatment earlier in the course of the illness. Another interesting feature of this case report is Dr. Hepworth's detailed presentation of how she dealt with the choreography of the family's presentation in the first session. This case illustrates how thinking contextually and intervening at the family level can have important payoffs for the medical system and for consumers of medical care.

A FAMILY'S HEADACHE

THOMAS J. GRAU
Family Practice Residency, Sioux Falls, South Dakota

Susan was an 11-year-old white female who was hospitalized by a neurologist for evaluation of headaches, nausea, and decreased vision. The neurologist performed an extensive workup, but could find no organic etiology for her symptoms. My colleague, Michael Bloom, PhD, and I were then consulted to evaluate the patient within the context of her family, which consisted of her parents and two brothers, ages 12 and 13.

The headaches had been occurring over the preceding 3 months, and had become especially bad the week or two preceding the evaluation. The headaches were of short duration, usually lasting less than an hour, although they occasionally lasted all day. They were occurring five to six times per day. There had been mild nausea without vomiting associated with the headaches, and Susan reported not being able to see as well during the headaches. In fact, her first medical contact for this problem was with an ophthalmologist because of her vision. The ophthalmologist had found decreased vision in the left eye (20/70) as compared to the right (20/20), and a constricted left visual field. These findings prompted the referral to the neurologist.

The headaches had not caused Susan to miss more than a couple of days of school, and she had not changed her activities to any great degree. Further questioning regarding medical history revealed stomach problems for approximately 9 months preceding the onset of headaches. These, too, had been evaluated, but no organic etiology was found.

The first description of the family came from Susan and her mother, and revealed some rather interesting findings. Over the past

---

I would like to thank Michael Bloom, PhD, for his assistance in treating this family.

year, Steve, the oldest brother, had had some rather severe behavioral problems and was getting into trouble frequently, both at home and at school. Susan had frequently been asked by her mother (who worked outside the home) to report on Steve's behavior during the day. For example, on three occasions he came home from school because of stomach problems and told Susan not to tell their mother, but Susan told her mother when she was asked. This caused a great deal of hostility between Susan and Steve, to the point that he threatened to kill her. Susan just recently told her mother that she was really afraid of Steve. Susan also told her mother that she was afraid her mother would leave, because of a comment her mother had made about a week before Susan was hospitalized: "Maybe I should just leave."

As the initial interview continued, many features associated with psychosomatic families were revealed (Minuchin, Rosman, & Baker, 1978). For example, anger was repressed. Susan said she never got mad at either of her parents, and that her parents never argued with each other. Also, the mother was overprotective; she saw her husband as being overly strict, so she frequently lied to him about the children's behavior to protect them from their father's discipline. The mother also stated that she worried about Susan and Steve's problems, at times to the point of being physically ill. There seemed to be a lack of generational boundaries in the family; the mother was deeply involved with her children, and rather distant from her husband. Finally, they were an inflexible family with rather rigid rules that were not usually altered during times of change, for example, when the children entered pubescence.

Another contributing factor was that the mother suffered from both headaches and constipation, but had never told anyone. She felt that her problems were related to stress. With this knowledge, we felt that involving the entire family in restructuring some interrelationships could improve Susan's condition. From this point forward, Dr. Bloom (our clinical psychologist) and I met with the family jointly.

Each session began with each family member having an opportunity to express his or her view of the problem, and to assess how things were progressing. This led to a period of interactive discussion in which we could observe changes in family interactions. Then, Dr. Bloom and I would excuse ourselves from the room to discuss privately our impressions and recommendations. We would then return to the room and relay our perceptions of the problems and our plan to the family.

Our first meeting with the family further clarified some of the relationships. Family members reported that there were two major problems: Susan's headaches and Steve's behavioral problems. Steve felt that Susan was always the good one, and he shed tears over the fact that he didn't seem to get any attention (he did, however, get a tremendous amount of attention from his bad behavior). The parents had tried various things to modify his behavior, all without success, and they were very frustrated. As mentioned, there was also some disagreement over discipline; the father was very strict, whereas the mother usually gave in to the kids. The father felt that it was his role to be the disciplinarian, although at times he wished he could be closer to his kids. When the kids wanted anything, they always went to their mother.

Our intervention objectives were to decrease the overprotection by creating more appropriate distance between the children and their mother, and creating more closeness between the children and the father. We also wanted to work toward helping the parents to be cooperative in their parenting, thus creating better generational boundaries. Working toward more cooperation between the parents required vigilance because we felt it could expose conflict in their marriage relationship, which would then require further evaluation.

We began the intervention by telling the children that whenever they were making any requests or complaints, if they went to their mother with them, she would tell them No, unless it was an emergency and their father wasn't home. The only way they could get things would be by asking their father. Now that she didn't have to worry about disciplinary concerns, the mother would spend a half hour with Steve on the days he behaved. This time was not to be disturbed by anyone. Steve and his mother could then have some quality time together, rather than their interactions only being negative. The explanation we gave for this was that all the kids fought for their mother's attention, and this was a way to break the pattern of Steve's getting his attention through bad behavior.

The parents were told that any major decisions were to be discussed and agreed on together, and then the father was to relay the decision to the children.

We tied this to Susan's headaches by saying that there was so much stress in the family, we doubted that Susan's headaches would get better. After the stress was reduced, we could then better deal with the headaches.

The second meeting with the family was 2½ weeks later. They said that the plan had worked well for the first week, and, in fact, for the first 3 days Susan had almost no headaches. However, the headaches slowly came back, and there was discussion about how they had slipped back into their usual pattern over the ensuing week.

We then discussed the dangers of improvement and went through what each family member had to lose (and gain) by the changes. We also suggested that to make these changes all at once would be very difficult. They should happen gradually, so we suggested trying the recommended changes for 5 days; then, for the next 3 days, they should try to go back to their old way of doing things; then try the plan for the next 5 days. They were somewhat reluctant to agree to intentionally act worse, but finally agreed. Paradoxically, we expected them to find acting "badly" somewhat difficult. (For explanation of therapeutic paradox, see Fisch, Weakland, & Segal, 1982.)

The family was seen on two more occasions, and each time each family member felt things at home were going much better. Interestingly, Susan's headaches had lessened markedly in frequency and severity. The only additional suggestion that was made during these visits was that Steve, since he was able to express his anger much better than Susan, be put in charge of teaching her how to do that.

Although Susan continued to have infrequent headaches, they responded well to subsequent relaxation training with Dr. Bloom. Susan returned to the ophthalmologist the day after our final session, and he found she had 20/20 vision in both eyes, and normal visual fields. The mother felt a shifted burden of responsibility, both parents felt closer, and Steve's behavior improved.

This case illustrates how involving all family members in dealing with what outwardly appears to be one family member's problem can be beneficial for the entire family. Without the insightfulness of each family member, as well as their cooperation, it would have been impossible to identify the significant interrelationships and to be able to suggest changes. This case also illustrates the need to view families as a system, and to appreciate how change of any kind in one family member affects all family members. When we suggest our patients change a behavior, we must be mindful of the adjustments the other family members will also need to make to maintain the change in the patient.

EDITORS' COMMENTS

How wonderful that this case was referred by a neurologist to a family physician for evaluation of the family context of the patient problem. We look to the day when many family physicians have the expertise, and are perceived by their colleagues as having the expertise, to evaluate perplexing illnesses in their psychosocial context. Dr. Grau made a perceptive family systems assessment of Susan's headaches and correctly saw that treatment was beyond primary care and would be done best in conjunction with Dr. Bloom, a family therapist. The therapy itself followed familiar protocols of structural and strategic approaches to family therapy (see the author's references). An important feature of this case is that the diagnosis was made and appropriate treatment begun 3 months after onset of the symptoms. The neurologist acted quickly, referring the family to a medical colleague who would not be as threatening to the family as a psychiatrist or other mental health professional. The family physician then acted quickly to initiate treatment before the family had become more dysfunctionally organized around Susan's symptoms. We suspect that the ease and speed of the therapy were the result of sound decisions by these physicians to face squarely the psychosocial context of the headaches.

CHRONIC HEADACHES AND A COUPLE WHO KNEW BETTER

GEORGIANNA S. HOFFMANN
MARTY BARTOLAC
University of Iowa

Mr. W, a 35-year-old executive, was referred to the Family Stress Clinic by his physician because of severe recurring headaches. For 2 years, Mr. W had suffered daily headaches; they were sometimes so painful that he could not function. The referring physician, after careful evaluation, could find no organic disease and had concluded that the headaches were caused by stress. He wanted Mr. W to learn stress-reduction techniques; hence, the referral.

The patient was married and had a 12-year-old son. We asked that his wife and son come with him for the initial session. Mrs. W agreed to take time from her very busy schedule to accompany her husband. However, neither parent wanted to bring the boy along because, "it might affect his grades to miss school." After discussion, we agreed to table, temporarily, our request to see the whole family together.

When Mr. and Mrs. W arrived, it was easy to see why their family doctor had thought of stress-induced headaches. Mr. W was a handsome man. Both he and his wife were impeccably groomed. Both were also extremely tense in physical posture, speech patterns, and affect. The attitudes they conveyed, together with the lifestyle they described, were strongly indicative of Type A personality and behavior.

In the initial session with husband and wife, we explored their family histories and their marital reelationship. Both adamantly denied any problems between them. Mrs. W was extremely upset about her husband's headaches. She cried when she discussed her fear that he had a brain tumor; she was very concerned that she might lose him. We asked that they bring their son to the next session, and reluctantly, they agreed.

In the one session that we were able to have with the whole family, the son revealed that he had had a great deal of trouble in school from the ages of 8 to 10 years—about the time his father's headaches began. Mark also reported that his mother was given to angry outbursts—which neither parent was willing to discuss. In fact, both of them looked horrified when he brought this matter up. We observed what seemed to be exceptional closeness between the boy and his mother, considerable distance between the boy and his father, and parental overprotectiveness. For example, the parents had moved their son from a public to a private school because he was "being picked on and bullied by the other boys." Following this session, the therapy team felt that a number of stressors had come into focus and suggested a family therapy approach. However, Mr. and Mrs. W refused, saying that, "Mark had been so upset by the one session he attended, he didn't get over it for a whole week." They wanted to get on with learning the relaxation techniques, which were recommended by their physician. Bowing gracefully to what we believed to be massive resistance, we agreed to their request.

We conducted two sessions. In the first session, we taught them progressive muscle relaxation; in the second session, we taught self-hypnosis to both husband and wife together. They were encouraged to practice at home, and Mr. W was particularly conscientious about practicing his progressive muscle relaxation exercises. At the close of the first relaxation training session, the suggestion was made that when Mr. and Mrs. W practiced at home they should try to use the post-relaxation state to recall what was going on at the time Mr. W's headaches began. The therapy team, believing that a combination of family dynamics and stress around the son's school problems were the precipitating factors, hoped that the family would recognize this and be motivated for family therapy.

Two weeks later, Mr. and Mrs. W returned looking far more relaxed and encouraged than before. In fact, they appeared jubilant. They told us they had solved the problem of Mr. W's headaches. They had followed the direction to think back to when the headaches began. Mrs. W had recalled that 2 years before, her husband had acquired extended-wear contact lenses. Coincidentally, she noticed that he did not have a headache the entire day while the contacts were removed for cleaning. Mr. and Mrs. W concluded then, that the contacts were the culprit. He had stopped wearing them, and his headaches ceased. At first, the therapy team was reluctant to accept this explanation, but after careful examination of Mr. W's experimenting with his contact lenses being removed, and the absence of headaches for 2 whole weeks, we had to agree that the patients were correct. They also told us that the relaxation techniques had been very helpful and they wished to learn more, so we continued on in that session teaching them self-hypnosis.

Mr. and Mrs. W did not feel any further need to return; they thanked us very much for our assistance and walked away arm-in-arm, extremely pleased with their experience in the Family Stress Clinic. It seems that sometimes the patient, not the doctor, knows best.

Mr. and Mrs. W responded very quickly to instruction and used the teaching they received in the Family Stress Clinic to discover for themselves what medical professionals were unable to determine in this case. It seems crucial to us that they were taught the relaxation techniques *together* and encouraged to practice them. In fact, it is our belief that Mr. W probably would not have been able to consciously remember the time when he got his contacts, because his eyeglasses had extremely thick lenses. He had been troubled all his life by feeling that his appearance was marred by having to wear such ugly glasses. His contact lenses were extremely important to him in maintaining his handsome appearance. It is our belief that Mrs. W's unconscious mind was able to recall the source of the difficulty—that was one of the beneficial things about training them both to relax.

It does still seem to us that this is a family in which each member shows Type A personality patterns. It seems likely to us that Mark, when he becomes adolescent, will have some difficulty with the high degree of parental control that his father and mother exert over him. Because of the parents' positive experience in the Family Stress Clinic at this time, it is our hope that if there is a need for family therapy in the future, they will return to us.

Postscript: In a follow-up phone call 6 months after termination, Mr. W reported that, in spite of having returned to the use of his extended-wear contact lenses, he was not experiencing severe headaches. He said, "I don't really know what my problem was. I think I just had too much free time. Now that we've had a major reorganization at work, I have twice as many people to supervise and a lot more responsibility. The extra load *helps* because I don't have time to think about myself or have headaches." Mr. W also told us that "a good night's sleep and keeping busy the next day is the best prescription for feeling better." Although he and his wife had not continued to use the relaxation exercises we taught them, Mr. W listened to relaxation tapes every night to help him fall asleep. He said that the sessions he and his wife had at the Family Stress Clinic were very helpful, and he expressed appreciation for the follow-up call as well.

We were dumbfounded to hear this patient's explanation for his continuing improvement, since our asessment had indicated that he was already overloaded at work, and we believed this to be a major stressor for him. In the follow-up call, he also told us that his wife had begun to see a psychiatrist for her "stress-level," and that this was helpful. We wondered if incorporating another person (the psychiatrist) into the family system in this way had relieved some pressure on Mr. W. However, in the absence of more detailed information, this remains conjecture. We were, of course, delighted to hear that the presenting problem continues in remission.

EDITORS' COMMENTS

We are as baffled by this case as the authors are. Until learning the follow-up information, which we asked the authors to obtain after they submitted this intriguing case, we were prepared to explain the case in this way: A misdiagnosis concerning the etiologic role of family stress nevertheless led to a family-centered treatment that turned up the correct diagnosis. What can we make of the patient's continued freedom from headaches when he went back to wearing his contacts and to working even harder, while his wife went into therapy? Our guess is that the brief family therapy and relaxation training, coupled with temporarily changing a physical stressor (the contacts), broke the tension/headache cycle for this patient. It appears that his wife is the new victim of stress in the family. Perhaps the son will have to develop symptoms in order for his mother to get better. But these thoughts are merely conjectures about a mystifying and humbling case. As G. K. Chesterton said, "I have seen the truth, and it makes no sense."

OVERUTILIZATION OF THE MEDICAL SYSTEM AND A TEENAGE SUICIDE ATTEMPT

THOMAS L. SCHWENK
University of Michigan

The S family, with whom I attempted family counseling, has five members: mother and father, married for about 25 years; son in his early 20s; a daughter in her late teens; and a daughter about 10 years old. The predominant feature of this family's medical care was their family-wide predisposition to somaticizing. Their medical records were each an inch thick—5 inches in all. The charts showed a variety of diagnoses, including diverticulitis with stricture, fibrocystic breast changes, abdominal hysterectomy, sialadenitis with stone, therapeutic abortion, and acne. What was most impressive, however, was the remarkable number of visits for minor problems of all sorts. Their ratio of illness events to office visits could not have been more than 2:1, compared to the usual 7:1 or higher. This somaticizing style was complicated by the fact that Mrs. S was one of my medical assistants, and she often asked questions about potentially important health problems—hers and others—in casual hallway conversations, or as I was walking into an exam room to see another patient.

My attempt at family counseling was precipitated by a suicide gesture/attempt by the teenage daughter. The significant relationship in this case was between this daughter and the father. The daughter was fairly rebellious and able to easily provoke her parents, especially her father, as with the suicide gesture. Her father projected a warm and generous image to the community, and, in fact, was the subject of a community "roast" for his many civic contributions. To his family, however, he was far less generous. Indeed, the daughter's suicide gesture was in response to the father's constant and escalating harassment about trivial deficiencies in her behavior. The daughter once said how unfair it was that her father seemed more pleasant to friends and neighbors than to his own family. About a week after the token medication and alcohol overdose, I suggested a family counseling session with the mother, father, and daughter, to which all agreed and were very appreciative. During the first, and subsequent three sessions, each about an hour long and held at night in their home, I attempted to build some clarity and honest caring into the father-daughter relationship, as well as to clarify the contribution made by the mother to the father-daughter difficulties. The family, as a whole, was quite invasive, with everyone's problems and feelings being everyone else's business. I assumed that the mother played some role in the perpetuation of the mutually antagonistic father-daughter relationship.

The sessions went smoothly—too smoothly. The father and daughter were willing to describe certain aspects of the other's behavior that bothered them and seemed willing to modify their own behavior accordingly. The mother indicated where her sympathies lay and seemed willing to try not to inflame the situation by intruding. Closure was reached after four meetings, with specific follow-up assignments, seemingly to everyone's satisfaction.

To my great disappointment, the subsequent several weeks showed no change in father-daughter behaviors. The reciprocal harassment continued, and the mother took sides on a random basis. I felt I had failed. There seemed to be no obvious opportunity or interest for further counseling or referral. Then, I noticed, over a span of many weeks a marked decrease in the number of trivial office visits. This has continued to some extent to the present. The number of clearly somaticizing behaviors dropped to a tolerable level, and my partners and I felt able to care for the family medically with greater enthusiasm.

I do not fully understand what happened with this family counseling attempt, but it would seem that my willingness to engage the family in counseling, and to examine the members' behaviors directly caused them to have less need to abuse the medical care system through somaticizing and trivial medical complaints. This was never discussed with the family, and I am not even sure if they were (or are) aware of the change. It may also be that the concern I demonstrated through my willingness to have intense nighttime sessions confirmed my interest and concern, and they had less need to test that concern through inappropriate utilization. In any case, there was an unexpected payoff from a family counseling attempt that otherwise seemed to fail.

EDITORS' COMMENTS

This fetching case has two important lessons in our view. First, it may be that the primary relationship dealt with here was the physician–family relationship. Given the family's remarkable overuse of the medical system, this relationship no doubt had been dysfunctional in the past. The daughter then called for special help by her suicide gesture. Dr. Schwenk, instead of medicalizing the problem, elected to deal with the underlying relationship problems in the family. Even though the family relationships apparently did not change much, family members seemed to become less apt to medicalize their distress. Second, because of the family's dependence on the medical system and the daughter's suicide gesture, we tend to regard this as a family therapy case instead of as a primary care family counseling case. Dr. Schwenk's straightforward interventions probably would have been helpful with a more adaptable family, but here it might have been wiser to bring along a family therapist consultant. From a family therapy standpoint, the husband–wife relationship would require sustained attention in order to allow the daughter her own life. We would also suspect an underlying problem in this family, such as alcoholism. At any rate, level four family counseling did achieve a positive transformation of the physician–family relationship. And the family's positive experience in the counseling sessions may prepare them for more intensive interventions later.

WHO'S ON FIRST: PROBLEMS IN PARENTING

MICHAEL A. CROUCH
Louisiana State University

I first met the H family in 1978 during a pediatric rotation the first year of my family practice residency. The 28-year-old mother, Christie, brought her 5-year-old son, Alan, to the pediatric clinic because she thought he was hyperactive. After evaluating him as a normal, bright, energetic child, I became their family physician.

Over the next year, I saw Mrs. H frequently for various somatic complaints that seemed to be related to anxiety about interpersonal relationships at work and at home. She experienced a major depressive episode and responded well to treatment with antidepressant medication and supportive counseling—listening to her concerns and gradually learning more about the complex history of her nuclear family (see Figure 1), which included four husbands.

Several months later, Mrs. H came in on an urgent basis saying that her oldest child, 11-year-old Candy, would have to be removed from their home immediately, at least temporarily. She felt that she could not deal with her anymore, and she was afraid that she might harm Candy physically if she remained in the home. She asked me to arrange a disposition for her daughter that day. After negotiating a contract with Mrs. H to not harm Candy, while she stayed in the home for the next 24 hours, I asked that she and the entire family return the next day, when I saw them with a faculty co-therapist.

Mr. H, whom I met for the first time, was pleasant and calm, in contrast to Mrs. H's usual intense hypomanic manner. The children were well behaved. The younger two were talkative, the older two very quiet. Candy looked depressed, and her voice was barely audible. She resembled her mother closely in facial features, hair, and slender build.

Questioning each family member about why they thought they

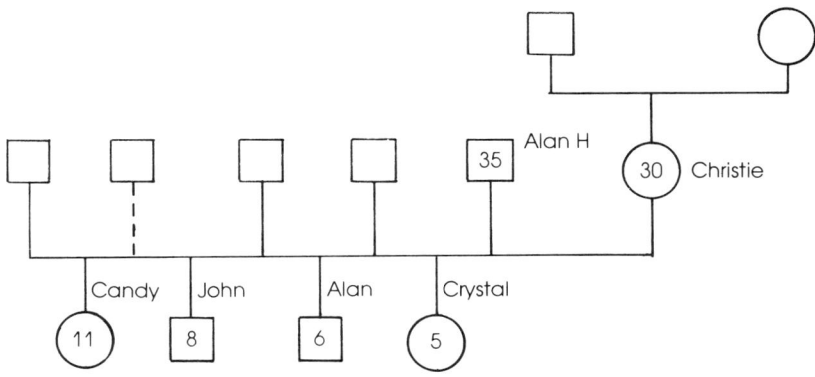

FIGURE 1. H family genogram (skeletal).

were there revealed that the parents had not clearly explained the reason for the visit. I asked the siblings and parents about the potential advantages and disadvantages of Candy's leaving home, which elicited ambivalent thoughts and feelings in everyone. Candy's behavior was described by the parents as increasingly surly and defiant. Candy spoke very little, and we did not push her to participate more, not wishing to worsen her already considerable anxiety.

Investigation of parental roles revealed a confusing picture. Mrs. H had decided she wanted her current husband to be an involved parent, so she turned the discipline over to him when they married. She set almost no limits on the children. She did, however, often undermine Mr. H's attempts to discipline them. Neither parent followed through consistently on various reasonable plans for discipline.

Mrs. H's parenting, as well as her life in general, had been heavily criticized by her mother, who had also abused her verbally and physically during her childhood. Mrs. H was chagrined to admit that she was reenacting the verbal abuse with her own children when she became upset, and she was afraid that she might repeat the physical abuse if things got worse.

Our approach to the family was based mostly on principles of structural family therapy and behavior modification. We told the family that we thought Mrs. H's desire to install Mr. H as a "real father" was laudable, but that she may have moved too far aside herself while including him fully in the family. We thought that their family needed a functional mother and father working together to be in charge, and said that we might be able to help them build a balanced parenting team.

At the end of the first session (90 minutes), the family seemed, at least partially, to buy our redefinition of the problem from bad kid to troubled family. They decided that Candy would stay in the home while they began working on the family problems. We met with them two more times for an hour each time. They selected a concrete area to work on—washing the dinner dishes in an acceptable way. When it was her turn, Candy had been washing the dishes slowly and poorly, and one of the parents had been angrily redoing them. This process was an epitome of the parents' inadequate enforcement of limits.

We helped the family negotiate specific new expectations and a system in which each parent had some responsibility for monitoring the children's behavior. A positive reinforcer (playing a game together) and a punishment (no television that evening) were selected by the family to encourage the desired behavior. Attention was also given to the need for each parent to spend time regularly with each child as an individual. Candy and Mrs. H chose to go window-shopping together as their first planned outing. Discussion of the different life-cycle needs of an adolescent led to negotiation of individualized rules for Candy, with some incentives for responsible behavior.

During the three weekly counseling sessions, the family mood changed from fairly negative to quite positive. Candy became more talkative and cheerful, and there was no more talk of her leaving home. She did well with her responsibilities after the second visit, and both parents felt good about the rearranged parenting roles.

During the latter part of the third session, we discussed the likelihood of future difficulties, particularly around issues of adolescent separation, independence, and sexuality. Reference was made to patterns in the previous generation that would tend to make dealing with these issues difficult. Since the family was happy with the progress they had made and did not wish to attend the fourth session we had initially contracted for, we expressed our willingness to meet with the family again in the future, if desired.

During the next year prior to my departure from the residency program, Mrs. H made very few visits, and she and the family did well. No long-term follow-up is available.

This family was my first experience with formal family counseling. It was scary, but exciting and enjoyable. The complexity of trying to observe, think about, and respond to so many simultaneous stimuli felt overwhelming at first. The positive outcome promoted me to read more about family therapy and encouraged me to try to work with other families. Having a cotherapist was reassuring, but I probably would have learned more by going it alone, with a supervisor behind the one-way mirror, and pre- and post-session discussions of the counseling process.

I think that most family physicians could work with the H family the way we did by using knowledge and skills acquired from residency training or continuing medical education. Many families' needs can be met very well with the problem-oriented approaches outlined in Doherty and Baird's (1983) first book. The multigenerational approach that I now use requires additional training available in only a few family practice residency training programs at present.

EDITORS' COMMENTS

For many family physicians who become actively involved in family counseling, a particular case provided the breakthrough experience. This was Dr. Crouch's. He aptly describes the experience as "scary, but exciting and enjoyable." He first survived the panic of having a mother tell him to take her daughter out of the home before she harmed her. He then got help for the family and himself in the form of a family therapist. Then, he and the therapist used structural family therapy techniques to help the family rapidly break out of its troublesome patterns. Dr. Crouch went on from this experience to get training after his residency in a different approach to family therapy—multigenerational (Bowen) family systems therapy (Bowen, 1976). Thus, this family started him down a new path in his medical career.

A TEENAGER WITH BRITTLE DIABETES

KARLOTTA L. BARTHOLOMEW
Philadelphia Child Guidance Clinic

I received information about Chris, a 14-year-old boy with brittle diabetes, and his family, whom I was to meet with for assessment for possible inpatient admission. Chris had had diabetes since he was 7 years old. The last 3 years, he had been hospitalized more and more often for ketoacidosis, about once a month over the last year. His hometown pediatrician had been carefully evaluating Chris, looking for the organic cause of these diabetic crises. He referred the family to Children's Hospital of Philadelphia (CHOP) for further evaluation.

The chief of endocrinology at CHOP reviewed the previous thorough medical evaluations and current results, determined that there was a major psychosomatic component, and referred the family to Philadelphia Child Guidance Clinic for assessment for inpatient treatment. The family's reluctance to hospitalizing their son 3½ hours away from home was broken when they were told that the situation was lethal.

When I first met with the family—mother, father, Chris, and 12-year-old Tracey—I was struck by how attractive, caring, and verbal they were. There was a lot of friendly bantering. The Children's Hospital pediatrician who attended the session stated that she was reluctant to think of the problem only as psychosomatic, and didn't want us to forget that Chris had a disease. This confused me. Also, in talking with the family about their perception of the problem, I became worried at how helpless the family felt and how the diabetes had gotten so much power. How had Chris gotten to such a lethal state? How could I get the family and attending pediatrician to see Chris's problem in a different way? How could I go beneath the pleasant exterior to see how this family really lived together?

It became clear to me during the assessment that Chris was overindulged by his mother. The father had accepted being pushed to the periphery of the family, and the mother and father had congenially "agreed to disagree" and had allowed their 12-year-old daughter to become the communication link between the father and the rest of the family.

I needed to break the mother's overprotective relationship with Chris. My major intervention during the 2-hour assessment was to support the father in challenging the mother to join him in expecting Chris to grow up, be responsible, and manage his diabetes. To do this, I had to prevent the father from withdrawing when the mother resisted him. Finally, the mother (in tears) felt his presence and embraced him. Holding hands, the parents, as a newly formed team, set goals for Chris's inpatient treatment: (1) to learn diabetic self-management; (2) to learn to settle daily conflicts without turning to his parents for protection.

The attending pediatrician developed and coordinated the diabetic program with Chris and the inpatient staff; she saw him several times a week. Chris, who was very knowledgeable, managed his diabetes, did well during the first week, but then started to complain and refused to follow the program, expressing anger at the disease. I was asked by the nursing staff whom to call in to deal with the problem: the inpatient treatment team, the parents, or the attending pediatrician?

I asked the nurse to call in the pediatrician. This is the thinking that guided my decision. I had found out that the pediatrician thought that I had been too challenging initially to the family, especially to Chris and his mother. She had been trained that a family suffering with a chronic illness needs support, education, and/or new technology. I noted that this represented a different problem-solving paradigm. I also noted that the pediatrician had been pulled into the protective relationship with "angelic" Chris, a role that had been removed from his mother during the assessment interview.

The intervention was successful. She saw that "angelic" Chris was defying her orders. She got angry at him for his blatant refusal to cooperate after she had spent hours going out of her way to be supportive and to accomodate to him in developing his diabetic protocol. She marked this as her turning point in allegiance to me and the treatment team. She now began to see how an overprotective relationship with

Chris kept him in his lethal medical state. She had never seen parental conflict in such congenial people exacerbate a severe medical problem in a child, as it was doing with Chris. She now held Chris and his mother accountable. This laid the framework for the major family treatment intervention in the 3rd week of hospitalization. At this time, I induced a crises in order to further dislocate the mother from her entrenched, lethal, overprotective relationship with Chris, by having the now active father push the mother to make a clear, unambiguous break with Chris, and form a more stable alliance with the father.

This marked the turning point for the family. Chris tested the mettle of the new relationship between the parents during his first 4 months back home; after initial discharge from the hospital, there were other hospitalizations until the parents stabilized their relationship and began working as a team. However, there has been only one hospitalization in the 2½ years since then, and Chris has not missed any school.

What has been striking in the follow-up is that the parents had to break the pattern of overprotection. It took several months for the family pediatrician to see Chris's problem as more than organic; the mother had to break her overprotective relationship with her diabetic son; and the parents had to teach the school nurse to send Chris back to class.

This case taught me that clinicians treating families with life-threatening illnesses need to keep a keen eye on all parts of the family ecosystem and understand the necessity for shifting patterns of overinvolvement not only within the family but also between the family and the major institutions.

EDITORS' COMMENTS

This is an example of the value and complexity of a family therapy approach to a serious medical problem that is nested in multiple systems. These symptoms included a specialized family therapist experienced in working as part of a well-coordinated medical team and empowered by a medical institution to have significant influence on medical therapy; a family that had been locked into counterproductive relationships with their diabetic son and with physicians; a primary physician who had become invested in viewing the problem in traditionally simplified terms; and a resident physician who temporarily became a factor in protecting the patient and family from change. By focusing on changing the closest interacting system in the hospital—the resident-patient relationship—Dr. Bartholomew ultimately influenced the patient-family relationship, the family's relationship to medical institutions, and the primary physician's relationship with the patient and family.

Dr. Bartholomew demonstrates here the unique benefits of working in a specialized environment that supports a family-centered approach to very different referral cases. Most primary care physicians and family therapists do not work in such an environment. However, by seeing the advantages of that system, perhaps we will find ways to engender more support in our own systems.

A HUSBAND AND WIFE WITH BACKACHES

STEPHEN TAPLIN
Group Health Cooperative of Puget Sound
University of Washington

SUSAN McDANIEL
ELIZABETH NAUMBURG
University of Rochester

The treatment and management of the P family was filled with mystery, challenge, frustration, and eventually, reward for the three of us. Initially, Dr. Taplin, a family physician, treated this family in his urban group practice (Treatment Phase I). After struggling for a year to diagnose Mr. and Mrs. P's various, and at times severe and unremitting, aches and pains, Dr. Taplin set up an evaluation session for the couple with himself and Dr. McDaniel, a family therapist. This session resulted in a referral to Dr. McDaniel for family therapy. In this phase, Dr. McDaniel tried to engage the somatically focused family, and Dr. Taplin worked to support the referral (Treatment Phase II).

Soon after, Dr. Taplin changed jobs and moved to another part of the country. He referred the P family to a family physician colleague, Dr. Naumburg, who continued to manage their care and collaborate with Dr. McDaniel (Treatment Phase III).

TREATMENT PHASE I: PURSUING THE MYSTERY

The P family presented to me on my first day in a four-person family practice group in an inner-city setting. The family consisted of 37-year-old Mr. and 31-year-old Mrs. P and three boys, 9-year-old Shawn, 7-year-old Aaron, and 4-year-old Todd. They lived in a nearby rural community where Mr. P was employed to run a dairy farm and Mrs. P tended to their own large collection of goats, horses, gardens, and hay fields. Treatment Phase I focused on a 10-month period when both husband and wife presented with low back pain.

Prior to this period, the P family had presented as an interesting and welcomed addition to the practice. Mr. P was seen for hypertension and other acute problems. Mrs. P brought the children to the office quite frequently, especially Todd, who had numerous visits for fever and tonsillitis, always strep negative. Just prior to Todd's tonsillectomy, Mrs. P presented as a patient herself. She came in for a complete physical exam, which was essentially unremarkable. A routine family history was obtained at this time (Figure 1).

Mrs. P presented with left adnexal cramping pain about 1 month after the complete physical. In her words, "Everything started going downhill after that." A 3- to 4-cm mass was present on pelvic examination. Over the next 3 days, the pain increased, then disappeared with the disappearance of the presumed ovarian cyst. Her gastrointestinal and genitourinary workup were otherwise unremarkable at the time of the initial presentation.

At that time, she also reported some low back pain, which increased over the next several weeks. It began radiating down her left leg, and she became a regular visitor to my office for a month, until one afternoon she called to report lower extremity weakness and urinary retention. She was admitted to the hospital and evaluated by a neurologist. However, the workup, which included a neurologic exam, repeat pelvic, routine blood work, and a multiple sclerosis profile on her cerebral spinal fluid, revealed no abnormalities.

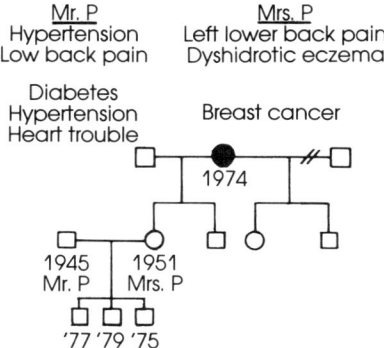

FIGURE 1. Routine family history.

Over the next 3 months, she saw me regularly for her pain, including an emergency room visit 2 days after hospital discharge. In the course of her visits, her complaints resulted in further diagnostic evaluation, including lumbosacral spine, barium enema, abdominal CT scan, and routine blood work, all of which were normal. This workup came in the face of mounting pressure from the patient, and within myself, to explain Mrs. P's pain. Despite a long philosophical stance that the mind–body split was false, I continued to investigate the potential organic explanations of her pain, and less aggressively pursued the family context. Mrs. P's pain eventually became tolerable on nonsteroidal, antiinflammatory medications. During her hospital admission, she had acknowledged that she had gotten some Tylenol with codeine from her husband, and that it appeared to her that she developed the urinary retention as a result. This was to be borne out by future experience. There was no evidence of addiction, and she did not require or seek other controlled substances.

For his part, Mr. P presented with nonradiating low back pain 4 months after Mrs. P's pain had begun, and about the time it had reached a steady state. He initially reported a persistent aching in his low midback without numbness, tingling, or radicular pain. Examination was unremarkable except for some minimal prostatic tenderness. His urinalysis revealed one to two white blood cells/high-powered field, and urine culture was negative. I treated him initially with aspirin, but he soon developed pain radiating to the left testicle and a blue discoloration of the scrotum. Examination by myself and a urologist could not document any abnormality, but the persistent mild prostatic tenderness led to a diagnosis of prostatitis. His pain decreased after prolonged antibiotic therapy, but did not resolve completely. No testicular abnormalities were ever found, but he continued to complain of intermittent problems and pain. Like his wife, Mr. P seemed organized, reasonable, and sincere. I was confounded by two family members with unremitting complaints, and hobbled by my narrow view that organized, reasonable, and sincere people only have organic problems.

I began to see either Mr. P or his wife every 2 weeks, and collected bits and pieces of their family history. At the time, I was participating in a Balint group that included the other authors as participants and focused on family factors in health care. That group encouraged me to pursue these factors. Stepping back to get a better sense of the context of their presentations became almost a defense for me against the onslaught of the P family's persistent vague complaints of pain.

The bits and pieces of their family histories became intriguing as I learned things like the fact that Mr. P had been abandoned by his parents in an isolated cabin at the age of 16 along with his four younger siblings. He had eventually found help and housing, but had to pay $20 a month to live with an aunt. He earned that money by working for a physician on a cattle ranch. He now considers that physician to be his adopted father. Mrs. P had been very close to her father and somewhat estranged from her mother. This information, and additional suggestions that Mr. and Mrs. P were suffering from some marital discord, led me to suggest they see a family therapist to explore the stresses involved in their chronic pain.

TREATMENT PHASE II: WIDENING THE PERSPECTIVE

With members of the Balint group behind a one-way mirror to consult, Dr. McDaniel and I met with Mr. and Mrs. P. Both of us were nervous to be working with each other in front of our colleagues, but curious to find out how family issues interacted with these patients' multiple and mysterious somatic problems. Mr. and Mrs. P also appeared nervous. Mrs. P acted inhibited, passive, and fearful. Mr. P acted dominant and protective of his wife, ruling out many areas of inquiry he said would be too much for her. Mr. P's anxiety was also apparent in frequent, inappropriate bursts of laughter.

Early on, it became clear that this couple was unusually scared about discussing family of origin issues. Over the 45 minutes, they loosened up and warmed to Dr. McDaniel, in spite of their hesitancy about seeing a psychologist. My previous work with them and mutual respect seemed to facilitate this process. In the beginning of the interview, discussion revolved around the extreme amount of work involved in farming, and the effect of Mrs. P's convalescence on the enormous number of chores at home. The ice was clearly broken when Mr. P told the story of his childhood abandonment, a story he claimed he had never shared with others except his wife. Soon after his disclosure, Mrs. P asked Dr. McDaniel for advice regarding her feelings of claustrophobia in dressing rooms or at home when trying to undress. The session ended with a review of their physical symptoms, and the couple accepting my recommendation that they follow up in family therapy with Dr. McDaniel. The Balint group and I agreed that Dr. McDaniel and this session were pivotal in shifting the focus for everyone to include the pain in Mr. and Mrs. P's families as well as in their backs. The family history had expanded from the one collected previously to one that better reflected the family dynamics (Figure 2).

Soon after the evaluation session, Mrs. P brought Todd in for a follow-up on his otitis media. At the conclusion of the visit, she sent him out and said, "Oh, by the way, I'm not sleeping much." In her two subsequent visits (prior to seeing Dr. McDaniel again), Mrs. P began to acknowledge her depression and related to me her guilt over

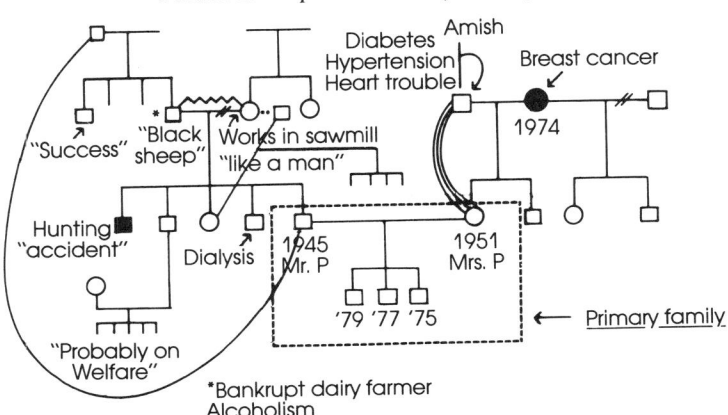

FIGURE 2. Expanded family history.

marrying against her mother's wishes. At the time of Mrs. P's marriage, her mother had metastatic breast cancer but had told no one. Mrs. P's mother warned her daughter that she "would pay" for marrying Mr. P. In the final sessions with me, Mrs. P developed this theme; by then, there was little mention of her back pain. At one point, she acknowledged offhandedly that she had not really wanted the medication for her back to be effective.

TREATMENT PHASE III: EASING THE PAIN

The last phase of treatment consisted of concurrent family therapy and work with the new family physician, Dr. Naumburg. Mrs. P seemed to accept the recommendations for this two-pronged treatment. Mr. P, however, let it be known early that he did not like "lady doctors," and that two at once was two too many. Dr. McDaniel handled this challenge by not asking Mr. P to be a patient, but rather asking him to consult with her on his wife's problems. Stressed by his usually energetic, caretaking wife's current debilitation, he agreed to come in every few sessions as a consultant. Dr. Naumburg, having been appraised of this case, saw Mrs. P and waited for Mr. P to decide how he would handle his new medical doctor. Mr. P threatened to change to a male physician, but slowly, through his wife, decided he could trust Dr. Naumburg. He once commented, "She's pretty good for a lady doctor."

The psychotherapy with this case consisted of individual and conjoint sessions, with occasional family sessions that included the couple's sons. Early sessions focused on Mrs. P's fatigue and physical symptoms by examining general lifestyle issues such as the enormous amount of physical labor this woman did each day. Her symptoms represented the first slowdown in a lifelong pattern of hard work. To allow her to slow down without symptoms, Mrs. P began a series of relaxation exercises. In conjunction with these behavioral techniques, marital work focused on helping Mr. P shift from rewarding his wife for excessive labor to rewarding her for relaxing and feeling better physically. Both members of the couple came to see the relation between amount of activity and Mrs. P's symptoms. Though never addressed directly, Mr. P clearly saw a connection with his own symptoms as well.

As Mrs. P began to work less and feel better physically, she began to experience first anxiety and depression, and then tremendous anger.

This stage of treatment focused on the importance of feelings, both negative and positive (a novel idea for this action-oriented woman). She worked to tolerate and understand her feelings without increasing her activity level. Slowly, lifelong pain regarding her childhood of abuse and deprivation surfaced and was integrated; much of this pain Mrs. P had never revealed to anyone. These changes in Mrs. P put pressure on the marriage. Mrs. P had never been expressive with her husband, and Mr. P had always kept feelings about his own childhood hardships under tight control. Discussion between the two of them about pain in their families of origin was welcomed by both parties. However, honest discussion of differences between them was much more difficult. Slowly, Mr. P was encouraged to convince his wife that he really could take her anger, since it was important to her health for her to learn to express these feelings.

In this stage, Mrs. P also worked hard to teach her children to be honest and expressive, "so they won't have to go through the same thing." She revealed that Todd was still sleeping in the couple's bed, and Aaron had only recently moved to his own room. While Mr. P had some difficulty denying his children any physical comfort or affection, he did want to be closer to his wife. So, eventually, Todd was moved to his own room. Soon after accomplishing the new sleeping arrangements, Mrs. P expressed concern about Todd starting school too soon because she feared she that he would have the same series of illnesses that Aaron had had when beginning school. From her description, it became clear that school phobia was behind many of these symptoms. Mrs. P worked to prepare Todd, and, after a few difficult days, successfully settled him in school.

The last issues of focus for Mrs. P were in the general area of feminine identity, sexuality, and feelings toward her mother. Mr. P supported this work by beginning to take his wife out on regular dates and by buying her a series of gifts, such as feminine clothing and jewelry. During this period, Mrs. P lost weight. Her new appearance and style of dressing stimulated questions and compliments from the staff when she came to see Dr. Naumburg. For his part, Mr. P made overtures to his maternal grandmother and his mother, ending 15 years of no communication with them.

Psychotherapy now consists of one session, usually with Mrs. P, every month or two. These sessions provide fine-tuning and support for the many changes Mrs. P has made. According to her description, the sessions are also part of the socializing she has never had. The time between her sessions has been increasing, and she has signed up for some homemaking classes to meet other women. The couple has increased their socializing with neighbors, family, and other couples.

Throughout this year and a half of family therapy, an important component has been the ongoing communication and planning with the P family's family physician, Dr. Naumburg. The coordination and dovetailing of treatment plans has allowed an integration of the somatic and psychological components of the systems experienced by various members of the P family.

When Mr. and Mrs. P first became symptomatic, they threatened to become a thorny problem for me. Taking a family approach, and collaborating with a family therapist allowed what could have become an incredible burden to become a fascination. Dr. McDaniel shifted the focus of our work, and in the process moved that burden back to the people who could relieve it, Mr. and Mrs. P themselves. With the responsibility for the hard work residing with the family, it seemed easier for the family physicians to assist in the process. This family will probably always be relatively heavy utilizers of health care services. However, this treatment was a positive experience for both patient and provider in that what began as incurable pain and frustration became productive interactions and mutual satisfaction.

Dr. McDaniel reports that for her, a case such as this is a rewarding collaboration with family physicians and permits a truly biopsychosocial approach that is intellectually stimulating for the caregivers as well as beneficial for the family. For me, it was amazing to see how much was going on in this family. I find it impossible to imagine that Mr. and Mrs. P could have made the progress they did without the collaborative efforts of a family therapist and family physicians.

EDITORS' COMMENTS

The authors said it well when they commented that taking a family approach and using a family therapist consultant turned a burdensome case into a fascinating one. The primary care task here was to disentangle the multiple, nagging somatic complaints from their web of serious psychosocial problems. Mr. and Mrs. P were "good" patients who had learned that the only way to ask a physician for help was to have a physical complaint. Dr. Taplin began to realize that he had dichotomized patients into "reasonable" people with biomedical problems and "unreasonable" people with psychosocial problems. Putting the biological and the psychosocial together in one patient and family is quite a challenge. In this case, the blending was accomplished by combining the efforts of family physicians and a family therapist working collaboratively. Outside an academic training center, the family physicians more likely would have referred the family to Dr. McDaniel rather than serving as cotherapists, at least after the initial family session. However, the same principles of coordination between physician and therapist would apply. Beyond the good done for the family, this kind of case can be a career-changing experience for the family physician. Once you have witnessed the dramatic marriage of biological and psychosocial approaches to diagnosis and treatment, your view of medical care is altered forever.

"BYPASS SURGERY" ON THE DOCTOR-PATIENT RELATIONSHIP

GEORGE W. SABA
University of California, San Francisco

PHYSICIAN: How long ago did you first have asthma?
JORGE: I first had the asthma 7 to 8 years ago.
PHYSICIAN: That was around the time you were married, right?
ROSA: No, it was just after Jorgito was born.
JORGE: Yea, I went to the doctor. I was having the same system, I mean, symptoms back then as I have now.

Perhaps Jorge meant to say "symptom" and the word "system" was accidently substituted. Perhaps Jorge was also insightfully presenting a systems analysis of his health problem. I will present a story of Jorge, his family, their family physician, and myself, their consultant. The family consisted of 45-year-old Jorge, the father, 35-year-old Rosa, the mother, 7-year-old Jorgito, and 4-year-old Maria. Jorge had complained of asthma for the past 7 to 8 years and Rosa had been experiencing pelvic pain for some time. Jorgito was also asthmatic.

Gerry McCallum, MD (a 2nd-year family practice resident), had been treating the family individually for 6 months. Lately, he saw his work with them resembling a game of symptomatic "hot potato." That is, one week Rosa arrived complaining of pain. As she improved, Jorge would appear the next week with increased asthmatic symptoms. On the heels of his improvement, his son's wheezing would exacerbate. Dr. McCallum decided that it was difficult for all members of this family to be healthy simultaneously. Once he had recognized this "turn-taking" pattern, he believed convening them would be more useful than dousing brushfires. He asked each of the parents, individually, if there were problems in their lives other than the medical ones. They each reported tension in the marriage, difficulties with finances, disagreements about where to live, and fears that the frustration would lead to child abuse. Dr. McCallum had never interviewed a couple, and decided to schedule them for a behavioral science clinic in which he could be supervised while conducting the session.

Dr. McCallum asked Jorge and Rosa if they would be interested in meeting as a family. They agreed, but wanted to come first without the children. Immediately prior to the couple's session, I met with Dr. McCallum and the other 2nd-year residents who comprised the training group. Dr. McCallum presented a brief history of his work with the family, and his assessment of the patterns. He described the aforementioned alternation of symptom and individual presentation to the physician. In addition, he himself often felt caught in the middle of parental decisions about how best to treat Jorgito's asthma. Specifically, Jorge and Rosa disagreed about the best method of administering Jorgito's medication: pills or inhaler. They continually abdicated to Dr. McCallum, who felt either method was fine and that the parents should decide. Hearing these common patterns, I suggested that Dr. McCallum begin the interview by gathering some basic information about the family, helping them become comfortable together, and that he be sensitive to interpersonal requests for abdication and triangulation.

Dr. McCallum brought the couple into the interview room, explained the one-way mirror and the team of consultants behind it, and the fact that he and the team would talk periodically during the session. They agreed to this arrangement. Rosa wondered if he would refer them to a psychiatrist after finding out what their problem was. Dr. McCallum stated firmly that he would help them come to a resolution about their problem. The couple seemed reassured with this degree of commitment.

Dr. McCallum began gathering an immigration and marital history of the couple. Jorge emerged as older, less educated, and had recently immigrated, while Rosa appeared more attractive and sophisticated, and had been living in this country since she was 12 years old. As mentioned in the opening transcript, the symptoms of asthma appeared around the time of the introduction of a third person into the system—their first child, Jorgito. In taking a work history, a clear difference in the roles of husband and wife unfolded. Jorge felt that Rosa should be working to help support the family. Rosa believed that Jorge should overcome his asthma, and get a job. Many difficulties surfaced, and Dr. McCallum and I decided to have them focus on one topic as a means of reorganizing their life, rather than feeling overwhelmed with a dozen problematic issues. I also suggested that Dr. McCallum begin to introduce a new pattern in the treatment system of the three of them and make it clear that the couple should decide the topic of discussion together rather than getting him to do so. He asked them to select, together, the most pressing problem they wanted to resolve. After some initial attempts to gain his help, they turned to each other and decided that emotionally they had the greatest tension around who should be the breadwinner(s). The amount of money earned was not as important as who made it.

Once they agreed upon the topic, I called Dr. McCallum out to consult. I suggested to him that the couple needed an elongated dialogue about this issue. The image I wanted to conjure in his head was one of performing bypass surgery on the doctor–patient relationship. In such a procedure, he was to remove himself from the interaction and have the communication flow directly between the husband and wife.

Returning to the room, Dr. McCallum prepped them for the operation. He found them reluctant to talk with each other. The only successful anesthetic that helped was their trust in him. That is, they and he were quite connected; he used this closeness to remove himself from the discussion by saying things like: "I want you to talk with each other." "Talk with Jorge like I know you can." "Do this for me." After several attempts, Dr. McCallum convinced them of his interest in resolving the issue, in his willingness to accompany them on this venture, but also of his unavailability when they needed to construct new pathways to each other. The content of the couple's discussion centered on expectations of each other as wage earners in the household. At times, they attempted to reengage Dr. McCallum by introducing events of which he had been unaware, such as a previous separation and a many-year battle about relocating in Los Angeles. However, Dr. McCallum continually refused involvement and returned them to each other.

Nearly 30 minutes had elapsed, and I called Dr. McCallum to come behind the mirror to decide how to bring a successful session to a close. In devising my supervisory intervention with him, I wanted to avoid replicating the family's pattern of abdication to an expert. To guide, yes, but not to infantilize was my goal. Dr. McCallum and I decided that he could first congratulate them for dealing directly with a very difficult issue. Next, it would be important to see if they wanted to resolve this problem, in other words to reexpress their wedding vows. If they wanted to resolve this, then he should ask them to decide what the first step in the change would be.

Dr. McCallum returned to the room, and my mind began to drift, preparing for the Chinese grandmother who was his next patient scheduled for a consult that afternoon. As I watched in the mirror for Dr. McCallum to wrap up the session, a remarkable pattern began to unfold. He had gone back in and said, "I want you to decide what the first step will be in making the change." He found them unwilling to discuss it, and Rosa brought up many objections. I called him out of the room and asked him if he had remembered that we decided to have *them* first choose whether or not they wanted to work on resolving this issue. He said he remembered when he left me, but in their presence was compelled to decide for them. I asked him if he wanted to return to the role of parenting them, and he said he was glad to resign. He returned, and asked *them* what *they* wanted to do. Rosa began, for the first time, to talk about how she wanted out. Jorge said, "Do you want out of the situation, which we can change, or do you want out of the marriage?" "Both," Rosa said. A session that was nearly over began a new phase.

I suggested to Dr. McCallum to hit this issue head-on and ask them to clarify with each other what was being said. As he helped them explore this issue, the tempting previous patterns of involving him began to reemerge. He continually refused reengagement in those ways. Jorge and Rosa danced around the topic of being married, separated, or divorced. Rosa said that every time she talked about divorce, Jorge would beg her to stay, and she would. She always suggested they move to Los Angeles, where extended family could be helpful, but he refused to discuss it. While many issues flew rapidly between the couple, they failed to near any resolution. As the conflicts intensified, they tried to reenlist Dr. McCallum's support.

I called Dr. McCallum out to decide how best to proceed. I suggested that he ask them to discuss whether they were talking marriage with some changes, separation, or divorce, and for him to remain completely out of the interaction until they decided, even if he needed to move back his chair. As he reentered the room, Rosa said, "I know you are running overtime. Will we finish?" Dr. McCallum replied, "We will finish!" This was an important statement of his commitment to a very intense process; it not only balanced his moves for greater distance but also reaffirmed his opening assurance that he would see them through this problem.

Dr. McCallum laid out the issue of marriage, separation, and divorce. To our surprise, he said, "I want you to discuss this, and I don't want to be part of it." With that, he not only moved his chair back, but turned the chair around completely. They took the hint, and began discussing the options. Once they were working at this issue, Dr. McCallum left the room and joined us behind the mirror.

We watched the couple enter new territory as they reached resolution. Rosa said, "I want a divorce." Jorge said, "Fine." For the first time, Jorge did not fight for her to change her mind. Rosa said, "This is the first time you ever listened to me. We never talked like this at home. You were always too busy when I would want to talk about these things, watching TV or something. You finally heard me."

Dr. McCallum returned to the room on this solemn, but resolved, note to have them decide how they wanted to use his services. They looked to each other, and decided to schedule another visit in 2 weeks to talk about the divorce and the children.

They arrived for the next session with the news that they were moving to Los Angeles that week. Jorge reported that on the night of the session, Jorgito had a serious asthma attack. The parents continued discussing divorce for a week, then Rosa agreed to remain married, and Jorge agreed to move to Los Angeles. They had reached a compromise. During the 2 weeks, there were no other exacerbations of the illnesses. Dr. McCallum felt he could no longer be helpful, and therefore had failed. They, however, were extremely pleased with how he had helped them; they felt he had facilitated a new lease on their family and marriage. I framed Dr. McCallum's disappointment as the kind of sadness parents sometimes feel after successfully helping their children leave home.

Six months after this last encounter, Dr. McCallum heard from Jorge and Rosa, who were still living in Los Angeles. They were doing fine, although Jorge still had asthma. However, Rosa no longer had pelvic pain, and Jorgito's asthma had vanished. A 2-year follow-up found a similar level of functioning. One session was not powerful enough to resolve all the difficulties this family faced. However, the goal of this session had been to help a family get unstuck from a problematic pattern and use the doctor–patient relationship to make the difference. Dr. McCallum's move from participating in a triangulating sequence to helping the couple work alone may have influenced the recommitment to a marriage, the exclusion of a child as a stabilizing part of an unhealthy pattern, and an improvement in the health of at least two family members.

EDITORS' COMMENTS

Sometimes the therapeutic triangle—the doctor, the patient, and the family—needs therapy focusing on the doctor's role in maintaining the patient's symptoms. In this complex case scenario, family therapist George Saba was helping family practice resident Gerry McCallum to extricate himself from a pernicious triangle with Jorge and Rosa. As long as they could turn to Dr. McCallum, Jorge and Rosa did not have to turn to each other. Physicians are continually at risk for becoming caught up in family interaction patterns that stabilize the patient's problems. Removing oneself from this pattern in a way that supports the family rather than rejecting it is a difficult task that is nicely demonstrated in this case. When called in to consult on a difficult case, we often find ourselves addressing first what Dr. Saba saw as the crucial initial step in helping the patient, namely, the doctor–patient–family relationship. Of course, this process requires a primary physician who is willing to look at his or her own contribution to maintaining the dysfunctional pattern. Dr. McCallum had the courage to work on his own behavior, and Dr. Saba had the insight to understand that physician change was the critical step in allowing the possibility of family change.

SEXUAL PROBLEMS AND UNRESOLVED GRIEF

JANET CHRISTIE-SEELY
Ottawa University

Fifty-two-year-old Joan and 43-year-old Bill were referred to me because of the delinquent behavior of Joan's son, which produced arguments and a deteriorating sexual relationship. This was Joan's third marriage. Bill, a laborer, had been divorced 10 years before, and had a daughter he rarely saw. Joan's second husband had died of carcinoma of the lung 6 years before. She had married Bill a year later. (Bill also smoked heavily). Joan's only son, 20 years old, had been imprisoned on drug charges during the past year, and was only now beginning to pull himself together. He and Bill did not get along, much to Joan's distress, and Bill felt Joan was much too easy on him.

Both patients had mild hypertension, and were on medication (Bill, 25 mg hydrochlorothiazide; Joan, 2 mg prazosin twice a day). Bill was followed with B_{12} shots for documented pernicious anemia. Joan had a host of physical ailments, including osteoarthritis, frequent bursitis, obesity, and esophagitis. Two years previously, she had also had dyspareunia following a hysterectomy. A sexual problem resulting at the time had been helped with advice on lubrication. Now Bill was complaining that Joan was losing interest in sex, and he was vaguely threatening to look elsewhere.

In the first session, I did a family genogram. I find genograms are a useful means of getting to know patients and their context.

Bill's mother had died 8 months ago in the spring. The sex problem, which he ascribed either to his wife or to the medications, had begun almost immediately thereafter. He admitted, "Things weren't quite the same after she died." He began to get tearful and spoke also of the death of his only brother 2 years earlier, which he felt had resulted in his mother's death. Joan's response was interesting—

when his eyes were full of tears, she would not look at him. Although it was she who complained that he was emotionally unresponsive and resistant to discussing problems, she shifted the topic away from sadness and death. I inquired into Joan's family history and discovered that her father had died 25 years earlier. Because she had had to be the support of her mother, she had never cried or grieved at his death. Bill said he had not cried for many years and had not cried at his mother's funeral or since. Joan said she felt she couldn't cry in front of him because he thought tears were weakness, but this was partly projection. Joan returned to her anger at Bill for picking on her son. There was some evidence, however, that he often did so in the evening, quite probably as a means of avoiding sex and then blaming her for this. Joan's son was a useful smokescreen for both of them.

Later, we focused on Joan's negative feelings about sex. Suddenly, she remembered an abortion that she had had 8 years before, a year after her second husband's death. This had made her feel enormously guilty, and she wondered out loud if it had anything to do with their current sexual problems. She then mentioned that when she was 20 years old she had had two babies who had died. Incredibly, they had died on the same day: a girl a month old, and a boy of 2½ years old. Both had died of the same congenital disease. Her young husband, presumably unable to cope, packed his bags that day and left her for keeps. Of the abrupt loss of her entire family, she said, "I put it in the back of my head," but on describing it she began to cry.

Still very tearful, she went on to describe her father's death, which occurred soon after. He had been her only support during the childrens' deaths, whereas her mother was much more distant. After telling her story for the first time, with a great deal of emotion, Joan said she felt "very relieved by opening up these skeletons." It was now apparent why Bill's mother's death and his tears had been such a threat to her. It was also apparent how many people she had lost, particularly males, and she seemed to be bent on a self-fulfilling prophecy of the fear of being left again. By denying Bill sex, which was so important to him, she was threatening to produce another repeat of the pattern of loss. She had also had a very repressed upbringing. Despite being raised on a farm, she never saw an animal born, and was banned from the barn. Whenever the cows or horses were breeding, the women were brought indoors.

A Sensate Focus program facilitated communication over sex, and stopped the constant triangulation of Joan's son. He never came to the sessions because he was unable to get off from work, and he had stated that "he was not the problem." He was now getting along better with Bill. They had been very friendly prior to the marriage. I explained to Bill and Joan the difficulties that stepparents often have when they take on the role of disciplinarian or are given it by their spouse.

The son frequently stayed with an aunt who had helped to raise him, a relationship that tended to make Joan jealous because she felt that he sometimes preferred the aunt to her. We talked about the empty-nest phase of family life, particularly difficult when a relationship was as close as hers with her son, and I encouraged her to think about her own resources and activities outside the home.

The two areas I focused on with this family were the tasks of this stage of the family life cycle: letting go a child who had been Joan's sole continuity and close relationship for years, and the uncompleted task of mourning for so many family members by both Joan and Bill. The added task of remarriage had been just too much for this system to bear, given the "stuckness" with previous tasks. Helping the stepfather make the transition from stranger to friend, rather than parental disciplinarian, and helping Joan realize that she could not force a father–son relationship on these two people who were important to her, but not to each other, coupled with the grief work that both had so vigorously avoided, was the key to solving the sexual problem. Although some sexual problems are relatively simple and respond well to the classic Sensate Focus therapy, I find many of them relate to anger or depression. The anger in this couple, which expressed indirectly through sexual rejection, was a displacement of anger at past figures and past events in their lives.

Delayed mourning was even more significant. Being able to cry in each other's presence was an important turning point. They needed permission to grieve without thinking that they were "falling apart." This took place with a physician who knew them and their medical history, which was very suggestive of underlying stress. I find that routinely asking about losses, particularly deaths in the past 3 years, is a high-payoff question. This applies particularly to patients who have frequent visits for organic disease, recurrent minor illness, relationship problems, or other family dysfunction. I have observed in many families that an unmourned death or distorted mourning precedes dysfunction or disease. There is now research literature to support this, along with new information about the neurological–immune–endocrine mechanisms linking family, stress, and illness. The resident who was with me during the initial interviews with this couple was amazed at the history of the death of Bill's mother and his emotional reaction to it, which came out in the first interview. It had never occurred to her to ask about it, though it was in the chart that his mother had died in the spring.

The second high-payoff area that I have found as a physician dealing with illness and relationship problems is the life-cycle concept. Systems theory is the underpinning of all this work. I suspect that more medical visits occur around the stage at which this couple was struggling—the adjustment to midlife with its changed roles, loss of children who are often useful scapegoats, and loss of the parental role—than any other life-cycle stage. Helping families successfully negotiate these stages, anticipating them when possible, and facilitating communication during the stresses are, I believe, more potent activities than much of what we do with medications or other medical therapies.

EDITORS' COMMENTS

This couple was ready to deal with their painful past when invited to discuss something other than their medical problems. The family genogram process was the gasoline that ignited the hidden, smoldering grief of both partners. Dr. Christie-Seely's greatest contribution here may have been her willingness to stay with this couple's intense feelings, neither trying to smother the flames singlehandledly by "fixing" the problem, nor fleeing the fire's heat. The middle ground between fixing and fleeing is staying with the family and moving forward through the flames of unresolved grief and pain.

PREMATURITY AND THE "VULNERABLE CHILD" SYNDROME

ANTHONY ROSTAIN
University of Pennsylvania School of Medicine

Jason was the third child and first son born into the F family. He arrived 2 months early and was hospitalized for the first 7 weeks of his life in our medical center's intensive care nursery. Jason's neonatal problems included mild respiratory distress syndrome (RDS), some feeding intolerance, and apnea and bradycardia of prematurity. His hospital course was relatively uneventful and he was discharged home weighing 3 kg, on oral theophylline, and with a home cardiorespiratory (CR) monitor to warn his parents of any severe bradycardic spells. Trained in cardiopulmonary resuscitation, Mr. and Mrs. F were resolved to stay close by their baby at all times, which they reportedly did for the first 6 months of his life.

When Jason was 4 months old, he developed a severe upper respiratory infection (URI) and suffered several cyanotic episodes at home that his parents successfully treated. He was admitted to the hospital for several days until the infection resolved, and although he suffered no sequelae from the illness, Mr. and Mrs. F were clearly unnerved by the entire experience. The next few months were filled with constant worry on their part that Jason was going to have another severe cyanotic episode that they would not be able to reverse. Both of them felt that they were "nervous wrecks" whenever their son developed a runny nose or an episode of diarrhea. Nevertheless, Jason outgrew his apnea spells and was taken off the CR monitor when he was 7 months old.

Shortly after he was weaned from theophylline, Jason developed a wheezing episode associated with a URI. The first bout was successfully treated in the emergency room, and he was restarted on theophylline, but when he was 11 months old, Jason had to be hospitalized again for an episode of severe bronchospasm. Over the next few months, Jason suffered recurrent bouts of wheezing associated mostly with URIs and with physical activity. He was rehospitalized several times, and remained on asthma medications until approximately his 2nd birthday, when it appeared that he was no longer prone to wheezing attacks.

Over the ensuing months, Jason remained healthy and symptom-free. He was growing and developing normally, and his intelligence appeared to be above average. Yet despite these good signs, Mr. and Mrs. F remained anxious about their son's health, and treated him as a vulnerable child. This affected the interactions they had with me as a pediatrician and the ways in which they parented him.

Mr. and Mrs. F's habit of overreacting to their son's health problems can be illustrated by an episode that occurred in my office when he was 2 years old. An active (at times even overactive) and curious toddler, Jason was constantly running and falling down. His parents claimed he bruised easily and were concerned that he might have a blood disorder. I tried to reassure them that he was fine, and that the bruising was par for the course at his age, but the couple were not quite convinced by my explanations. I showed them that he had no signs whatsoever of any blood disease, and I insisted that the bruises were completely normal given their characteristic distribution on his upper and lower extremities, especially his knees. Yet they were still genuinely worried. Exasperated by their insistence, I finally obtained a spun hematocrit in the office. It proved to be within normal limits.

As Mr. and Mrs. F appeared only slightly reassured by the results, I gently suggested to them that they were overly concerned because of Jason's earlier medical problems, that they had no reason to remain so anxious anymore, and that they should be careful not to turn their son into a hypochondriac.

The following week, Jason developed a URI with swollen glands, and he was taken to the emergency room by his parents, who were convinced he had leukemia. The emergency room physicians, unable to persuade them otherwise, obtained a complete blood count with differential, which again proved completely unremarkable. The couple phoned me the next day to say that they were still concerned. "What if the blood test was wrong?" they asked. After learning he was afebrile with only a slight sore throat, I agreed to see Jason in 2 weeks. If the lymph nodes were still swollen, I would "work them up," I added. On the return visit, Jason was completely recovered. I used the occasion to restate my belief that they were in danger of burdening their son with their own anxieties. I offered them the opportunity to return the following week to talk more about their fears and their concerns.

Mr. and Mrs. F were an unlikely couple. She was portly and fair-skinned, with an attractive smile, a relaxed appearance, and a pleasant conversational style. He was thin, dark, and nervous, with rapid, slightly stammering speech and a look of uncertainty on his face. It was clear from the start that Mrs. F was the spokesperson for the couple, so I took great care to give Mr. F a chance to express his ideas and feelings. Over the next half hour, I learned that the family was struggling financially; Mr. F was studying computer programming and working nights in a bank, while Mrs. F was looking for a job. They had recently moved away from their hometown in order to be closer to the medical center, and were as yet without many social supports. Their other children (two girls, 3 and 4 years old) were in generally good health, but lately they had started fighting with each other over toys, books, and other trivials.

With all their other problems, Mr. and Mrs. F were most worried about Jason. They repeatedly expressed the fear that he would die, and they were petrified by every little cold or sniffle he developed. After they recounted some of their worst memories of his infancy, it occurred to me that they were having a hard time seeing him as just a little boy who had once been a premie but who was now healthy and normal. I asked them how long it would be before they were convinced that he was going to be fine. When Mrs. F answered, "Probably never," I asked her what it would take to prove it once and for all. She couldn't say, nor could Mr. F. After a few moments of silence, I suggested that although they would always have vivid recollections of the early days and that this was a natural thing for parents of premature infants, it would be a shame if they couldn't enjoy their son the way he was. It would also be unfortunate if they continued to indulge him and overprotect him because he would surely turn out to be a spoiled brat.

At this point Mr. F smiled at me, turned to his wife and said, "He's right. We're too overprotective with him, and we're letting him get away with murder. We have to stop this right away or else he'll really get out of control." I encouraged them to pick a behavior that they truly disliked and to discuss some ideas for disciplining him. They decided to ignore his temper tantrums and to refuse to give in to him if he threw one. I warned them that it was going to be difficult at first to assert control over Jason, but that if they were patient and consistent, they would see results in a few weeks. I enthusiastically endorsed their plan, and asked them to return to see me in a month.

When I saw Mr. and Mrs. F again, Mrs. F had found a job and was working during the day while Mr. F stayed home with the kids and studied. In the evenings, Mrs. F would care for the children while her husband attended classes. Although they were still having some problems disciplining Jason, the couple felt that things were going better for them. They thanked me for listening to their concerns, and they admitted to feeling less worried about Jason's health since that conversation. It was obvious they were more relaxed and more optimistic than before. I commented on the positive change in their attitudes, and I cautioned them that there were new challenges in store now that Mrs. F had taken a job.

About 6 months later, Jason and his parents came to my office for a well child visit. His physical health continued to be excellent, but he was still throwing tantrums at home, particularly when his mother tried to direct his behavior. Mrs. F and her son were having tremendous battles over picking up toys, putting on pajamas, taking baths, and brushing teeth. She sadly confessed to giving in to him rather than continuing to hassle; she was tired from a full day's work, and she felt guilty about not being home more.

Although Mr. F had tried to talk with her about it, the pattern had continued and, if anything, had been getting worse with time. Part of the problem was that Mr. F wasn't home when the two of them would fight. I asked him what he thought his wife should do when Jason threw his next tantrum. "Stick to your guns; don't give in. Make him do what you're asking him to do. If you really insist, eventually he'll stop his screaming and he'll do what you say." Mrs. F shook her head as if to say "Easier said than done. . . ." I acknowledged this by remarking that it must be hard to listen to Jason screaming. I asked Mr. F to explain how he managed to ignore it. At this point he admitted that his son never seemed to give him as hard a time as he did his mother.

After commenting that this was a fairly typical pattern in families where children are throwing tantrums all the time, I encouraged the couple to exchange a few more ideas about how to handle their son's misbehavior. Since the time was running late, I suggested that they return the following week to continue the discussion.

When Mrs. F handed Jason his shoes to put on so the family could leave, he refused to do so and asked her to put them on for him. As she was about to give in to him, I remarked that now was as good a time as any to start changing her approach with her son. I instructed her not to leave the office until she succeeded in getting him to put on his shoes, and I told Mr. F to remain nearby to help his wife, but *not* to take matters into his own hands. He could offer ideas or words of encouragement and support, but he was absolutely not to get directly involved. I left the family to see my other patients.

Over the course of the next 45 minutes, a loud shouting match ensued. Mrs. F began by trying to reason with her son, and when that failed, by threatening him. When Jason began to cry, his mother almost gave up, but Mr. F reminded her that she had to make him listen to her. She got angry at her husband and refused to continue. I returned to the room, gave them both some encouragement and repeated Mr. F's statement that Mrs. F needed to learn to "stick to her guns" or else Jason would continue to disrespect her. I left them alone again.

For several minutes, the screaming grew louder and more insistent; Mrs. F was getting very angry at her son. Yet Jason refused to budge, and instead began to cry so loudly that his chest was hurting and that he couldn't breathe. At this point, I heard Mr. F start to yell at his son. I returned to the room, looked Jason over, and reassured his parents that he wasn't having any trouble breathing. I asked Mr. F to step out of the room, and once outside, I stated that since it was hard for him to stay out of the conflict, it would be better for him to stay away. After all, his wife and his son needed to learn to settle their differences without him. I urged him to sit in the waiting room for another 10 minutes.

Within 5 minutes, the crying stopped. Mrs. F walked out of the office and very proudly announced that she had succeeded. Jason sullenly followed her into the waiting room, staring down at his shoes and sniffling quietly. I congratulated Mrs. F on her determination and strength, Mr. F for his ability to offer his wife the support she needed, and Jason for being such a big boy. I expressed a great deal of confidence that an important milestone had been reached here, and that things would go smoothly from now on. Since then, Mrs. F has had no trouble disciplining her son, and Jason's tantrums have all but disappeared.

This case highlights several features about vulnerable children. The recurrence of medical problems early in life often leads parents to view these children as frail and sickly. If there have been frightening events at home (such as cyanotic spells or episodes of bradycardia), parents may be left traumatized. Several close calls in which the child almost dies right before their eyes is enough to cause parents to become constantly frightened and worried about their child's survival.

Beyond the first few months, if the child continues to have medical problems (or develops new ones) requiring hospital stays, the parents will have a harder time accepting the fact that their child is essentially healthy. They will often begin to look for problems if the physician's attempts at reassurance fail. Unwittingly, I was drawn into this pattern when I succumbed to their anxiety about the bruising. In retrospect, my obtaining a hematocrit when it was not really indicated only served to heighten their anxiety. Although it was something of a catch-22 situation, it would have been better if I had challenged their convictions a bit sooner.

Along with the persistent fear of losing the child to some terrible illness, these parents tend to have an extremely hard time setting limits. Either both parents indulge the child, or one parent will and the other one will collude with this behavior so as to avoid conflicts. Once I got the parents to recognize the effect this was having on their son, it was easy for them to use a different approach.

Perhaps the most interesting aspect of this case was the spontaneous manner in which the overdue confrontation between Mrs. F and Jason came about. The perfect opportunity presented itself just at the end of the visit, and instead of allowing it to pass (as would likely happen at home), I was inspired to make full use of it. Once the scene was set, I was able to leave the room and go on seeing patients while keeping one ear tuned to the argument. At certain points, it was essential to reenter the room and provide support to the parents; otherwise they would have given up. My intermittent presence was a reminder that I approved of what was going on, and that I believed they could succeed if they stood firm. This event proved to be a milestone in the family's development.

I wonder how many chances to foster change are missed because physicians are worried that they don't have enough time to spend with a family. Perhaps we need to learn new ways of setting things in motion, remaining nearby to monitor the process, and intermittently intervening at critical moments when we are needed. This would enable us to be more flexible in our work, and more creative with our scheduling. Who says therapy has to take place in 60-minute sessions?

EDITORS' COMMENTS

To casual observers, Dr. Rostain's case may appear to be an example of spontaneous good luck: the family just decided to change. However, the ultimate beneficial outcome occurred in a supportive clinic environment, with parents who had grown to trust their physician, and with the skillful assistance of a confident and creative physician. Setting the stage for the final act of this drama required patience and creating a clinic milieu tolerant of loud parent–child confrontations, respectful of patients and struggling parents, and receptive to unplanned interventions in the office.

Dr. Rostain could have succumbed to the temptation to scapegoat one or the other parent for not sticking to the original treatment plan. With a few angry, critical remarks to Mrs. F about not cooperating, coupled with a knowing glance to her husband, this physician might unwittingly have locked the mother into a prolonged role as an overwhelmed parent. It would have been another example of "inadequate mothering." This physician, who is trained in family therapy skills, chose another plan. Everyone benefited from his decision. A creative second effort helped a family readjust and move toward new levels of development. Indeed, therapy does not necessarily require 60-minute sessions, or even a couch.

A PATIENT WITH APHASIA

SUSANA SEGRE
National Institute of Mental Health
Private practice, Buenos Aires, Argentina

For 3 years, I worked full-time in the Research and Rehabilitation Center for the Aphasic. By carefully studying and observing the traditional therapeutic methods, fundamentally derived from the biomedical model, I was determined to develop a new scheme based on the biopsychosocial model.

Angel was a physically and intellectually well-endowed, single man, who studied in the university toward a career in teaching. When he was 43 years old, an ischemic vascular accident in the middle cerebral artery area produced a right paraplegia and total aphasia. The damage was very acute, with an almost complete loss of speech function although comprehension was relatively intact.

When the critical phase of the patient's condition was over, he was admitted to the rehabilitation unit of the hospital. After 6 months, a complete review was done of the progress of the patient, and during a meeting with the neurology staff, the team decided to move the patient to a private clinic that specialized in aphasia.

Angel was admitted to the Research and Rehabilitation Center for the Aphasic as an outpatient. The professional staff planned a treatment of speech therapy complemented by physiotherapy sessions and occupational therapy. A very difficult and slow process of recovery was expected, but there was hope for some limited progress. The treatment was followed as initially planned for 3 months without any improvement.

In the phonoaudiology sessions, the patient was depressed and discouraged, and therefore new and different experimental techniques were applied to better treat his speech problem. There was some reactive speech provoked by chance or by external stimulation, but it did not become voluntary. The patient could not express himself by his own initiative. After 6 months of frustrated attempts, he was classified as an "irreversible patient." He was going to be discharged soon, as his symbolic system did not function and his verbal expression was purely automatic and useless for communication. He was considered incapable of participating in the treatment. It was very difficult for the treatment team to accept this fact. The impossibility of treating this patient caused institutional problems, because the severity of the neurologic injury was not a sufficient explanation for the vicissitudes of the rehabilitation. There was a psychologist with the therapeutic team, but as long as the patient did not have any speech, the psychologist's intervention was considered impossible.

I had been on staff at the Center for a while but had not been part of Angel's treatment team. I was looking for new channels of investigation with aphasics, hoping to enlarge the treatment options. I was very much interested in Angel's case, and at my initiative was put in charge of it. I knew the magnitude of the task with such a difficult patient, but because of my research interests, I wanted to work with him even though he was considered untreatable.

Together with the neurologist, I reviewed the clinical history and the therapeutic plan. I was surprised by the amount of information gathered related to the aphasic syndrome and its cerebral location compared to the lack of personal references about the patient. This situation made me ask the doctor how it was possible to work with a patient when no one knew who he was and who he had been. The neurologist said that the level of Angel's aphasia made it difficult to question him, so no personal information was gathered, and, according to the neurologist, was not necessary. However, I considered this lack of information a very significant omission.

Reviewing the therapeutic treatment, I observed that the functional problems were treated in a disconnected way, which established a distance between the team and the patient as a person. During 6 months of therapy, the therapist used very rigid techniques that served to emphasize the patient's deficits. Over the course of treatment, some techniques were modified, but the therapist always followed the prescribed protocol.

My impression was that this case was handled in such a way that the psychosocial problems associated with the disease were reinforced and probably added to the patient's confusion and dependency. I planned to work with the family not only to enrich our perception of the problem but also as a therapeutic strategy, capable of counteracting the patient's dismal situation.

Angel and his mother, Mrs. R, came to the family interview, and they impressed me as a crippled couple, one in which it was difficult to determine which of them was the patient. It was a surprise to know that they were mother and son. Mrs. R spoke for the patient. She told me that he had always been an aloof person, with no men or women friends. The father, who was always an absent figure, had died when Angel was an adolescent. The patient was an only child. In name selection, parents usually look for a story that depicts their own wish for the child. I asked about the name, and Mrs. R said, "He will be my guardian angel." I associated the name Angel to the Greek meaning—messenger—really a paradox for an aphasic!

The two had lived in a situation of extreme isolation that was exacerbated after the death of the father. Angel had remained devotedly dedicated to his mother.

During the first session, the following situation was revealed: Angel was aphasic, without speech, but his silence was not empty. It had the function of allowing his mother extended speech without questions, without openings, but closed to my intervention. When I focused on the subject of the cerebral-vascular accident and its vicissitudes, the problem became inaccessible. All information ceased, and neither expressed feelings of abandonment or anguish. I asked myself, what problem are they trying to handle with that behavior? I believed that in reality the aphasia came to close an unconscious deal between both of them, guaranteeing their narcissistic ties.

"Only I understand my son and can do something for him," said Mrs. R. And the patient seemed to surrender his vital strength to his mother while she defined herself as his unique guarantee for being.

All of this partially clarified the failure of the rehabilitation. Neither doctors nor therapists could work with Angel. There was no place for third parties, but the therapeutic context contributed to maintaining the pathological ties.

In the following sessions, I proposed to Angel the utilization of other than verbal ways of expression that could serve as transmission channels, and that I would try to understand. His choice was paper and pencil, and he started to draw. His drawings were his way of writing. Among the different shapes Angel drew, I was able to see into Angel's broken world. I started giving sense to his drawings verbally, as well as using his same code by modifying his drawings or designing new drawings. In this way, we inaugurated a relationship method that thawed something that was frozen, opening a dialogue and emission–reception that went both ways. His attitude improved as he was able to actively communicate, not just react rigidly to his surroundings. As a consequence, there were also positive changes in his mother's attitude. I understood that my function was to act as a regulator in this primitive family relationship. By introducing myself into this paralyzing mother–son relationship, I facilitated a more dynamic bond, thereby allowing the patient to recover his self expression and his awareness of himself as a human being.

I involved Mrs. R in her son's treatment with four goals in mind.

1. To help her understand the reasons why her participation in Angel's rehabilitation was absolutely indispensable by providing miss-

ing psychosocial information, and through concrete therapeutic action aimed at helping her understand her son's disease. This means that I looked for the development of a rational behavior, and not just a purely intuitive behavior, on the mother's part.

2. To help Mrs. R resolve the everyday problems that arose in the family group as a result of the chronic disease of her son's behavior modification. This had a restoring effect on Mrs. R because it was she who promoted the change through a sort of autorehabilitation.

3. To help Mrs. R to be able to express the depression caused by Angel's aphasia. To do this, I presented myself as an attentive listener who issued no judgments about Mrs. R or Angel. I validated her feelings and helped her to see that even though she and her son were bonded by his disease, she would not lose him if he improved.

4. To preserve the family homeostasis. I worked with Mrs. R and Angel and provided a continuity of care for this family during follow-up interviews and tried to promote the conditions that would establish a healthier mother–son relationship.

This was a very significant case for me because I was able to apply not only my scientific and technical expertise, but also my spiritual and cultural knowledge as well. Each session with Angel was resolved in an increasingly creative way. My purpose was to give more and more light, and more and more life to Angel.

In my opinion, a rehabilitation program should have been developed that could respond to the changes that occurred in the patient. I had talks with the institutional staff, and I understood that they were not prepared to establish a link of larger contact with the patient because deep inside they were all afraid of the madness and death associated with aphasics. The staff had to cut themselves off from Angel and his disease, so they concentrated only on the speech pathology. This way they could protect themselves from the pain of experiencing the patient as a human being.

Carefully and softly, I presented my impressions about this case and found great resistance at first. Nevertheless, I persisted with my efforts to help the therapeutic staff help this patient. I was admired by some and rejected by others. My way of working was certainly daring, since I questioned the traditional approaches to treatment. Eventually, my success with Angel gained acceptance, and was even considered exemplary, so my clinical duties were extended to other cases. The institutional staff have now begun a more comprehensive approach to patient treatment and care, and they have accepted my suggestions for starting a Balint group.

EDITORS' COMMENTS

We will comment on just one aspect of this lovely case from a family therapist in Argentina. Taking a biopsychosocial approach and involving the family in the treatment of an obviously biomedical problem is likely to stir up considerable resistance in the health care team. This is especially true when, as Dr. Segre points out, the staff are defending themselves against the frightening aspects of problems such as brain damage conditions. However, if the physician or therapist shows the same patience and systemic understanding with the staff as with the patient and family, then success in initial cases can lead to changed minds and hearts among the staff. The most significant evidence of this change in the present case is the staff's openness to starting a Balint group for exploring personal reactions to their relationships with patients. Sometimes, cases such as this one can be watershed experiences for the whole therapeutic system, and thereby influence the care of innumerable patients to follow.

TRIANGULATION, FEAR, AND UNCERTAINTY IN TREATING AN AIDS PATIENT

JOHN S. ROLLAND
Yale University
Center for Illness in Families, New Haven, Connecticut

Mr. T was a 30-year-old, married executive with a lifelong history of hemophilia. He was diagnosed with acquired immune deficiency syndrome (AIDS) in February 1984. Four months later, he and his wife were referred to me for couples therapy through the psychiatric consultation–liaison service of a major university hospital. At the time of referral, he had been admitted for workup of gastrointestinal bleeding. Diagnostic tests revealed a small gastric ulcer. Concern about the relationship between the psychosocial impact of AIDS and Mr. T's ulcer led to an initial request for psychiatric evaluation.

Mr. T's past history with hemophilia had been relatively benign; he had required occasional factor VIII infusions after trauma. In December 1983, 15 months prior to his diagnosis, Mr. T had received an infusion of factor VIII pooled cryoprecipitate. Eleven months later, he began to experience increasing malaise, fatigue, decreased appetite, a 35-pound weight loss, recurrent sore throats, low-grade fever, night sweats, and lymphadenopathy. In February 1984, he developed shortness of breath, pleuritic chest pain and clear-yellow productive sputum. Subsequent hospitalization revealed *Pneumocystis carinii* pneumonia and reduced peripheral blood T-cell lymphocytes. A presumptive diagnosis of AIDS was made based on these objective findings and complex of symptoms. In the ensuing months, Mr. T required readmissions for persistent headaches and fever of unexplained origin in March 1984; for a thymus transplant to his left forearm in June 1984; for a workup for his gastrointestinal bleeding in July 1984; for a second thymus transplant and esophageal candidiasis in October 1984; and a follow-up 2-week intravenous infusion of interleukin II in November 1984. The admissions for thymus transplant and interleukin II were elective experimental protocol procedures designed to regenerate and stimulate new T-cell lymphocyte production. None of these experimental trials had succeeded.

I would like to focus on a series of consultations that occurred during Mr. T's admission in November 1984. To provide a context, let me first give a backdrop of the couple's relationship, their relationship to the medical center, and their prior therapeutic work with me.

Mr. and Mrs. T had been married for 3 years, after a courtship of 1½ years, and had no children. Both were engaging, intelligent, thoughtful, and very successful in their young careers working for large organizations. Both come from families of divorce in which their fathers were viewed as being prone to emotional weakness under stress. Mr. T had a strong internal sense of self-control and mastery over all facets of his life including life-threatening illness. He disdained dependency and lack of personal control. This complemented his wife's wish for a strong, self-sufficient partner. Mr. T was meticulous about details and had voraciously sought and assimilated information related to his medical condition. Since his diagnosis, he had attempted, in a perfectionistic manner, to control his personal environment through diet modification, graded exercise, elimination of environmental hazards, and general stress reduction.

Mr. T expected precise, coordinated, first-rate care from the medical team. His intensity and his demanding style had frequently intimidated or alienated members of the medical team, especially nurses and less experienced house staff. Mr. T had a keen sense for noticing and pointing out individual or hospital system weak points. His presentation with AIDS and hemophilia, combined with difficult-to-manage complications and experimental treatments, had led to the involvement of many physicians. He had frequently complained of the lack of physician coordination and a consistent, identified medical team leader. When dissatisfied, Mr. T freely showed his anger and frustration. The couple's view that medical negligence was directly responsible for Mr. T's developing AIDS is critical to understanding their demanding, angry, and somewhat distrustful stance towards the medical team. They maintained that the original infusion with pooled factor VIII (drawn from a number of donors) had greatly multiplied his risk of contagion.

By contrast, Mrs. T was mild mannered, but actively supported her husband's feisty "go-for-it" attitude. However, her fear of his anger often led her either to protectively placate him while swallowing her own feelings, or to act as a softening buffer between him and others. Part of my therapeutic work had focused on his finding other appropriate outlets for his anger, and her assuming a less protective posture while also taking more risks expressing her own needs.

Many AIDS patients in the region seek treatment at this medical center because of the university's prestige and the presence of an internationally respected immunologist who takes a major interest in serving AIDS patients and doing research. An outpatient AIDS clinical service with a psychosocial component has been established. A number of mental health professionals and leaders in the gay community have formed a volunteer organization to provide additional supportive care to patients and their families. They work in close cooperation with the AIDS clinic. However, inside the hospital, AIDS patients are admitted to a variety of clinical services depending on the reason for admission (type of complication, treatment, etc.). Both the fear of contracting

AIDS in an atmosphere of uncertainty as to *all* the modes of transmission, and the strain of coping with terminally ill, hopeless patients contribute to a tense, emotionally volatile environment among unit staff. In particular, nurses who have to work in frequent, close contact with these patients seem among the most distressed.

When Mr. T was admitted in November for his 2-week interleukin II infusion, he stayed on a clinical research unit that had had little prior contact with AIDS patients. Fortuitously, I had an informal liaison relationship with this unit. At their request, I had provided the nursing staff with a miniseries on family systems and medical illness, and then continued, on a biweekly basis, to discuss with them family-oriented psychosocial management of difficult cases.

On this occasion, knowing my involvement with the couple, the nursing staff launched into an animated discussion that centered on three main issues: their growing intolerance of his demanding and intimidating style, their fears about getting AIDS themselves, and their concern that the couple were continuing sexual intercourse and intimate kissing despite recent reports of virus transmission through semen and saliva. One nurse, in the process of talking informally with the couple, had discovered their ignorance on this issue despite the fact that published reports had appeared months earlier. The couple denied being informed of this risk by any of the physicians and were distrustful and angered to get this kind of news through "second-line" medical professionals.

In the same vein, several nurses vented their own fears of contracting AIDS and endangering their own family members. Mr. T had, in an irritated and intimidating fashion, confronted nurses about the superfluousness of their following and sometimes augmenting (e.g., wearing two pairs of surgical gloves) standard hospital contagion precautions. To dramatize concern, one nurse threw down on the table a newly published report of a 70-year-old woman who had contracted AIDS from her spouse. Nursing staff complained of their own sense of isolation and of the lack of consistent support and coordination from physicians within the hospital community in working with AIDS patients. During the discussion, I became painfully aware of my own fears, my sense of isolation as a private practitioner providing my piece of the care, and the couple's denial and isolation. There was an unusual drawing together as we saw our commonality with the couple in vulnerability and confusion—an ad hoc larger family that had become fragmented. The physicians, nursing staff, and couple constituted a triangle of stressful relationships, in which expression of these tensions were occurring primarily between the couple and the nursing staff. The several physicians involved in his care resembled a distant, workaholic spouse/father. I encouraged a more assertive but nonblaming stance by nursing staff vis-à-vis the physicians. Their providing a protective buffer for the doctors under high-stress circumstances was heightening distance and resentment. In this regard, the physicians' and nurses' relationship was isomorphic with the couple's. Also, I supported the need to define appropriate limits on Mr. T's expression of anger in the context of other necessary unit functions.

Using the issue of the couple's high-risk sexual contact as a focus, we strategized a unit staff conference that would include nursing staff, the medical resident, Mr. T's attending physician (the immunologist), and myself. It was felt that the couple needed to hear of these risks from the most authoritative person on the team, the attending physician. As a physician, I assumed responsibility for calling my colleagues to arrange a meeting at their convenience. This was accomplished at the end of my meeting with the nurses while we were still gathered in the conference room.

Immediately following my meeting with the nursing staff, I met with the couple and included the unit head nurse for part of the session. The couple seemed genuinely relieved and hopeful about the planned medical team meeting. I shared my formulation of some of the larger system issues stressing the common themes: fear of contagion, fragmentation of care, and overprotectiveness. I stressed that intimidation would only further undercut the nursing staff's ability to provide professional help. Mr. T softened, and a fruitful discussion ensued with the head nurse. Following the nurses' lead in expressing their fears of contagion and their suggestion of a team meeting to work toward a less protective stance toward the physicians, Mrs. T was more frank about her fears of catching AIDS and her own emotional needs. Fears about lack of control over the illness and possible loss were expressed more candidly. This undercut the denial in the couple's relationship, and they began a painful but open, supportive dialogue.

The medical team case conference went smoothly. The attending physician and resident listened attentively to nursing staff concerns about the couple and what the nurses felt they needed from the physicians. Since the attending physician took care of a majority of the

AIDS patients seen at the hospital, his advice and reassurance about contagion control were very helpful in reducing anxiety. More frequent and coordinated communication was agreed upon. I discussed my concerns vis-à-vis the couple, and their need for clarification and direct advice about how to alter their sexual life. We briefly discussed a strategy for the attending physician's meeting with the couple that included my views of their relationship dynamics. The following day, the physician met with the couple and they agreed to the recommended changes. Then, I met with the couple to discuss further the emotional impact of the proposed changes.

I feel that this series of consultations and interventions had an effect on a number of interlocking subsystem relationships: (1) the couple's, (2) the nurse-physician medical team's, (3) the medical team and the patient-spouse, leading to a more balanced supportive system. particular, my role as a liaison-consultant allowed me flexibility to propose change in the triangle involving the physician, nursing staff, and the patient-spouse, leading to a more balanced supportive system.

EDITORS' COMMENTS

Dr. Rolland's creative interventions demonstrate his unusual skill in providing support and therapy at multiple levels of systems. Contextual understanding of the patient's problem of AIDS inexorably led to involving all the different groups in the treatment plan. An intervention excluding any of the major characters in this drama might have been futile. After careful orchestration by Dr. Rolland, the patient and family were able to express their feelings directly to the physicians, and the physicians were able to communicate accurate information directly to the patient and his spouse. Fear and anger were dissipated to manageable levels.

In this case, a family-centered approach to the patient demanded from the therapist a sophisticated multifaceted plan affecting all levels of health care providers. A psychiatrist trained in family therapy, Dr. Rolland provided therapy to the larger medical and family systems. We may need to look to this example for guidance as the AIDS epidemic unfolds.

CONCLUSION

THE STATE OF THE ART IN FAMILY-CENTERED MEDICAL CARE

The cases in this book are like detailed photographs of many encounters with patients and families. In this chapter, we will assemble the photographs into a collage that expresses the patterns and themes we see in the cases. We will also attempt to describe the current state of the art in family-centered medical care in North America. By "state of the art" we mean the practices of physicians who are actively committed to understanding the patient's psychosocial context and to involving families in the care of patients. Although they do not represent all family-centered physicians, nonetheless many of the authors in this casebook work at the creative forefront of biopsychosocial, family-centered medical care. By analyzing their cases and summarizing the survey information they gave us about their training, experience, and everyday clinical practice, we hope to distill the essence and the variations of family-centered medical care in the mid-1980s. This discussion will be in two parts: first, the foundations of family-centered medical care as we see them expressed in the cases and authors' surveys; and second, the practical aspects.

THREE PILLARS OF FAMILY-CENTERED MEDICAL CARE

Problem Solving by Expanding the Context

A common theme in these cases is the physician's desire to better understand difficult patient problems. The perplexing diagnostic presentation, the failure to respond predictably to conventional therapies, the patient's or family's surprising level of emotion—these situations stimulate the physician to seek more information through expanding the context of the problem beyond its biological dimensions. The physician accompanies the patient on a journey leading to more complex understanding about the psychological and social issues intertwined with the biological ones. In some cases, exploring these wider issues with the individual patient alone reveals the likely sources of the medical problem, as in Dan Rains's case of the sexually abused patient with headaches. In other cases, only a meeting with a couple or family can unlock the door to the secret, painful issues underlying the problem. Either way, the physician has an "aha" experience at the moment when grasping the larger context of the problem makes what was puzzling understandable, and what was hopeless from a biomedical perspective suddenly hopeful from a biopsychosocial perspective.

Even when the patient and family do not share this problem-solving journey with the physician—when they hold to narrow biomedical understandings, offer contextual information begrudgingly, and decline to work on psychosocial issues—the physician may derive satisfaction from at least having better understood the problem. In Dr. Rains's case cited above, when the physician realized that the woman's medical problems were probably related to the abuse she had experienced, he could proceed with more clinical wisdom than before he knew this information, even though the patient was not yet willing to work on her own problems. Clinical wisdom can mean that the doctor and the patient avoid taking an expensive biomedical journey that neither will find satisfying.

Family physicians spend most of their time figuring out clinical problems. They enjoy the intellectual challenge of making sense out of an apparently unrelated complex of symptoms that have not been analyzed by another physician. Even when they feel sad about diagnosing a life-threatening disease in a patient with puzzling symptoms, they often feel a sense of satisfaction that their diagnostic skills made sense out of the ominous uncertainty. Similarly, the physician who pursues the psychosocial dimensions of a problem frequently achieves satisfaction derived from having a clearer picture of "what's really going on." As a final example of this phenomenon, consider a situation in which the physician discovers, through contact with the family, that a patient whose hypertension is chronically uncontrolled despite adequate medication compliance is an active alcoholic. Even if the patient and family are not willing to pursue treatment for the alcoholism, the physician now understands the medical problem in its context. The patient and doctor now may be able to agree that it would be useless and possibly dangerous to pursue more potent medications while the patient continues to use alcohol.

Physicians, then, are practical problem solvers, and pursuing the larger context of a patient's problems seems to help solve problems. This appears to be a major reason why the authors of the cases in this book decided to involve families in their clinical practices.

CARING FOR THE PATIENT ENOUGH TO CARE FOR THE FAMILY

Balancing the intellectual problem-solving pillar is the emotional investment that case authors so clearly made in their patients. For a physician curious about the psychosocial context of the patient's problem, caring is the only doorway to this information. When people become medical patients, they hand over their physical privacy to a physician, but most will not permit a physician to explore their painful psychosocial interior unless they sense that the physician's care for them as a person is genuine. Patients usually safeguard their psychological privacy and family privacy, and let down these barriers only with the physicians who seem humanly concerned.

There is nothing new about this idea. Caring deeply about patients has been an axiom as long as medicine has existed as a profession. However, the corollary we derive from reading the cases in this book is as follows: Caring for the family is an extension of caring for the patient. There are two important implications of this corollary for family-centered medical care. First, even in a family-centered approach, the physician's relationship with the patient who seeks medical help is still the cornerstone of the therapeutic system that includes the family, the patient, the physician, and others. It is only through a caring and problem-solving relationship with the patient that the physician gains the *right* to explore the psychosocial interior of the patient's family. Second, care for the patient naturally spills over into care for the family. Caring about the patient's pain over an unhappy marriage suggests the step of asking the patient to invite the spouse to the office for a consultation. Caring about the stroke patient who is fearful about going home suggests meeting with the family to work through everyone's fears, and to make plans for the homecoming. Caring about a dying patient suggests caring about the already grieving family. Furthermore, as Ransom (1985) has observed, a family-centered approach can make the doctor–patient relationship healthier than a relationship in which the doctor's caring gives the illusion that the doctor can be all things to the patient.

From this perspective, there is no necessary contradiction between patient-centered medical care and family-centered medical care. The latter builds upon the former, and the former is limited without the latter. Both in turn are aspects of inclusive biopsychosocial medical care (Doherty, Baird, & Becker, 1986; Engel, 1977). Every experience in training or in practice that helps the physician achieve emotional connection with a patient and a family is a powerful contribution to the development of a patient-centered physician, a family-centered physician, and a biopsychosocially oriented physician.

This is not a book about teaching students and residents. However, we want to observe that the deck is stacked heavily against students and residents learning to practice family-centered medical care in hospital settings where they are not encouraged to form close relationships with patients. On most hospital services, patients have no personal context visible to the students and residents; that is, they have no personal past or future, nothing that makes them unique. These patients appear suddenly in a resident's life for biomedical assessment and treatment, and will vanish forever within a few days or a few weeks. In this environment, it takes extraordinary efforts to connect personally and caringly with the patient. A family-centered approach in a hospital setting will be successful only to the extent that students and residents are helped to relate to and eventually care about patients as complex human beings. The next step of family involvement then becomes achievable with encouragement from faculty, because care for the patient tends to spill over into care for the family.

EXTRA EFFORT AND EXTRA COURAGE

In reviewing the cases, we were struck repeatedly by the fact that the physician walked the extra mile with the patient and family, sometimes over treacherous terrain. Sometimes, the physician made a home visit when an office appointment or emergency room contact would have sufficed. Sometimes, the physician persisted in encouraging the family in their resolve to have the patient die at home, even when the family members were saying that they felt like giving up. After encountering resistance from the patient or family about the possibility of a family problem contributing to the medical condition, the physician gently but steadfastly brought it up again, and then again. Although we do not want to depict these physicians as heroes, nevertheless they frequently went beyond what is routinely expected of physicians in our culture in caring for patients.

Ironically, many of these physicians told us in their surveys that the extra effort involved in talking in depth with patients and families pays off for them in more job satisfaction and in subsequent savings in time and effort spent on the case. For example, the Saturday morning family meeting that Terence McCormally and Katherine Cole had with an alcoholic family may have significant payoffs over many years through fewer emergency room trips for the physicians. To paraphrase the television commercial for oil filters, for complex patient problems, the motto seems to be "Pay me now in extra effort for awhile, or pay me later in routine effort that may never end."

Accompanying the extra effort put into the cases was personal courage in the physician. In our view, the greatest courage in patient care is to feel the patient's and family's pain and anger, and not to run or hide. Dennis McCullough, when faced with a hostile, miserable family, stayed with them long enough to uncover the guilt and resentment surrounding the mother's injury. The second-greatest courage is to be vulnerable enough to admit to a patient and family one's own confusion, uncertainty, and unhelpful behavior. Jim McCoy told his female patient that he was allowing himself to get too close to her and thereby was replacing her husband. The third-greatest courage is to bring up issues with a patient and family that are redolent of secrecy and anxiety for everyone. Steve Spann did this by talking with a teenage boy and his mother about incestuous feelings and behavior.

Family-centered medical care, then, sometimes involves significant personal risk and unusual personal effort. It is not just another tool in the physician's bag of techniques. Getting close to patients and families means running risks that should not be approached lightly.

HOW FAMILY-CENTERED CARE IS PRACTICED

Here we present a summary of the experiences of our casebook authors as communicated in a survey we conducted of their experiences with family-centered patient care. The survey was a simple homespun questionnaire rather than a carefully developed and validated instrument; the goal was to compile an overview of the authors' training and practice experiences. Although we also surveyed the family therapists and other authors who were not family physicians, this discussion will be limited to the family physician respondents.

The 50 family physician authors ranged in clinical experience from 1 year to 37 years, with a median of 8 years. Eleven are in full-time private practice; another 20 had private practice experience before moving to teaching positions. The rest have been based primarily in teaching programs. Twelve physicians had formal family therapy training after residency; the rest learned from a variety of sources, including residency curricula, readings, continuing medical education workshops, and work with therapy consultants.

When asked what initially attracted them to a family-centered approach, most replied with some variant of the theme that exploring the family context of the medical problems helped them to find answers to puzzling questions. Some of the physicians came to this realization in training, while many others experienced a shift in their framework after several years of practice when they found themselves frustrated with the limitations of the biomedical model. Attending to family and other psychosocial contexts helped them cope with the perplexing patient problems they faced in practice.

How do these physicians practice medicine in a family-centered way? In most cases, they see individual patients while being attuned to the patient's psychosocial context. The family-centered approach is first of all a *way of thinking* for these physicians. Secondarily, meeting with couples and families is a way of gathering data and intervening in selected cases. The typical physician in the survey meets with couples or families 3 to 5 times per week for 30 to 45 minutes in the office or hospital; a few have 15 or more family conferences per week. These meetings are in addition to routine contacts with family members who bring patients to the office or who visit them in the hospital. Although we did not ask specifically about how often the physicians tend to meet with particular families, the cases in this book suggest that from one to a few sessions is the norm. The most common charge for these conferences is the regular fee for an extended office visit.

The physicians in this book are most apt to convene family conferences around serious or chronic illness and the dying process.

The majority deal with psychosocial issues insofar as these issues interact with medical illness. The exception is the 10 family physician/family therapists who are more apt to treat families with problems traditionally viewed as psychosocial, for example, marital conflict and depression. Some of these physician/therapists carry formal family therapy caseloads in addition to their medical practices, with many of their referrals coming from other physicians.

Finally, 26 of the 50 physicians surveyed have family therapy consultants available to them. Some physicians in private practice expressed frustration about problems obtaining third-party reimbursement for family therapists who worked in their offices. Maintaining an in-office family therapist on a fee-for-service basis without third-party payment appears to be quite difficult.

IMPACT OF WORKING WITH FAMILIES ON THE PHYSICIANS

In the survey, we asked the physicians about how their work with families has influenced their attitudes, practices, and satisfaction as a physician and person. Because this is a self-selected sample, and because we were asking for testimonials, we want to avoid implying that family-centered medical care is akin to a toothpaste that will eliminate decay and renew your sex life. Nevertheless, the respondents' statements impressively document how central the family perspective is to most of them.

The overall impression we derive from the physicians we surveyed is that working with families helps them to do a better job as physicians in treating medical problems. They engage in lots of routine medical work, but are alert to expanding the context of the problem when that seems appropriate. Here is how Leonard Roberts states it:

> People come to the doctor with a problem. Many are common and easily managed issues that are strictly biomedical—no family understanding required (or invited), no context beyond the obvious needed, diagnosis clear, management clear. But a significant number of presenting issues (and all patients over time) are best understood in context of that human life (family, job, daily routine, etc.) and how the problem affects it. To understand and explore these issues requires skill and training of the physician and the permission or mandate of the client.

After practicing with this framework for a number of years, many physicians experience it as central to their way of practicing and to their professional satisfaction. As Stephen Taplin writes, "I can't imagine practicing any other way. It's at the core of who I am and what I have to offer as a physician." After 25 years of private practice experience, Milton Seifert states, "It is more satisfying to include family factors because I cannot practice as competently without a family approach. There really isn't an alternative." Reflecting on both the risks and the gains in working with families, Roger Bermingham wrote, "When I first started working with families I was quite scared. I figured I was going to screw up somehow. I still feel that way, but I get a great deal of satisfaction out of helping families out." A number of physicians also commented on the positive influences of family work on their own family relationships.

What are some of the frustrations? It is difficult to practice contextually-sensitive medicine in a culture and a medical environment that is frequently not geared to this perspective. As Godfrey Ripley states, "[Working with families has] increased my perception and satisfaction—but *some* patients have not appreciated my interests!" This kind of patient care can feel like an intrusion to some patients, although Baird's experience is that most patients come to value the approach over time (Doherty & Baird, 1983). A second problem concerns the fit between talking in depth with patients and the demands of a busy medical practice. Quoting again from Stephen Taplin, "There are frustrating times when I have to 'put the blinders on' and forge ahead because of time pressures. This may happen in the course of a day when my schedule is backed up and a difficult patient, an alcoholic, a behavioral problem or some red flag goes up which I address on a strictly biomedical level. It feels superficial, like I've cheated the patient . . . but kept on schedule." The physician's own context, then, is as important as the patient's context. Some days the physician's context constrains the exploration of the patient's context. Fortunately, in primary care physician–patient relationships, there usually comes another day and another opportunity.

The third problem, brought up primarily by physicians with private practice experience, is reimbursement. Although most charge an extended office visit fee for a couple or family conference, sometimes this amount only partially compensates for the physician's time. The Canadian physicians appear to have the easiest experience with compensation, since provincial health insurance plans reimburse them for family conferences. For many U. S. physicians, the challenge is whether to charge fully for time spent with a family, often without third-party payment in the outpatient setting, or to reduce the fee routinely. We have several observations about this problem: First, since the average number of specially arranged couple or family conferences among even committed physicians is likely to be no more than one per day, the financial impact is not likely to be significant for the physician's overall income; second, since the average number of sessions a particular family would attend is quite low, the financial impact on most families should be small; third, we have found that physicians who are confident in their family counseling skills tend to charge fully for their time and receive the payment (Doherty & Baird, 1983); and fourth, lowering or waiving fees for patients who are financially strapped is no different for family conferences than it is for regular medical visits.

Because of these observations, we view the physician compensation issue as a nagging but not disabling problem for family-centered physicians. Compensation for in-office family therapists, especially in low-income areas, is a tougher problem. (Michael Glenn has struggled with this problem in his private practice.) Family therapists, unlike family physicians, spend most of their time delivering psychosocial services. These services are inadequately reimbursed by insurance and are likely to be costly to the patient because of the greater frequency of sessions for therapy than for primary care family counseling. Since having a family therapist consultant close by seems to help family physicians work effectively with patients' psychosocial context, this problem of compensation for therapists requires serious attention.

CONCLUSION

We believe that the case reports and experiences of the physicians and therapists presented in this book help to bring the area of family-centered medical care to a new level of sophistication and practicality. As editors, we certainly have met our initial need for more understanding of how family physicians who are interested in families actually work with them. What is most striking and reassuring is how these physicians have learned to integrate a family perspective into their everyday work, not as would-be family therapists but as family physicians who use biopsychosocial perspectives to understand and engage their patients.

How much is this approach the "wave of the future"? No one can say, but the movement seems to be gaining momentum in family medicine, as demonstrated by an increasing number of books, articles, and workshops. Obviously we welcome this growing trend toward family-centered medical care. However, we find it useful to recite a number of warnings to temper our own enthusiasm. First, we must avoid the myopia of viewing the family systems perspective as the only useful way to view complex psychosocial phenomena. As Howard Stein (1985) has argued, there are no royal roads to truth in complex human affairs, and the "family" perspective will get us nowhere if it becomes a constricting ideology. Second, we must avoid dichotomizing patient-centered care and family-centered care; as stated earlier, they are aspects of each other. Third, we must continue to develop an integrative biopsychosocial framework for family medicine, and not stop short at more narrow family systems theories that do not incorporate biological variables and sometimes shortchange psychological variables (Doherty et al., 1986). Fourth, we must honestly acknowledge the paucity of research data on the process and outcome of family-centered approaches in medicine, and we must support careful studies in this area. Finally, we must resist the temptation, common in "movements," to splinter into rival factions practicing their own brand of family-centered medical care while denigrating the other brands. On this point, we are happy that many of the creative leaders in family-centered medical care contributed cases to this book.

We close with a quote from William Miller, whose cases read like poetry. His survey ends with these words:

> Once you have joined with a family, shared your candlelight, and together found a path through the dark clouds of illness, the attachment that results between that family and you is at least as powerful and beautiful as the bond that forms when you have the privilege of participating with a family in the birth of a new member. This privilege is not free; it creates a special covenant. It means you feel tragedy more deeply, cry more often, never take your own family for granted, greet each sunrise with more gratitude. It means you celebrate life. The pressures and responsibilities that frequently seek to overwhelm the practicing physician and convert hope into cynicism are transformed back into hope when you expand the presenting problem to include the family living the problem. This is the special joy of being a family doctor.

REFERENCES

Baird, M. A. (1985). Chemical dependency: A protocol for involving the family. *Family Systems Medicine, 3,* 216–220.

Baird, M. A., & Doherty, W. J. (1986). Family resources in coping with serious illness. In M. A. Karpel (Ed.), *Family resources: The hidden partner in family therapy.* New York: Guilford Press.

Banahan, B. F., & Abbott, L. (1983, May). *The keeper syndrome.* Paper presented at the Society of Teachers of Family Medicine Spring Conference, Boston, MA.

Bowen, M. (1976). *Family therapy in clinical practice.* New York: Jason Aronson.

Christie-Seely, J. (Ed.). (1984). *Working with families in primary care.* New York: Praeger.

Doherty, W. J. (1985). Family interventions in health care. *Family Relations, 34,* 129–137.

Doherty, W. J., & Baird, M. A. (1983). *Family therapy and family medicine: Toward the primary care of families.* New York: Guilford Press.

Doherty, W. J., & Baird, M. A. (1986). Developmental levels of physician involvement with families. *Family Medicine, 18,* 153–156.

Doherty, W. J., Baird, M. A., & Becker, L. A. (1986). Family medicine and the biopsychosocial model: The road toward integration. In W. J. Doherty, C. E. Christianson, & M. B. Sussman (Eds.), *Family medicine: The maturing of a discipline.* New York: Haworth Press.

Engel, G. L. (1977). The need for a new medical model: A challenge for biomedicine. *Science, 196,* 129–136.

Fisch, R., Weakland, J., & Segal, L. (1982). *The tactics of change: Doing therapy briefly.* San Francisco: Jossey-Bass.

Friedman, E. (1985). *Generation to generation: Family process in church and synagogue.* New York: Guilford Press.

Glenn, M. (1985). *On diagnosis.* New York: Brunner/Mazel.

Haley, J. (1976). *Problem-solving therapy.* New York: Harper & Row.

Huygen, F. J. A. (1982). *Family medicine: The medical life history of families.* New York: Brunner/Mazel.

Laing, R. D. (1969). *The politics of the family and other essays.* London: Tavistock.

Mace, N. L., & Rabins, P. V. (1981). *The 36 hour day.* Baltimore, MD: Johns Hopkins University Press.

Madanes, C. (1982). *Strategic family therapy.* London: Jossey-Bass.

Minuchin, S., & Fishman, C. H. (1981). *Family therapy techniques.* Cambridge, MA: Harvard University Press.

Minuchin, S., Rosman, B. L., & Baker, L. (1978). *Psychosomatic families: Anorexia nervosa in context.* Cambridge, MA: Harvard University Press.

Preker, S. A. (1984). *The symptomatic aged: Family dysfunction expressed through symptomatic behavior in the elderly.* Paper presented at the International Association of Gerontology, New York.

Ransom, D. C. (1985). Random notes: The unconventional future of family medicine. *Family Systems Medicine, 3,* 120-126.

Ruberman, W., Weinblatt, E., Goldberg, J. D., & Chandhary, B. S. (1984). Psychosocial influences on mortality after myocardial infarction. *New England Journal of Medicine, 311,* 552-559.

Sawa, R. J. (1985). *Family dynamics for physicians: Guidelines to assessment and treatment,* Lewiston, NY/Queenstown, Ontario: Edwin Mellon Press.

Seelbach, W. C. (1978). Correlates of aged parents' filial responsibility expectations. *Family Coordinator, 27,* 341-350.

Selvini-Palazzoli, M., Boscolo, L., Cecchin, G., & Prata, G. (1980). The problem of the referring person. *Journal of Marital and Family Therapy, 6,* 3-9.

Stein, H. F. (1983). The case study method as a means of teaching significant context in family medicine. *Family Medicine, 15,* 163-167.

Stein, H. F. (1985). The hazards of driving on royal roads: A modern parable. *Continuing Education for the Family Physician, 20,* 553-554.

Zuk, G. H. (1975). *Process and practice in family therapy.* Haverford, PA: Psychiatry & Behavioral Science Books.

INDEX

Abandonment, childhood, 270-273
Abdomen, carcinomatosis, 50
Abdominal pain
  boy, stress-related, 170-174, 244-248
    hostile, absent father, 172, 173
    parents' divorce, 245, 246
  girl with infant brother, stress, 205-207
  woman, 185-189
    irritable colon, 185
    psychological asepcts, 187-189
    strict Catholic upbringing, 186-188
  see also Ulcer, peptic, adolescent male
Adenoma, parathyroid, 137
AIDS patient, hemophiliac, 296-301
  factor VIII infusions, 297
  and staff
    demands on, 298-300
    fears of infection, 299, 300
  unsafe sex, 299, 300
Alcoholism, 17, 18, 304, 305, 307
  compared with dementia, elderly man, 133-136
    depressed wife, 133, 136
  father and daughter, 149-152
    father, hypertension, edema, and stasis ulcers, 150, 151
  father and husband, woman with alopecia, 229-231
  suicide attempt/gesture, adolescent girl, 259
Allergies, infant, 107, 108
Alopecia areata, woman with marital problems, 228-231
  abusive alcoholic father and husband, 229-231
  headaches, 228
Alzheimer's disease, 53-57
Alzheimer's Disease and Related Disorders Association (ADRDA), 55
Amputation, diabetes, 36, 37

Amyotrophic lateral sclerosis, 112, 113
Anaplastic adenocarcinoma, metastatic, 87-90
Anemia and colon cancer, 145; *see also* Myeloid metaplasia and myelofibrosis
Aneurysm, high aortic, 11, 12
Anger, repressed, 250, 272, 273
Ankle fracture, 119, 120
Antithrombin III deficiency, inherited, 79-81
Anxiety
  and depression, 19-28
  divorce, 130
  gastrointestinal problems and hyperventilation, adolescent boy, 92-94
  Ménière's disease and spastic bowel syndrome, elderly widow, 155, 156
  peptic ulcer, adolescent boy, 194-196
Apert's syndrome, 43-46
Aphasia, 43-year-old man, 291-296
  depression, 292
  drawing, 294
  lack of information, 293
  mother, close relationship with, 293-295
  reinforcement of psychosocial problems, 293
Argentina, 8
Arteriovenous malformation, 111, 112
Asthma
  and hypertension, 64, 65
  man and son, 275-280
    marital problems, 278, 279
    turntaking pattern in family, 276
    wife's pelvic pain, 275, 276, 280

Back pain, lower, husband and wife, 267-275
  childhood abandonment, 270-273

315

Back pain (continued)
  genograms, 269, 271
  hypertension, 268, 269
  prostatitis, 269, 270
  repressed anger, 272, 273
  school phobia, children, 273
Bed wetting. See Enuresis
Belching, paroxysmal, 90-93
Birth defects. See Apert's syndrome;
    Down's syndrome
Birth to inexperienced couple, 178-182
  epilepsy, 178, 179
  genogram, 180
  low socioeconomic status, 179
  paranoid grandmother, 179, 181
Bone cancer, 80, 81
Breast cancer, 160-164
  anaplastic adenocarcinoma, metastatic, 87-90
    problems with daughter, 88, 89
  German woman, 119-121
    dependence on daughter, 119-121
  openness about death, 161-163
    desire to return home, 161, 162
    elderly mother, 162, 163

Canada, 8, 310, 311
Carcinomatosis, abdomen, 50
Cecum carcinoma, 64-67
Celebrant role, family therapy, 82
Cerebral palsy and mental retardation, son, 79-82
Cerebrovascular accident, aphasia, 43-year-old man, 292, 294
Cesarean section, 43, 44
Chiropractic, 19
Choanal atresia, Down's syndrome baby, 102, 103
Colon
  cancer, 13-15, 49-53, 143-149
  irritable, 185
Congestive heart failure, 68-70, 232, 235
Contact lenses, 255, 256
Craniosynostosis, 44

Day-dreaming, 153, 154
Death, 62, 63
  at home, 51, 78, 79
  mother's, 80, 81
  talking about, 147, 148, 161-163
Delinquent son, 281-283

Dementia
  compared with alcoholism, 133-136
  presenile, 182-185
    wife's cancer, 183, 184
Depression
  anniversary, 111, 112
  and anxiety, 19-28
  aphasia, 292
  breast cancer, 119-121
  fibromyositis, 216
  Ménière's disease and spastic bowel syndrome, 155, 156
  mother's, and suicide attempt, adolescent girl, 240, 241, 243
  osteoporosis, 95, 96
  wife's, and husband's affair, myocardial infarction, 83-85
Diabetes
  brittle, adolescent boy, 264-267
  and complications, 35-39
    amputation, 36, 37
    loss of independence, 36
  congestive heart failure and pulmonary edema, 68, 69
  and myocardial infarction, older man, 165
  newly diagnosed adolescent girl, 125-130
    exercise, 125-127
    guilt, 127
    independence, 126
  uncontrolled, adolescent girl, 209-212
    incest, 210, 211
    vaginal/perineal irritation, 209, 210
Diplopia, boy, 70-73
Discharge planning, colon carcinoma with metastases, 13-15
Discipline, 199, 200, 261, 262
Divorce, 130-133, 245, 246
Down's syndrome, 101-104
Drawing, aphasia, 294

Edema, 150, 151
  pulmonary, 68-70
Educator, health, overweight adolescent girl, 74, 75
Emotional investment, family-centered medical care, 305, 306
Endometrial leiomyosarcoma with metastases, 183, 184

Enuresis
  daytime, after car accident, 198–201
  divorce, 130
Epilepsy, 178, 179; *see also* Seizure
  disorder, girl
Exophthalmos, 44
Eye melanoma, 77–79

Factor VIII infusions, 297
Failure-to-thrive, infant boy, 223–227
  behavioral problems, brother, 224–227
  genogram, 224, 225
  lack of contact and attention, 223, 224
Family-centered medical care, overview,
    5, 303–312
  celebrant role, 82
  emotional investment, 305, 306
  expansion of context, 303–305
  impact on physicians, 309–311
  physician's effort, 306, 307
  questionnaire results, 307–309
  references, 313, 314
  reimbursement, Canada versus United
    States, 310, 311
Fever
  and fatigue, adolescent boy, 122–124
    father, myocardial infarction, 122–
      124
  myeloid metaplasia and myelofibrosis,
    58, 59
Fibromyositis, 215–219
  depression, 216
  insomnia, 215–217
  retarded daughter, 216–218
  stress, 216
Fracture
  ankle, breast cancer, 119, 120
  compression, osteoporosis, 95
  T_{12}, 11–13
Friedman, E., 3

Gastrointestinal problems and
    hyperventilation, adolescent boy,
    90–94
Genogram
  baby's birth to inexperienced couple,
    180
  failure-to-thrive, infant boy, 224, 225
  intracranial hemorrhage, 112
  and low back pain, husband and wife,
    269, 271

parenting roles, woman and fourth
    husband, 261
  renal cell carcinoma with metastases,
    175, 176, 178
  ventricular tachycardia, woman, 233
Gonococcus, pelvic inflammatory disease
    secondary to incest, adopted girl,
    192
Grief, unresolved, 112, 113

Headaches
  abused child, 304
  alopecia areata, 229–231
  chronic, 47–49
  nausea, vision disturbance, 11-year-old
    girl, 249–253
  stress-induced, man, 253–257
Health educator, overweight adolescent
    girl, 74, 75
Hemodialysis, 69
Hemophilia. *See* AIDS patient,
    hemophiliac
Hyperactivity
  parenting roles, woman and fourth
    husband, 260
  10-year-old boy, 139–143
    child as common focus, 140, 141
    unresolved parental conflict, 140,
      141
Hypertension, 150, 151
  and asthma, 64, 65
  and hyperparathyroidism, 136–139
    28-year-old son at home, 137, 138
  and low back pain, husband and wife,
    268, 269
  sexual problems, married couple, 281

Incest, 307
  and pelvic inflammatory disease,
    adopted girl, 189–193
  uncontrolled diabetes, adolescent girl,
    210, 211
Incestuous feelings, mother for
    adolescent boy, 195–198
Independence, loss of, 36
Insomnia, fibromyositis, woman, 215–
    217
Intellectualizing, ventricular tachycardia,
    woman, 236
Intercourse, pain during, 47–49

Intracerebral hemorrhage, death of
  teenage girl, 110–114
Involvement, levels of, 4–9, 33, 105, 221

Keeper syndrome, Alzheimer's disease, 56
Ketoacidosis, 264
Kübler-Ross, E., 146, 163

Laing, R. D., 188
Larynx cancer, elderly man, 85, 86
Leukemia, hairy-cell, young mother,
  115–118
Liver cancer, wife's, and myocardial
  infarction in older man, 164, 165
Lung adenocarcinoma, 27–31
Lupus erythematosus, systemic, 90, 91

Manic-depressive daughter and
  ventricular tachycardia, woman,
  233–237
Marital problems
  alopecia areata, woman with, 228–231
  asthma, man and son, 278, 279
  and infant's nasal stuffiness and dry
    cough, 107–109
  Ménière's disease and spastic bowel
    syndrome, 157, 158
  peptic ulcer, adolescent boy, 195–198
  seizure disorder, girl, 154
Melanoma, eye, 77–79
Ménière's disease and spastic bowel
  syndrome, elderly widow, 155–160
Mental retardation
  and cerebral palsy, son, 79–82
  daughter, and fibromyositis, 216–218
Miller, W., 312
Myeloid metaplasia and myelofibrosis,
  57–61
Myocardial infarction
  class IV inferior, 82–85
    wife's depression, husband's affair,
      83–85
  father, 112, 113, 122–124, 167–169
  older man, 164–167
    wife's death, 164, 165
  renal cell carcinoma, metastatic, 61

Nasal stuffiness and dry cough, infant,
  107–109
  marital difficulties, parents, 107–109

Nausea, headaches, vision disturbances,
  11-year-old girl, 249–253
Neuritis, ulnar, recent widow, 212–215
  problems with daughter, 212–215
Nightmares and daytime enuresis after
  accident, 198, 199

Obesity. *See* Overweight, adolescent girl
Organization of cases, 3–8
  family therapy, 5
  levels of involvement and skills, 4–9,
    33, 105, 221
  need for change, 5
Osteoporosis, 91–98
  self-help group, 96, 97
Ovarian cyst and low back pain, 268
Overindulgence/overprotection, 250, 251,
  265, 266, 287–289, 291
Overweight, adolescent girl, 73–76

Paranoid grandmother, baby's birth to
  inexperienced couple, 179, 181
Paranoid schizophrenia and divorce, 130,
  131
Parathyroid adenoma, 137
Parenting roles, woman and fourth
  husband, 260–263
Parkinson's disease, 98–100
Pelvic inflammatory disease and incest,
  adopted girl, 189–193
Pelvic pain, wife's, asthma, man and
  son, 275, 276, 280
Perineal irritation, uncontrolled diabetes,
  adolescent girl, 209, 210
Pregnancy
  Cesarean section, 43, 44
  hairy-cell leukemia, 117
  see also Birth to inexperienced couple
Prematurity and vulnerable child
  syndrome, 285–291
Prostate cancer, elderly man, 85, 86
Prostatitis and low back pain, 269, 270
Psoriasis, nummular, 16–18
Psychotherapy, referral, 22, 23, 26–28
Pulmonary edema and congestive heart
  failure, 68–70
Pulmonary embolism, breast cancer, 119,
  120

Questionnaire, 307–309
Quinlan, Karen Ann, 65

References, 313, 314
Reimbursement, United States versus Canada, 310, 311
Relaxation techniques, 254–256
Renal cell carcinoma, metastatic, 61–63, 174–178
Renal failure, 69
Respiratory distress syndrome, 285
Respiratory failure, renal cell carcinoma, 61, 62
Resuscitation
 Down's syndrome baby, 101, 102, 104
 elderly man, 85, 86
Roberts, L., 309
Roman Catholicism, 186–188

Schizophrenia, 130, 131, 175–177
School phobia, 273
Seizure disorder, girl, 152–155
Self-help group, osteoporosis, 96, 97
Sensate Focus therapy, 283
Sexual problems
 married couple, 281–284
 painful intercourse, 47–49
 ventricular tachycardia, woman, 237, 238
Skills, level of, 4–9, 33, 105, 221
Smoking, 82–85, 122, 123
Spain, 8
Spastic bowel syndrome and Ménière's disease, elderly widow, 155–160
Stress
 fibromyositis, woman, 216
 -induced headaches, man, 253–257
  contact lenses, 255, 256
  relaxation techniques, 254–256
  son's school problems, 254, 255
  type A, 254, 256
 management, mother, overweight adolescent girl, 74, 75
 -related abdominal pain, boy, 170–174
  hostile, absent father, 172, 173
 20-month-old girl with infant brother, 202–208
  abdominal pain, 205–207
  absent father, 206, 207
  tantrums, 203, 204
Suicide
 attempt/gesture, adolescent girls, 239–244, 257–259
  alcoholism, 259
  bullying by brothers, 240, 242
  depressed mother, 240, 241, 243
  family overuse of medical services, 257–259
  father antagonism, 258
  father's accident, 239–242
  threats, 236
Syndactyly, Apert's syndrome, 44
Systemic lupus erythematosus, 90, 91

Tantrums, 203, 204, 287–289, 291
Thrombocytopenia, 59
Tongue cancer, elderly man, 85, 86
Tranxene, 92–94
Type A personality, 254, 256

Ulcer, peptic, adolescent male, 194–198
 anxiety, 194–196
 incestuous feelings of mother, 195–198
 parents' marital problems, 195–198
Ulcers, stasis, 150, 151
Ulnar neuritis, recent widow, 212–215
 problems with daughter, 212–215
Unemployment, son's 157–158
United States, 8, 310, 311
Upper respiratory infections, prematurity and vulnerable child syndrome, 285, 286
Urinary tract infection, overweight adolescent girl, 73, 75

Vaginal irritation, 209, 210
Ventricular septal defect, Apert's syndrome, 45
Ventricular tachycardia, woman, 232–238
 angry explosions, family members, 233, 234
 congestive heart failure, 232, 235
 genogram, 233
 intellectualizing, 236
 manic–depressive daughter, 232–237
 sexual problems, 237, 238
Vertebra T_{12} fracture, 11–13
Vertigo, acute, 39–43
Vision disturbances, 11-year-old girl, 249–253
Vomiting, 90–93